Communications and Culture

Communications has been defined as the conveying or exchanging of information and ideas. This wide definition is taken as the starting-point for this series of books, which are not bound by conventional academic divisions. The series aims to document or analyse a broad range of cultural forms and ideas.

It encompasses works from areas as esoteric as linguistics and as exoteric as television. The language of communication may be the written word or the moving picture, the static icon or the living gesture. These means of communicating can at their best blossom into and form an essential part of the other mysterious concept, *culture*.

There is no sharp or intended split in the series between communication and culture. On one definition, culture refers to the organisation of experience shared by members of a community, a process which includes the standards and values for judging or perceiving, for predicting and acting. In this sense, creative communication can make for a better and livelier culture.

The series reaches towards the widest possible audience. Some of the works concern themselves with activities as general as play and games; other offer a narrower focus, such as the ways of understanding the visual image. It is hoped that some moves in the transformation of the artful and the scientific can be achieved, and that both can begin to be understood by a wider and more comprehending community. Some of these books are written by practitioners – broadcasters, journalists, and artists; others come from critics, scholars, scientists and historians.

The series has an ancient and laudable, though perhaps untenable, aim – an aim as old as the Greeks and as new as holography: it aspires to help heal the split between cultures, between the practitioners and the thinkers, between science and art, between the academy and life.

P. W.

The Politics of Information

Problems of Policy in Modern Media

ANTHONY SMITH

© Anthony Smith 1972, 1976, 1977, 1978,
Sage Publications, Inc. 1976,
Acton Society Press Group 1978,
International Institute of
Communications 1976

First published 1978 by
THE MACMILLAN PRESS LTD
London and Basingstoke
Associated companies in Delhi Dublin
Hong Kong Johannesburg Lagos Melbourne
New York Singapore and Tokyo

Printed in Great Britain by
LOWE AND BRYDONE PRINTERS LIMITED
Thetford, Norfolk

British Library Cataloguing in Publication Data

Smith, Anthony, b. 1938
    The politics of information. – (Communications
    and culture).
    1. Mass media
    I. Title   II. Series
    301.16′1   P90

    ISBN 0–333–23610–6
    ISBN 0–333–23611–4   Pbk

For Suzie

Contents

Acknowledgements   ix

Introduction   xi

Part 1   BROADCASTING

1 The Audience as Tyrant – an Elitist View of
   Television   3
2 Television as a Machine of Social Regulation   11
3 The Management of Television in a Democratic
   Society   24
4 The Finance of Television   38
5 Social Accountability and Television   45
6 The German Television Producer and the Problem
   of 'Internal Democracy'   54
7 Management and Creativity in Television   74
8 A Maturing Telocracy – Observations on the Tele-
   vision Coverage of the British General Elections of
   1974   84
9 Television Coverage of Northern Ireland   106
10 Community Conflict and the Media   129

Part 2   THE PRESS

11 News Values and the Ethic of Journalism – a View
   of the Western Tradition   143
12 State Intervention and the Management of the
   Press   157

13   The Long Road to Objectivity and Back Again – the
     Kinds of Truth We Get in Journalism   177
14   Technology, Distribution and Editorial Control:
     their Interactions in the Evolution of Journalism   199

     Conclusion A TELECOMMUNICATIONS FUTURE?

15   Needs, Wants, Demands, Luxuries and Scarce
     Natural Resources   227

Notes and References   239

Index   248

Acknowledgements

I wish to thank the Warden and Fellows of St Antony's College, Oxford, for harbouring me during much of the period in which these articles were being written; in the same breath I must thank the Trustees of the Leverhulme Trust Fund, whose generous grant made this work possible. My gratitude is due to Stephen Graubard of Harvard, Editor of *Daedalus*, for acting as impresario of one chapter and for thinking of the title for the whole. The Acton Society, through its Press Group, has been the sponsor of several pieces published here and I am grateful to Edward Goodman (the Society's Chairman), Pauline Wingate, James Curran and Jacky Lebe for their various roles in the work of this most useful study group. I am deeply conscious of the debt I owe Lord Annan's Committee on the Future of Broadcasting for commissioning one of the pieces published here and other papers published elsewhere; the Committee's existence between 1974 and 1977 served to focus and encourage public and academic discussion of media policy in Britain. Acknowledgements for individual chapters are made at the beginning of each.

Introduction

The essays in this book came originally into existence to serve quite different purposes but all of them share a single mission – to examine the field of force in which the modern media of communication operate. There was a time when it seemed possible to study the new mechanical devices which provide society with information as objects in themselves. The technology arrived as the end-product of an activity known as 'invention'; the institutions which owned and operated the machinery were thought somehow to be the inevitable concomitants of the inventions; the joint impact upon society of machines and institutions was thought to be capable of inspection in conditions analogous to those of a laboratory. Ever since television became the dominant means of communication in the majority of developed societies the relationships between media and people have come to be seen in a different light. Technology itself arises from the demands placed upon inventors; institutions arise out of the fears of loss of control by powerful sections of society. Within the many-layered world in which radio, television, the press and the newest electronic devices exist a new physics of society is perceptible, in which the day-to-day function of placing words and images before an audience entails the drawing of those very lines along which the forces of society travel. All decisions concerning information, from deciding where to place telephone circuits to deciding which jokes to excise from a comedy script, are part of the field of social forces which may be crudely termed 'communications'. This book consists simply of fifteen different assaults upon the same fundamental issues.

The 1970s, as far as the information media are concerned, may come to be seen as the age of enquiries. All developed societies –

and many others – have endeavoured to take their bearings, as it were, in the uncharted ocean of communication issues by holding one or more public investigations. Many of them have been directed simply at deciding how to reorganise radio and television; others have been directed at the more speculative problems posed by modern telecommunications developments. All of them have been aware of the likelihood that any conclusion reached will be quickly overtaken by events. But the speed of change, and its shifting directions (not all of them forwards), have only encouraged further acts of investigation.

The holding of two enquiries in Britain into the future of broadcasting and the press has quickened the pulse of debate in this country. Many aspects of the political and economic convulsions of Britain have posed special communication problems, including, in particular, the situation in Northern Ireland. These problems have sparked off many of the essays I have chosen, and so have specific situations in other societies including America and Germany. The Helsinki Agreement provided the starting point for a discussion of the nature of news values in western society. There is, however, a single unifying principle to the new politics of information and to these attempts to deal with it.

We are gradually evolving in the late twentieth century an altered view of the place of communication and of cultural activity in general within society. Whereas traditionally these were seen as a congeries of essentially private acts, over which governmental processes were to have no authority, we are coming now to realise that the whole panoply of communication media are inexorably public institutions dependent upon decisions taken by or on behalf of society as a whole. This book is an attempt to work out some of the implications of this growing realisation.

Oxford   A. S.
July 1977

Part 1

Broadcasting

Chapter I

The Audience as Tyrant – an Elitist View of Television*

It was the mass-produced newspaper at the end of the last century which gave rise to the notion that there exists a public right to be informed. Television has converted the notion into a right to be entertained. The new medium, from the start, was set in a competitive mould, and for that reason it has come to seem natural – *in the nature of the medium*, as they always say – that all programmes must be directed at a median audience, hour by hour. The programme-maker, in the very process by which he is professionalised and trained, is made to believe that his audience must be 'held' hour by hour, that it must be 'grabbed', that it must be addressed within the compass of an area of common allusion created by the medium of television itself. The programme-maker, the audience and the medium are *assumed* to be locked together within the same plane of meaning; all other meaning is excluded as lying outside the nexus. Inevitably, the terms in which the audience is addressed are derived from the world of entertainment. In other words, the television producer has to believe that he may speak to the audience only at the level of a public which has paid for a seat in the cinema, not at the level

*Published originally in *The Listener*, 26 August 1976.

of a public which has filed into a lecture hall, or queued for the Strangers' Gallery, or crowded into a church. It is fundamentally the music hall which has won. All the other audiences and publics have been rammed into a single hall, and all the different ranges of communicator hand over the audience from one to another, each one of them having to make do with a public which has been previously assembled by someone else for some other purpose.

It is this phenomenon which lies at the root of the quarrels over broadcasting which have taken place in the last ten years, not merely or even principally in this country, but in virtually every nation in which the medium of television in the 1960s reached a statistical and technical maturity. Even in the Soviet Union in the early 1970s there took place a drastic reduction in the quantity of ideological material carried on television; radio and the press have continued to fulfil the role of political instruction which was previously thought to be the proper function of all the media in socialist societies. Ever since the Soviet public in the major cities has been able to choose between two or three channels, the pressure has been felt on the broadcasting authorities to provide material which the audience – now being measured, channel by channel, day by day – will be willing to watch in large numbers. In most countries – not excluding the Soviet Union – the forms and methods by which the vast audience is hooked are largely of American origin. It is the vast engine of American peak hour television which has discovered the techniques which arouse and compel that weary giant which can be counted but never seen. It is like some distant galaxy, the existence of which is known to exert great influence upon our own world, but which cannot be seen with the naked eye, only registered electronically in an observatory.

The great official re-examinations of broadcasting which broke out like a rash in the 1970's are a response to the tensions produced by the strange democratic aberration of mass television. The 1960s saw a leap in the importance and dominance of television, relative to other forms of communication. It did not displace or even dislodge the theatre, the cinema, the newspaper, the music industry, but, in its search for material, it invaded every available field of information and entertainment to the extent that all the other media were obliged – successfully on the whole – to redefine their functions and their publics. Television by 1970 throughout Europe (east and west), America (north and south), Australia and large parts of Asia was acknowledged as the master of the general audience. Theatre, cinema and press had after that point, to offer their publics something which could not be obtained from television: there no longer existed, over roughly half of the world, an audience which was a non-television audience.

Television didn't just transmit, it transformed. To the surprise of many of the earlier prophets, it found the economic basis for creating its own infrastructure of content: it has its own newsrooms and schools of writers; its own genres and its own literature. Because of its unique grasp of the new, vast, median audience (almost coterminous with society itself), it came to exercise a power of arbitrage through all the fields of human culture, which became the underlying source of conflict with politicians and moralists, every group in society which felt it had a legitimate function to lead a segment of society from which it was now cut off. Moral conservatives turned with fury against television and its masters because they saw their flocks being led into alien pens. Marxists battled with it because they saw it as a machinery for subverting consciousness, a psychic counterpart of capitalism's means of production. Television had become the one well from which society now drew its common allusion; all other media, and all who wished to say anything to the society, found that they had to start with the same reference points selected by television. No wonder that the 1970s are left to struggle with a long series of unresolved problems of power in the field of the media.

What most societies which have tried to tackle this problem have resorted to is to tinker with the institutional mechanisms which were constructed, in the main, fifty years ago to deal with the infant medium of radio, and which have been successively adapted in the intervening years to cope with television. What makes the task of reforming the structures of the medium so extremely difficult is that the tools for making changes consist only of a small group of institutions, in Britain, the B. B. C., the I. B. A. and the Post Office. The greater forces which shape the behaviour of those institutions lie, of course, outside the scope of media-reformers, who are like doctors with excellent diagnostic equipment, but only different kinds of aspirins in the medicine chest.

The French found themselves, when the old Gaullist machinery for running radio and television collapsed in 1972, with an excellent opportunity for trying out something quite new. They reformed by stages, and, by 1975, had created an elegant model of internal competition within a monopoly which would have satisfied Descartes for symmetry and coherence. The director-general of each channel is chosen by the government. The three channels have prescribed, but slightly overlapping, roles; their share of the collective income (from licence fees and advertising) is partly dependent on their winning the race for the ratings. The heartland of the old O. R. T. F., however, is still intact, organised as the French Society for Production (S. F. P.); it is responsible for the main entertainment and dramatic programmes which it sells to the three channels, which, in effect, become commissioning agencies for all the nonfactual programmes. It is all like a piece of seventeenth-century French clockwork. It is a device of administration, by which French television can try to maximise the audience without running out of ultimate political control. Some would see the system as a transitional one, preceding a more complete 'democratisation' along the lines of Anglo-Saxon competitive entertainment. Others see it as a disastrous example of France's failure to separate television from its political élite.

Perhaps the most interesting attempt to escape from the trap has been that of the Dutch. In the Netherlands, broadcasting has always been run by the major confessional groups in Dutch society – Protestants, Catholics, socialists, liberals. Each has its own broadcasting company and is editorially sovereign; each company is responsible primarily to the hundreds of thousands of individuals who have chosen to subscribe, and only secondarily to the general audience, upon whose licence fees the whole system lives. But to retain its status as a major company (with a large share of radio and television time), there must be a minimum of 400,000 paid-up members, and it is becoming increasingly difficult for the traditional companies, based as they are upon traditional ideologies, to reach, this figure. V.A.R.A., the socialist group, lives in constant danger of falling below the figure and thereby losing most of its time. There has been a growth of 'general programme' groups operating within the Dutch system; one of the former pirate radio stations, Veronica, came ashore in 1970 registered as a candidate broadcasting group, and started signing up members. A few years earlier T. R. O. S. made the same journey, and is now the largest of all the companies, dedicated as it is merely to mass-audience programming, with no ideological overtones. Europe is in danger of losing its one really maverick system with the arrival of a generation which has simply sloughed off the old religious and political beliefs, upon whose assumed durability the broadcasting system had been based. The Dutch are, as it were, invited by their system to fulfil two separate functions—first as members of an opinion-oriented public and, secondly, as members of a mass-audience: the latter identity is threatening the existence of the former.

What needs to be brought out of the present discussion about systems of broadcasting and ways to reform them is the long line of unargued assumptions about television which underlie the medium as we know it. First, the idea that the audience is one, and must be served at all times, laughing at the same jokes, adhering to the centre in politics, cheering on the same teams. Second, the idea that, because it pays for its sets and its programmes, the audience must be given programming end-to-end – television abhors a vacuum. Third, the idea that a single channel must belong to a single control. These assumptions have precluded great divisions of the audience into the natural, historical audiences of which it is really composed; they have also necessitated the way in which television has grown up in slots or strands, endless series which belong to single production teams, which make for a certain type of mass production and easy budgeting. Fourth, they have prevented the development of an open publishing system via television, by which the editorial control becomes the responsibility of some organisation which does not control the technical transmission. All of these assumptions, had they not been made, would have laid the way for quite different developments in the content of broadcasting, but, of course, different assumptions could only have been made in a society moving in rather different general directions. One must avoid the fallacy of technological determinism; television does not escape the society it serves.

A variety of expedients has been adopted to 'mix' the strands of content to enable large audiences to be held with one kind of material, while being fed dutifully with another, surreptitiously. The magazine programme was born of this need. *Britain's Nationwide* and other regional programmes adopt this approach. The American breakfast show – one of the few American forms never to have been imported to Europe – is an inventive effort in the field. In Brazil, there is a two-hour weekly musical programme, *Fantastico*, which contains a good deal of current affairs material, slotted into a superbly presented musical extravaganza, which must surely be one of the greatest regular technical feats of television in the world.

But the fusion of entertainment values goes much more deeply into the culture of the medium than the mere mixing of forms in 'magazine' formats. The development of the long news programme – first in America, then in Europe – occurred only after styles of news presentation had been evolved in television which succeeded in hooking audiences large enough for advertising. The development of *News at Ten* in the late 1960s marked an important stage in the development of an entertainment form designed to convey news: the viewer's attention was directed, for the first time in Britain, to the personality, of the presenters. The constant repetition of the title of the programme by the reporters in the field helps to build the audience into the supporters of a kind of team; the promotion of later items before the commercial break helps to emphasise the structure of the programme in a way which constantly reassure the audience that lighter material is on the way. The constant effort to humanise the stories, to dwell on familiar themes (strikes, crises, catastrophes, human interest stories) were techniques derived ultimately from entertainment and the popular press. Television in its maturity achieved a perfect fusion of pill and sugar. But, at that point, the medium – internationally – let loose a series of political hurricanes, the force of which is not yet spent. Television found itself on the defensive simultaneously on a series of fronts. There was trouble with politicians, and trouble with moralists. Wilson, Agnew, de Gaulle, Kreisky – all of them were affronted fundamentally by the political implications of the establishment of a public entertainment apparatus which was being made to carry the burden of political communication (or so it seemed).

But there was a more far-reaching disquiet in all those other areas of society which were accustomed to addressing special constituencies (religious, ideological, regional) within that society; there was a small section of vocal people who were used to ploughing the audience in lone furrows, and who were either refused permission to reach the new general audience, or who had to do so within formats which made them ridiculous or ineffective. Television could not afford to assist them on any terms. It is the collective feeling of dissatisfaction created by all of these that has led to a spate of reorganisations, commissions and other inquests. The list of countries which have put themselves through this particular trauma since 1970 is now very long: Canada, France, Austria, Germany, Holland, Switzerland, New Zealand, Australia, Ireland, Sweden and many others including Britain.

It is difficult to prise open a discussion of this kind because all those involved in broadcasting have come round to accepting the notion of a public right to be entertained at all times; it is built into the system, into the scheduling, the training, the recruitment, the management. It leads to extremely good results in terms of the satisfaction derived both from watching and making programmes. It helps to make broadcasting into a separate estate of specialised services, into a public service of professionalised mediation between communicators and audience; it gives broadcasting its mystery, and enables it to speak of its cares and responsibilities as special ones, involving a different range of considerations from other communication activities, like industrial management or education. It is behind the institutionalisation of the 'public service in the private world', of which Tom Burns speaks in his sensitive examination of the B. B. C. conducted in 1963.[1] The right of entertainment is also sanctified as a manifestation of democracy, instead of being regarded as an example of the deepest paternalism; to oppose the communication values which it entails is to earn the label of élitism.

Apart from the rare examples of pay-TV, there exists no transaction between viewer and broadcaster, no exchange of tokens by which audiences could define themselves cumulatively in the minds of the programme-makers. If they could do so, it would be possible theoretically for the audience to manifest itself in terms of all the smaller 'real' audiences of which it consists. So long as control over broadcasting is unitary, the service it

provides will be treated as a unitary service, keeping within
median taste, following the contours of work and leisure which
define the peak and non-peak hours. Within television technology as it exists (i.e. excluding the things which might happen
when cassettes develop fully, and cable and other broad-band
services, which could be anything from a decade to a generation),
the only hopes lies in the separation, in certain channels at least,
of the publishing and transmission functions. The right to publish
via television would create lines of communication between
broadcaster and audience much more localised in content than
anything possible within services which try to guarantee the right
to be entertained. It took from 1695 to 1865 for the press in
Britain to establish a right to publish, untrammelled by government interference at the point of production or the point of
distribution. From then on, the freedom of the press, such as it has
been, has been guaranteed by market forces, by the establishment of economically viable audiences for particular products.
Television began its development at the opposite end; the
medium belongs not to the communicator, but to the audience,
invisible, a faceless tyrant; in television, all the 'rights' are vested
in a mysterious entity known by its number but not by its face, a
private public, as it were, isolated, but vastly numerous, powerful
but helpless.

Chapter 2

Television as a Machine of Social Regulation

Much if not most of the critical literature of the mass media in the 1960s dwells upon an alleged superimposition upon society of a world of illusion, an enforced unreality, at variance with the more solid world of 'reality', which television had finally – apparently – extirpated from the realm of cognition. Daniel Boorstin, who wrote in 1961, opens his influential essay 'The Image', which, if any text ever did, stuck the label upon the bottle of prevailing notions (the lees of which are just now in evidence), with a sentence designed to stun: 'In this book I describe the world of our making, how we have used our wealth, our literacy, our technology, and our progress, to create the thicket of unreality which stands between us and the facts of life.'[1] The decade was beckoning us into a world in which we could no longer know what things were 'really' like, because our emotions and our learning processes were now forever intermingled in that variety of experience which we imbibed from a contraption standing between all reality and all perception. After all, in the 1960s we had already passed through a full decade of such vicarious experience. The principal writers on the topic continually emphasised the fusion of 'emotion' with 'cognition' in the output of the electronic media.

McLuhan and his followers explained that 'I – thou' thinking

was over. Political scientists discovered that the opinion poll and
the television campaign had brought about what radio engineers
would describe as a 'howlround' in the political sphere: the
messages passing between communicators and audience were
passing through the same circuits and the result was mere noise.
The American politician and political manager were among the
first to grasp the new vision of the media's part in society. The
cognition–emotion duality was easily exploitable by politicians
competing for votes; politicians had of course always exploited it,
but one could now ascribe the blame to an external compulsion.
Television became a major object of attention for political
managers and the resultant trend towards the 'packaging' of
political leaders and their messages only served to give broader
credence to the new critique. The lessons learned from Boorstin,
McLuhan and many others applied more than anywhere else in
the political sphere.

The last Jeffersonian voter was given a decent burial, entirely
on subscription from the new media mysticism. 'Voting in the
traditional sense is through', McLuhan told the readers of
Playboy, 'as we leave the age of political parties, political issues
and political goals and enter an age where the collective tribal
image and the iconic image of the tribal chieftain is the over-
riding political reality.'[2] There was an underlying patrician
element in the critique, a disdainful rejection of the idea that the
voting millions should actually get what they had paid for –
namely, entrance to a more complete citizenship via their
television sets. Harold Mendelsohn and Irving Crespi were
certain that what they saw on television could not possibly
represent things as they were, as they had always been deemed to
be; one has to register their vocabulary to obtain the full flavour,
the references to 'ritual', 'reality', 'pseudo':

> With the advent of television as a major means of political
> communication came a ritualistic, stylized orientation to
> national political campaigning, the product of which looks
> like the genuine, honest-to-goodness real thing, but in essence
> is not. The pseudo-campaign as presented by television merely
> simulates political reality, but is as far from the real thing as
> the girl in the Revlon ad is from the bucolic young creature
> next door.[3]

In a way, the 1960s approach to the study of television, especially in the United States (whence emanated every influence and trend in the media, about the media and against the media) was the result of a kind of exasperation which had set in after several fruitless decades of searching for direct 'hypodermic' media effects. The academic world had assumed in the decade before the Second World War that the advertising industry could not fundamentally be wrong, indeed that all other forms of communication influence must be susceptible to forms of research parallel to advertising and market research. They had not, however, fully appreciated the differences of genre between advertising and other forms of mass message-sending. Modern advertising is a branch of production, it coaxes a product, the relevance of which to its market has been established in advance, through its last journey from the counter of the store into the possession of the customer. It is quite a different matter to examine the *ab initio* effects on an individual of violence seen on the screen, or of political argument. None the less a tremendous amount of skilled effort went into the study of direct effects (some of this work continues) for a whole generation before Klapper's masterful and devastating summary of the state of knowledge which he published at the end of the 1950s: 'Mass communications *ordinarily* does not serve as a necessary and sufficient cause of audience effects, but rather functions among and through a nexus of mediating factors and influences.'[4] The disappointment seeped slowly through the media research community; every now and then a smile burst through the tears as a sudden chance result would reignite the old hopes of isolating within the content of a medium some factor which produced a significant and provable behavioural response; like doctors who had spent their lives trying to isolate the virus of a killer disease to be told that the symptoms could be cured with an aspirin, the effects – researchers turned aside from their graphs, to dedicate their remaining efforts to the elucidation of 'indirect effects' or 'gratifications'. A new school was, however, ready to infiltrate the void; its interests lay in the observation of the professionals and in the attempt to set out the special 'constraints' which operated upon the content of the medium, that host of social, institutional, ideological and occupational influences which made 'Bonanza' what it was.

At this point in the evolution of general disquisition about the media, the audience itself lay outside the zone of certainties; it watched television for over twenty hours a week without evincing specifiable and separable kinds of impact and therefore one was led to making a much broader kind of statement about the influence of television in society. The whole media – society model needed to be changed, and indeed the notion of causality itself, if anything meaningful was now to be said about the state of Man in the presence of the Box. In the political sphere especially one could descry a veil of deception spun by television through which national leaders now had to make their appeal. The deception itself was the supposed cause of fundamental changes in the stance and behaviour of the political élite, and perhaps too in the identity of that élite.

The researchers, therefore, who got to work on the media professionals saw themselves as investigators of a machinery of obfuscation if not illusion, which was widely believed to have already hoodwinked society. Open generalised impact was more amenable to analysis than particular personalised persuasion. Kurt and Gladys Lang had already in the 1950s in a series of sensitive and persuasive studies[5] shown the transformational power of television in altering the 'reality' which was allegedly being observed; they had shown how at that time the camera altered the behaviour of the people it photographed and how the producers and reporters always brought out the archetypal (that is, preconceived) elements of crowd behaviour. The camera which cannot lie photographed that which it looked for. Now television had become a dominant instrument of social communication and the camera took on a more sinister guise. 'The candidates make their progress through engineered crowds, taking part in manufactured pseudo-events, thrusting and parrying charges, projecting as much as they can with the help of makeup and technology, the qualities of youth, experience, sincerity, popularity, alertness, wisdom and vigor.'[6] Thus wrote Robert MacNeil, a reporter who worked on both sides of the Atlantic. Television was making completely revised demands upon the democratic politician; his image had to shine through a cloud of unknowing, he had to reach his electors through a technology of malfeasance. Again, it was the machinery which had to be blamed, together with the people who provided its professional and bureaucratic superstructure. Indeed the techniques of television helped to excuse the cynicism of those who were coming to condemn traditional democratic politics. The new technology, however, was also peculiarly suited to the new anti-politics of the 1960s students; the Vietnam moratoria were mass graduation ceremonies in television politics.

There was nothing essentially new in the prevailing analysis of television's impact on society. Walter Lippman in the 1920s had written of the secondary environment in which the mass press now enveloped every citizen; the reality of news was a surrogate reality to which politicians had now to respond, dangerous but inexorable. Graham Wallas, even before the First World War, had examined the new situation from the perspective of the politician. The politician of the mass age, Wallas had observed, had to behave as if the electorate were a photographic plate on which his image was to be implanted; if he rushed his electorate with too many or too rapidly developing ideas and policies, it would have the effect of a bird flying across the plate, only a blur would be registered. The modern man of politics needed to work through signs and symbols; he needed to carry an umbrella, or an old bag or a distinct form of headgear with which the voter would identify and which would be assimilated in the mass mind with the ideas of its owner. Several (but not many) politicians of the pre-television age were quick to sense what was in the air, even before television came to dominate political communication: de Gaulle, who had broadcast all over the French-speaking world during the war years was astonished to discover how his 'image' preceded him. On a visit to the newly liberated French Cameroons in 1946, when he heard the crowds at the quayside chanting his name, he realised he would have to get to know this 'de Gaulle', the man created by the radio broadcasts, a secondary self more potent than his primary self. It was not, however, the medium which had 'created' this secondary self but the audience. The packaging of the politician was a phenomenon which occurred within society, the attribution of qualities to an individual which the audience as much as the politician required the latter to possess. The radio and the newspaper chose the forms in which this process occurred, though the forms themselves were borrowed from the traditions of political communication; the leader was seen as teacher, or magician or priest or master, he was the product of what the audience remembered of politics and leadership as much as of what they wanted. The forms selected by the media were memory systems which related the data concerning the new leader with the transmitted needs of the society.

The observers of the media of the 1960s had seized upon the process by which television fused the needs of entertainment and the needs of information within a new set of genres. So firmly separated had the two become in the traditions of political communication set during the preceding century that a kind of sacrilege seemed to be involved in the process of television itself. The Presidential debates of 1960 presented the American voter with a formal contest for national leadership and established an inward picture of two-way conflict as the underlying structure of political life. It was a picture which lent itself easily to the world of entertainment. The mass media had built up America's entertainment industry, vast even before the coming of television, and its outpourings belonged to the secular sphere. Until television dominated the attention of the audience politics took place in a non-secularised realm; the audience was there by duty rather than simple inclination. Once the political process was secularised and placed in the same arena, as it were, as entertainment, it had to be judged by the same criteria as other kinds of public performance. Politics now took place within the same kind of permanent emergency, within the same orbit of incessant risk, as entertainment; the audience had to be grabbed and held, without stint, without relaxation.

A tug of war developed between rival versions of public affairs. The politician would tell the story one way, the media would tell it another. Both were essentially 'trying out' their competing accounts. Three Presidents, Kennedy, Johnson and Nixon, tried to recount the story of Vietnam in a gradually changing but essentially similar set of stock plots: limited war, repelling of aggression, the domino theory, backing up our troops, imminent victory. The media tried out a rival set of plots: unacceptable scale of loss of life, an unwinnable war, a diversion from domestic politics. Some of them worked, some of them did not, some of them coincided with the President's plot, increasingly they did not. The media placed the story in the context of the scenes which it was able to focus on, from battles overseas to riots at home, from the burning of villages by American troops to street executions.

Both sides were trying out parts of the story on the audience, both sides were adept at grabbing the audience for differing purposes. The politics of the society lay in the pictures and the pictures expressed the producers' and reporters' preconceptions as to what the audience at any single moment would respond to. Each half of the new political world was trying to catch up with the influences exerted by the other. There was a *reality* after which both were striving, but the genres in which both worked could only grasp it in segments. A debate would bring out one aspect of it, a dramatically timed address to the nation another; the talk of political commentators broke the spell of the patrician discourse delivered straight to camera; the denunciation of the press by a Presidential straightman would help to apply an anti-magic to lower the credibility of the media. What had seemed to be a wicked 'packaging' of men and issues by the media, a series of deceits conducted by technology, was a series of feints, none of which could ever come off completely. In a society in which one by one the traditional systems of regulation, the historically accumulated means by which society worked out the terms of social order, had collapsed, television now became the principal system of social regulation. Television offered a form of knowledge which society as a whole could be presumed to share; other carriers of knowledge henceforth automatically became 'specialist', partial, not the bases of assumable common allusiveness. Ignorance of the televised was no excuse.

What the viewers, producers and observers of American television were experiencing was a stage in a process which had in fact begun a century before, as soon as media of communication had begun to develop in such a way as to maximise social spread in their circulation. In the late twentieth century the information upon which society relied for its proper governance was being unpacked from the media which had borne it for several generations and rearranged in a new medium in a new set of social circumstances. The symbols and imagery of politics were changing and a larger audience was participating (in a different meaning of that word) at different levels of their lives. The mass press of Europe had long ago become fundamentally a press of entertainment, and still the carrier of the bulk of political information. Whether this in itself meant that the whole apparatus of cognition had withered as a result was doubtful. The imagery of society has to conform to the media which carry it; the media too inevitably conform to the imagery which they are obliged to carry. What Nixon tried to do was interfere with the process by which the genres are made. There is no shock so great to the audience of a game as the realisation that one of the players is cheating according to the implied rules of the game; it renders the game pointless. In the television world it is vital that the key moves are made in public; you have to see a convincing development of the plot. Out-of-character behaviour must be explained or altered; each stage of the story must be credible. If there are areas which are necessarily out of vision they must be accounted for in the rest of the story. Motiveless behaviour inexplicable reactions, consequenceless pieces of action are *ipso facto* deceptions of the audience, breaches of procedure. The conspiracy conducted off-stage is unsatisfying to the audience, unless it is brought into the plot later and helps to explain the story so far. Television forces the events of politics into a story-line, a structure which encompasses the socially prescribed rules of narrative, which leave plenty of room for privacy of a kind for certain of the characters, but which leave little room for behaviour out of tune with the role of the character and no room at all for activity irrelevant to the plot. The audience participates in the sense that the actors and producers know that its attention must be held, all of the time. Nixon (and Johnson before him) thought that the cosmeticians were at fault. The successful politician of the television age realises that the story-line is everything, the scene shifters and makeup artists can only help a tired actor through a difficult bit of the performance. Only a bad actor dreams of blaming them. The politics of spectacle is not the same as the politics of television: Nixon staged his dramatic flight to China to divert attention as his Presidency slithered to an end; but that was the response of the nineteenth century politician not that of the late twentieth: Disraeli offered circuses with his bread but knew that these were mere sub-plots and additions to the main narrative. In the television age there is hardly room for a sub-plot. The story must go on and on around the main characters.

True, one can argue that this is indeed the politics of the 'image', entailing and encouraging an element of illusionism. But it is not fundamentally a politics which is different from that of tradition, it is merely applied through the mass media of today. Television has become the theatre of politics in both senses of the term. Like the theatres of classical times its structures combine into a memory system, its disciplines incorporate the moral norms of politics as these apply at a given moment in history. American television has become more totally a medium of politics than the television of any other society and it is disputable whether this has led to a greater level of deception. The most powerful and memorable pictures generated since 1960 on the American screen – the assassinations, the state funerals, the wars, Chicago, Watts and Watergate – act as caskets containing the normative serum of those events. Each scene is a clay tablet into which other forms and types of statement have been mentally impressed. Television presents an official world, or several contending official worlds whose reality has to be adjusted by the citizen. The regulatory processes which govern the multitude of institutions, all existing within a state of mutual tension, which constitute American television (stations, networks, F.C.C., pressure groups, production companies), force television content into a deliberate form of statement; whatever is seen has been permitted as well as conceived by someone, and is presented with many self-justifying artifices. The promotion, pre-emption, introduction, presentation, titling, structuring of all television involves an element of self-defence. Television was quickly made to realise that it was indeed a form of government as well as a usurper of powers. It is a pressured message which emerges, laden with conceptually impossible but symbolically important ordinances such as objectivity; the great row which followed the exposure of the quiz scandals back in the 1950s helped television into that attitude of mind which it has in most societies, of being as it were weighed down with awesome responsibilities, both in the commercial sphere and towards the audience in a moral sense. It is not always a universally attractive morality which the networks pursue, but it reflects the most powerful forces at work in American society. Television is a conditioner because of its careful relationship with power, because of the marginal nature of the regulatory mechanisms. The literature of the medium is weighed down with pieties and counter-pieties of Stanton and Friendly, Nicholas Johnson and Dick Salant. It is a regulatory medium in itself, a parallel constitution, separated from the

Constitution of the United States by the First Amendment, that
ark of the franchise-holder's covenant, in which the network
chiefs keep their profits.

In the last fifteen years, as a result of the spread of television
almost everywhere, America has become the most abundantly
observed society in history. No single society has ever revealed
itself so completely to its friends and enemies, or employed self-
revelation as a principal means of social change. It has meant, as
Jean-François Revel has pointed out in *Ni Marx, ni Jesus*,[7] that
the rest of the world has been invited to judge America according
to what American standards are imagined to be rather than
according to the standards of the judge. America is condemned
for the violence of its policemen even though the speaker lives in
Paris or Santiago. America is condemned for its internal tensions,
though the speaker live in Brixton or Beirut. America is
condemned for its wealth and for its poverty, for the way its
politicians try to manipulate the media, for their corruption and
ignorance of the rest of the world. The images which American
television presents to the world arrive prepacked in hostile
judgements. For most of the world America is now a preoccupation rather than a reality. We watch our own societies
develop the indigenous appurtenances of mass consumer society
(the motel, the supermarket, the paperback) and label the
process 'Americanisation'. To Americanise is to destroy tradition, to force American messages into the inherited memory
structures of our own societies. It induces in the observer the sense
of being quaint, of being the inheritor of a shabby collection of
cultural furniture, unusable, 'unreal'.

Naturally, the colossal scale on which all the strands of
American society have developed in the last half century has
resulted in creating this sense of provincialism – especially in
other parts of the English – speaking world; however, the
controlling structure of that relationship is today contained
within that area of allusion created by television. This is in
itself not altogether new; relationships between societies have
generally been fostered by media content created originally for
the internal consumption of the societies concerned. Each
generation of communicators has had to acquire a new set of skills
to fit the prevailing media, which register in return the
dominating images and stances of the society. In nineteenth-

century European politics there was constant recourse to government pressure on the press to control the impressions it generated about relationships between societies. The media tend to set the distances between different societies, which are entailed in the particular accounts of events which they transmit. The models and metaphors implied in the descriptions of foreign or international phenomena are an important element in setting the norms for a given society. The image of the Cold War, for instance, or that of the Middle East implied in most of the coverage of these topics on British television is quite different, far less stark, more susceptible to nuance, than the counterpart material made for American television. At the centre of television is something further-reaching than the transmission (or distortion) of information; it is a testing ground, a sifting mechanism, for the dominant assumptions of a society. It is part of the regulatory equipment of a modern nation.

The forms of television provide the main guide to these dominant norms, these inward structures of meaning present within material and resulting from the pressured nature of work in the mass media. The interview, the standard mode of political discourse on television, pioneered by the American television news of the mid-1950s, implies an equality of being between politician and interlocutor. The interviewer is raised much higher than the newspaper interviewer of the journalism of fifty years ago. The interviewer has become much more of an interrogator, validating his task by emphasising its representative nature; the politician (elected) is by implication a vested interest; the interviewer, by implication, a delegate of the viewers, putting the questions 'which they would like to ask'. There is a presumption of non-responsibility on the part of the politician, embedded in the genre of the political interview itself. If you close your eyes and think of all the political coverage of television in the last decade or more you see a man trying to justify himself before another man, who begins every fresh question with a 'but'. How different from the standard political communication of, say, the late nineteenth century, where the printed speech was the standard form, the recovery, via shorthand, the telegraph, the train and the press of the *ipsissima verba* of a politician standing upon a platform: the platform presented a totally different icon of the political situation. The platform inherited certain overtones from the pulpit and certain from the classroom; the politician was half-preacher, half-teacher, distanced both from his audience and his opponents. His speeches were delivered, as if to the audience in the hall, but in reality, to the buyers of the newspaper. Today the politican speaks as if in conversation with a 'neutral' confessional, as if with an acquaintance, but in reality to the viewing millions. The Presidential debate is a special form, a public testing of stamina, in which the participants are involved in a kind of joust. When the sound went down on Ford and Carter they were obliged to maintain the standing position, the stance which most tested their strength and will; to move to a sitting position would have seemed to cause a shift in genre: the characters in an icon must adopt the poses expected of them and retain them. The forms of television are, as it were, extensions of devices available in the Constitution into symbolic forms. The choice of the electors is *likened* to a duel which is *likened* to an intellectual disputation and the result is a televised debate between Presidential candidates. In other countries the metaphors have been different, unadjustable (as yet) to the form of public debate.

All this does not amount to a world of dream or unreality. The forms of political television are merely typical examples of the working of all television forms, as devices for testing moral norms. It is the presence of the mass audience, an undifferentiated audience identical with society as a whole, which turns the programme device from a game into an emblem. The quiz programme, the game show and the dramatic forms of soap opera and western have moved into a kind of official sector of the entertainment business, they take on the work of mediating values. Mediating not inculcating. The media are not instruments of propaganda; the whole system of contact with the audience is severed as soon as they drift towards a propagandistic mode of address. Their power lies in the impreciseness with which each programme, each genre aims at its moral statement. Television operates in the subjunctive rather than the indicative.

Television in its most highly developed state, where it is least overlaid with competition from other traditional social institutions dealing in values, that is to say, in North America, operates in a manner similar to the medieval trial by ordeal. A supposed miscreant was subjected to one of a series of available traditional tortures, the physical effects of which were examined in full public view. If, half a minute after being thrown into a pool of water, the subject floated, then he was guilty, if he sank, then innocent. If his arm, after being placed for a prescribed period in boiling oil, began to heal after three days, then he was deemed to be guilty, if it did not heel, then he was innocent. The tests were *objective* in form; they removed the necessity for other forms of investigation. In any case the activities of a witch were inscrutable, the precise results of an act of witchcraft inaccesible. Modern medicine has shown that all the tests used in trial by ordeal can only produce results which are ambiguous; after the prescribed period the human body neither sinks nor swims, the boiled arm has neither withered nor healed. Medieval society had created a mechanism by which a judgement about an important social issue (whether the suspect's withcraft had *caused* the current misfortunes of the community) as transferred into a judgement about something else. Society could therefore reach a judgement about an imponderable, imprecise, changing set of problems, in the form of a judgement made about something precise, objective. The free exercise of prejudice or presupposition or suspicion could be elevated into a process of detection. The countless reactions of a society towards one of its number could be transmuted, no doubt in a form 'biased' by those with most power in the community, into a single verdict.

The central element in the trial by ordeal was its irrelevance to the real topic under discussion. Political television, as it has developed in the American networks since 1960, reveals a certain similarity to this medieval model. The electorate is invited to shape its electoral judgements around its judgements of television performances. The contenders for power spend much time and money in acquiring the skills necessary for success. The real question being asked is unanswerable, whether X or Y will *cause* certain desired developments in society, or whether the reign of X or Y has already succeeded in producing certain consequences in society. This is not a sudden abrogation of rational thinking, a sudden decision to make political judgements on the basis of emotion rather than cognition. It involves a vigilance of its own, its aim is a kind of precision. What the television screen offers is an arena for a form of transferred judgement, a living means for a society's self-regulation.

Chapter 3

The Management of Television in a Democratic Society*

Very few societies have escaped a major internal ruction within their broadcasting institutions, or between their broadcasters and their politicians. In many cases there have been major explosions of internal or external discontent which have led to the complete reconstruction of broadcasting systems. In some countries there has been more than one crisis. The more liberal the society concerned, the more complex and tortured the debate about broadcasting, about the appropriate pattern of duties and responsibilities for broadcasters, management and politicians. By a strange and unpredictable irony, the medium of television is raising in new forms the whole range of issues which we thought had been settled under the rubric of freedom of expression. What we thought was a settled set of social rights turns out, in the context of this mass medium, to be a series of undecided dilemmas.

The electorate, the great audience of politics, has become one with the great mass audience of entertainment. Politics is carried through society by the same instrument which carries the bulk of

* Originally delivered as a paper to the Committee on Education and Culture of the Council of Europe at Munich, June 1974.

its entertainment, its drama and much of its education and information. We have acquired a double conundrum: What happens to freedom of communication when the necessary instruments are concentrated inside a small élite of professionals? What obligations has society towards policing its mass culture when that culture can exercise an influence over the attitude, the morals, the emotional security of the mass audience? We have already lived with this debate long enough now to know that these are not simple organisational questions capable of simple organisational answers. The problems are buried very deep inside our culture and like such problems in past generations they cannot be solved, only replaced with new problems and new formulations of old ones. We have been left wondering about the effects of television long enough to realise that the only un-disputed effect is the dilemma which it poses for all modern societies.

Our subject is the *management* of television in a democratic society, and we should pause to consider the paradox buried in the question. If the medium is to be *managed*, how can there be any democracy? We are using as the main means of political communication a one-way medium which is supposed to func-tion in a two-way or pluralistic society. We have persuaded ourselves that technological exigency alone has forced television into being dominated in most countries by one or two state semi-monopolies. But historically radio and television developed from telephony, a technology developed in the last century for two-way communication between individuals and groups. In the course of the 1920s the technology took a decisive turn away from pluralism and the two ends of the telephone, as it were, were separated; the speaking end was placed in a sacred temple situated somewhere near, though not too near, the parliament house; the listening end was placed inside millions of wooden boxes, which were distributed at low cost through the selling organisations of the mass furniture industry, to every home in every nation. The results of that great splitting of microphone from loudspeaker we have come to call broadcasting and we have gradually come to treat all the cultural and political assumptions which go with the monoplisation and nationalisation of broad-casting as if they were inexorable laws of nature. We believe that there is one great mass audience of the whole society which demands non-stop material throughout the main hours of viewing. We have now created a vast international market for the software of mass entertainment. Increasingly today the television product is directed at one great international median viewer. We assume that this mass audience is the 'natural' audience for television and a discussion has developed about how television should deal with 'minority' taste; anyone who is not part of the non-stop median audience is deemed to belong to a 'minority' whose needs must indeed be supplied, although only at great inconvenience to the system.

Only in very recent years has any important debate developed, still at the radical fringes of the broadcasting world, about the possibility that television organisations could somehow undergo a separation of powers between transmitting and controlling; this would mean that writers, producers, pressure groups, politicians, could somehow be enabled to use the medium in their own names, unmediated by members of the tiny professional élite. It would be very difficult to accept the demands of this new 'access' lobby, in the context of a medium which claims as its *basic* public, an audience equivalent to the available population. The complex and unwieldy machinery of simultaneous mass entertainment inevitably creates an appalling series of responsibilities for all who are set to govern the institutions of broadcasting. Many of those responsible for television pretend that the problem results from the physical technology of television, rather than from the assumptions and institutions in which it happens to be enwrapped.

Of course there is a terrible problem involved in 'managing' television. Too much decision-making has been concentrated in too few hands. The media system of a society is its central nervous system; to control it opens up the immediate possibility of social manipulation of various kinds – the opportunity for social edification, for mass political education, for encouraging the good at the expense of the bad in a culture, for political tyranny or simply for gentle sustained ideological bias. In fact the system does more than this – it makes a set of national choices obligatory, it forces those in charge to operate the cultural nervous system according to some centrally enunciated rationale. If you are in charge of a mass broadcasting organisation you cannot operate within the rules of John Stuart Mill; the traditional liberal model of total freedom of argument and total creative freedom just cannot operate. A single social institution, responsible for its decisions to a Parliament or a whole society, is obliged to make choices, to make decisions between good and bad, between biased information and objective, between mass viewing material and minority. It must arbitrate between minorities, make the best decisions it can within the resources available on behalf of the vast majority.

Many decades ago some English wag gave a name to this process. He looked at the B. B. C. and called it 'Auntie' and Auntie has been the nickname of the B. B. C. ever since. We have been lucky to have an Auntie; some nations have had to put up with a Big Brother instead, which has been far less pleasant. But in the context of this decade in which there is a general demand for autonomy in many sectors of society, and in which the medium of television has come to be felt to be more powerful than any other medium of the past, it is no longer acceptable to many people – including many of those professionally involved in broadcasting – for so much media power to remain so centralised.

Television, whether publicly financed or commercial or based on a mixture of both, is always prone to influence by politicians, whether liberals or dictators. But it is also prone to interference on the part of paternalists and I would argue that all are versions of the same aberration. Broadcasting is prone to a special kind of distortion, which results from its institutionalised nature rather than from its technical nature. Every television organisation operates according to a central philosophy, however tacit it may be. The central rationale may be founded upon a desire simply to make as much money as possible from advertising and where that is the case the organisation inevitably acquires certain views about how it can best avoid any high authority interfering in its inalienable right to exploit the airwaves for financial gain. It develops a central view which helps to validate and legitimise its attitude towards the strands of material which pass through its programme schedules. Its employees develop a view of the world which may not correspond with its dominant institutional philosophy but which at least enables them to function within it in a negative way. They may simply alienate their emotional lives from the central organisation, they may sacrifice conscience and live by the rules of the organisation.

The organisation may be committed to a central philosophy of simple obedience to an outside political élite, the rulers of the country. It will therefore develop a hierarchy of values consistent with the function which it is obliged to perform within society.

The broadcasting organisation may be committed to a totally liberal ideal, of allowing the greatest possible variety of expression, of exploiting the greatest range of entertainment and information available within the transmitting society. But even in this case it is committed to ensuring that its programmes correspond to a view of what that total variety is. An organisation dedicated to the ideal of liberal democracy is not in itself dedicated to freedom, to allowing itself to be used as a common carrier for the propagation of the ideas of any individual or group within society. For it is committed – by logical necessity – to the task of understanding its society as best it can and bringing about a reflection of that understanding. It has to create, as it were, a simulated model of the cultural intercourse of the society in which it operates. The problem is that the broadcasting institution is master of the airwaves, the basic resource of broadcasting, as well as master of the broadcasters. Imagine that there were, for example, a single monopoly of newsprint, whose controllers were dedicated to the pure ideal of freedom of expression, but in a society in which there was a scarcity of newsprint. The controllers of the newsprint would be obliged themselves to decide whether, through their distributive decisions, they were helping to advance one cause at the expense of another; they would be obliged to explain to the society what principles they employed for the distribution of newsprint and if it happened to be a very liberal and open society there would inevitably be generated demands from a larger number of groups to participate in the decision-making of this newsprint monopoly. This situation is exactly what has happened in broadcasting; the original decisions made concerning the housing and development of the technology of broadcasting created a shortage of the basic resource involved – the wavelengths. Since this resource is nationally controlled it became inevitable that governmental agencies would handle the fundamental decision-making, the allocation of the wavelengths, and would decide the basic cultural principles by which any recipient of the wavelength would be judged when the moment arrived for his franchise to be renewed.

Some nations created stable liberal institutions, which are now beginning to run into trouble because, with the proliferation of channels and the decline of other media, the power concentrations are becoming too great for liberal societies to tolerate. Where broadcasting grew up in less liberal communities, an opposite problem has developed: the power concentration around the wavelength has helped to emphasise the dominance of the élite which controls broadcasting and has exposed, as in the case of France, the proximity of that élite to the general apparatus of government. In both extremes broadcasting has simply developed, almost accidentally, more power than it was intended to have. To diminish this power, to limit it in any way, raises the whole question of cultural freedom all over again. No one is very clear where else the controlling authority over broadcasting should lie if it is to lie neither with the politicians governing the society as a whole, nor with the existing broadcasting authorities. Germany, in inaugurating its second channel, ran into a particularly fascinating version of this problem, because of the need to avoid dominance both by the federal government and those of the *Länder*. Holland met up with this problem and solved it, in a spectacularly original manner, by decentralising editorial power into a profusion of confessional and ideological organisations. In Britain, the symbol of the independence of broadcasting from government control was the licence fee – a source of finance mediated by government but outside government; the viewers and listeners purchased their viewing directly. Britain is large enough for the licence fee to support two television channels and many radio stations; the pressure for ending the monopoly of the B. B. C. was fed into a successful campaign for commercial broadcasting and now the discussion over the future of our fourth channel has brought out all the underlying paradoxes once again. Under the impact of broadcasting the ideal of liberty of expression, the ideal of individual political liberty and the dream of cultural democracy are strained to the limit.

There is a tragedy, a peculiar late-twentieth-century tragedy at the heart of all television. In every broadcasting organisation of the world, the problems of what to say and what to show, the fundamental cultural, artistic decisions, which should be taken at the very roots of a man's being, become institutional decisions, taken along the chain of a hierarchy. What I, as a broadcaster, want to do is transformed into what I may do. The professionalism of broadcasting, which we often like to speak about with an exclusive pride, is a body of practice partly composed of an inherited wisdom in evading or complying harmlessly with the rules of an organisation. All broadcasting is vested in hierarchies and the lines of command stretch upward through society. The editorial decisions of broadcasting are not made in the heart. They are made somewhere between the office next door and the Post Office or the Prime Minister, nobody knows exactly where. The position of the producer or editor in broadcasting is not similar to his counterpart in newspapers or in publishing, nor even in the cinema. The ultimate decision is taken somewhere in social space.

Almost everyone involved in this medium is involved in a long process of pondering over 'how far' he can go. But freedom of expression lives only at its own frontiers and the frontiers shift from country to country. In Ireland at present, for example, it is forbidden by law for broadcast journalists to do anything which might assist any illegal organisation and that prohibition is bringing about a slow corrosion throughout the journalistic departments of Irish broadcasting; one inhibition begets others. The same prohibition could exist in, say New Zealand, without being an important infringement of the scope of journalists. In Ireland, illegal organisations are at the centre of political events; in New Zealand, where for all I know, there are no such organisations active in political life, the same prohibition would be marginal and harmless. I am not judging the Irish politicians who may well regret the necessity of the prohibition; I am merely saying that any interdiction, applied within a medium, hampers the function of journalism. If I am free to say anything I want to say, except the one thing I want to say, then I am not free. In broadcasting, because of its highly institutionalised nature, a single prohibition imposed on a national broadcasting authority or within it, tends to corrode the whole output. A man who is sick in only one part of his body is a sick man. An organisation which can be trusted on any matter except the one vital issue of the moment, will gradually cease to be taken seriously.

The memoirs of prominent broadcasters of the past are studded with references to suppressions, to struggles for freedom from various restraints; radio and television were born in a nest of thorns. The whole culture of broadcasting has become corroded with problems of permission and prohibition. Yet I believe that at this moment in history, as we are becoming more fully aware of the problems posed by broadcasting and the threats which exist towards it, we can see a new series of opportunities arising to deal with these problems. We are reaching a turning point and it has now become feasible as the cable, the cassette and the communications satellite gradually turn from possibilities into realities, to re-establish broadcasting outside these traditional besetting anxieties.

If you examine any broadcasting institution today, you will find three points of frustration, at which, though differing in degree from country to country, conflicts and confrontations occur. There is in all cases an overall governing administration of civil servants, of politicians, or of distinguished lay men and women whose responsibility it is to lay down the long-term policy of a nation's broadcasting; in Britain, where we have two separate broadcasting systems, the B. B. C. and the Independent Broadcasting Authority, there are two such governing structures, which between them possess complete editorial power over all the broadcasting of the country, in radio as well as television. They form a kind of unelected double parliament making decisions on behalf of the entire society over the whole of the professional world of broadcasting; they can decide what resources to assign to drama, or to politics, or to competitive sport. They decide to what extent the scheduling of their organisations shall be competitive, to what extent the broadcasters are to aim at majority or minority audiences. Their powers are laid down by Act of Parliament. Every broadcasting organisation possesses such a body and it is the chief focus of power within broadcasting. I believe the time is coming when the decision-making processes of these bodies need to be opened up; their internal deliberations should henceforth be made public. It is as intolerable for a society to be kept in the dark about the long-range policy discussions in its broadcasting as it would be for it to be kept in the dark about the discussions of its national parliament. These are public processes and should be seen to be public. I go further and propose that the governing bodies of broadcasting organisations should be partly representative in nature; their members, or some of them, should be chosen as representatives of various national constituencies, regions, national minorities, trade unions, industry, the broadcasting professions themselves. I believe that at this highest level broadcasting decisions should be taken by people who are, to some extent at least, socially accountable. That would help to mark out the division between media power and political power in a society. We should know what pressures are being exerted by the politicians upon a broadcasting organisation and we should know how these pressures are being responded to. The pressures are perfectly legitimate if they are public. Indeed we all have the right to exert pressure upon the supreme governing bodies of our broadcasting organisations, as much as upon legislative bodies.

The second point at which the managerial structures of broadcasting should be opened up is the editorial level. Producers and editors require clearer definitions of editorial responsibility than exist at present in most broadcasting organisations, where important decisions are taken at ever higher points in the organisation. This is especially the case in Britain at the present time. A producer's independence – or clearly defined area of responsibility – is not a personal privilege accorded to the individual; it is a responsibility exercised on behalf of a public to whom those responsible for any programme should be clearly identified. That is why there must be a countervailing set of obligations alongside independence. The producer needs to be accountable for his actions within his programmes and there is therefore a powerful argument for the setting up of national communications councils where points of principle arising from editorial practice can be adjudicated. In Britain we have a Press Council which, despite its faults, has helped to improve the quality of our journalism in the last fifteen years. I believe that each society could benefit from having a Communications Council, stretching across all the media, which can hear cases of complaint and where producers and editors can explain themselves. A Communications Council needs to be utterly and completely outside the managerial structures of broadcasting and newspaper organisations. Producers and public should have equal recourse to it. It should have no power other than the eloquence of its own judgements. It is there to enable an aggrieved citizen, who might himself be a broadcaster, to make a point against those in the world of communication who might have deliberately or inadvertently wronged him. It would be a media parliament, not a media Government. Bodies of this kind are only in themselves conducive to an atmosphere of media freedom if they are themselves free and if the other elements of broadcasting control are also open to the society. In the case of the B. B. C. a kind of private court has been set up within the organisation of the B. B. C., known as the Complaints Commission, which is exactly – it seems to me – of the wrong variety; the producer has no individual right to put his case to it – he has no opportunity to dissent from its findings. The exact formulation of the rules and structure of a Communications Council are extremely important. The label itself is no guarantee that the body concerned is working towards a media democracy; set up in the wrong way, it can tend to cripple journalistic practice, rather than render it socially accountable.

The third point at which we should reconsider our broadcasting structure is at the point of entrance – of access to – the studio, the camera, the microphone. The time has come for us to recognize a citizen's right to broadcast as much as a citizen's right to speak in the open air or to publish. Of course, there are enormous practical problems in bringing this about. Who, after all, will decide who is to have or not to have access to the television studio? Does not the question of access merely beg all the questions of broadcasting control? I think not. I believe that every society now requires a broadcasting structure which is open to groups and individuals to use outside the professional canons of control and mediation of normal broadcasting. I believe also that this new 'access' which we need to provide should be access to the whole society, at peak hours on national networks, not only for a few odd moments on small cable networks or local radio and television stations. The real resource to which people require access is not only the studio and the wavelength but the professional experience and talent which is locked up inside broadcasting organisations. I think we might see a day when it will be possible for a group that wishes to transmit journalistic material, or educational or pure entertainment material, to hire the professional expertise necessary to turn their intentions into viewable programmes. We need to develop in all our societies healthy freelance broadcasting enterprises, outside the mainstream broadcasting organisations. They can make their own programmes or make them under contract for others. The time has come when people in all walks of life who find they want or need to participate in national discussion over economic questions, social problems involving national priorities of one kind or another, should be able to have direct access through television to the particular part of the public concerned.

We have a great series of opportunities opening up in the next decade of increasing the facilities for transmission in cable television, in local television and in some cases in extra national networks. In Britain we could have a fourth national network in this decade, two more in the 1980s, and five satellite channels in the 1990s. I believe we should ensure that wherever a new technical resource of this kind becomes available, we should create a new institution, with an entirely new structure to run and control it. Tidiness in media matters is tyranny. We need many different kinds of organisation, committed to differing policies, with different sources of finance. There is no essential sin in financing television through advertising, or through the licence fee, or through sponsorship, or direct government grant. We should draw on many different kinds of finance in television – because each is suitable for a different branch of the broadcasting culture. No broadcasting structure in any nation is ever complete, final, irrevocable. The organisational structures should always remain tentative, experimental, available for further change as the patterns of the society and its cultural and political priorities shift. At the same time, there need to be large national organisations with a good deal of finance at the centre of a nation's media life which provide a certain stability in the long term.

In Britain, I see a time when the B. B. C. would exist as the senior member of a group of national media corporations and a much larger group of small professional programme-makers. There would be one commercial network as now; there could be a separate local radio corporation; there could be a national federation of local cable franchises; there could be a national corporation involved in educational television empowered to negotiate with the other broadcasting organisations for transmission time. There could be a kind of television publishing authority free to experiment and commission in every area of television, with access to the new fourth national channel – the authority would operate at regional as well as national levels. We are fortunate in Britain in that the one commercial network brings in a vast sum of cash every year, most of which – it is now about 67 per cent – is mulcted by the Treasury. In Britain we could therefore very easily set up a Communications Revenue Board which would receive this special levy on the advertising revenue and redistribute it, or part of it, to the new media enterprises, as these are formed. In local radio, there is a new kind of advertising revenue available and this could be collected at a central point and distributed to local radio enterprises all over the country; the ability of a particular station in a large city to raise a great deal of revenue should be in no way related to the amount of cash available to that particular station for making programmes. There is scope for decades of institution-building in broadcasting. Our broadcasting structures should be as inventive as our programmes, and as varied.

I have arranged the three points at which I believe broadcasting should be democratised in reverse order of the priorities, as I see them. I think that access to the studio is more important and more urgent than the task of making producers socially accountable and more clearly independent; I think that latter development is more urgent in its turn than the task of making whole broadcasting organisations accountable at the level of the boards of governors. I believe, however, that steps forward should be made in all these areas. There is also, however, a fourth area in which progress needs to be made in this decade if we are to ensure that broadcasting develops in ways which help to develop democracy rather than retard it – and this fourth area I believe to be more important than all the others. It is also the hardest to explain.

The great debate about broadcasting has largely been conducted by politicians and broadcasting managers. A few academics have joined in from time to time. If you examine any other important area of social decision-making, you will find that there is a large, expert, though non-professional intermediate public involved in the discussion. If you discuss law reform, for instance, or problems of the medical service or the prison service, there are in every society, hundreds or even thousands of people well educated in the issues concerned and eager to discuss them. They work in quite different professions themselves, but they have long-term well-informed interests and preferences in these areas. The press, radio and television provide discussions of an increasingly sophisticated level on these matters. Schools teach children and adolescents the rudiments of the issues involved. In the case of the media this vital intermediate public is missing. Very few people apart from the politicians, the engineers and the broadcasters themselves (and sometimes very few of them) are aware of the nature of the problems we have been discussing today; very few are aware that we are approaching some important turning points in matters of media control and organisation. It seems to me important that in future we should encourage our universities to intensify their interest in the study of the media; we should attempt to create a branch of the humanities, parallel to social science and political science and sociology and involving elements of all of these, which would be concerned with the problem of the media in modern society. There should be far more research at graduate level into problems arising from the mass media. There should be far more learnt by students at schools and universities of the problems of media organisation. I am not here referring to journalist education which is spreading very rapidly even in Britain today. That has its limited uses. I am speaking of something at a much deeper level. I am speaking of the need for our societies to come to a realisation that in dealing with the media we are dealing not with problems of a few little organisations in London, or Paris or Amsterdam or Madrid, but with age-old problems presented in a new guise, problems which must be addressed with the same seriousness as problems of political organisation or of religious organisation in the past.

We stand today facing towards a half-closed door through which we can see, still clearly delineated, the ideals of a past age. We still can see the value of cultural freedom as this was enunciated in the last century. We are committed as a civilisation, whether we are pro-socialist or pro-capitalist, to the notion that ideas should circulate in society between individuals and groups without the mediation of state power. We do not always practise the theory but we all at times measure our practice against that purist model. I believe that we must do all we can, in all media, and in all political institutions, to prevent that door finally closing upon the ideal of freedom. It is a strange and terrible enigma which we face in broadcasting. We do not know precisely how to translate our own intentions into action. We do not know how to exercise the strange and vast new power which has grown up within our societies or whether it should be exercised at all. The only useful guide, in my belief, is the pure ideal of cultural liberty, to which we must constantly return as we construct and reconstruct our broadcasting institutions.

Chapter 4

The Finance of Television*

About ten years ago, people began realising that television lay at the centre of the debate about the nature of power in consumer-oriented societies. In looking back over that decade of discussion, one can pick out several quite different layers within the controversy, each of them having an important bearing on the way in which it seemed right for broadcasting systems to be set up, financed and managed.

The first discussion was essentially about the level of taste on which radio and television operated; it was still widely believed that television could, in a direct way, alter and improve – or degrade – the cultural condition of the people, provided that it was not permitted to seek out the lowest common denominators of taste. The audience could be grasped by the coat-collar and slowly hauled up the ladder of culture. It was the residue of a late Victorian vision of an educated, involved, popular democracy, and it had reached us via the Pilkington Report of 1961. But the underlying social optimism was disappearing, and the Manichaean opposition of high-brow and low-brow similarly evaporated. For a time it seemed that the problem had been settled, with television addressing its audience at a rather higher level than the popular press and the cinema had traditionally done. That was the case in Europe, at any rate; in America, it seemed,

* Published originally in *The Listener*, 2 December 1976.

television was irremediably corrupted by a process of irreversible commercialism. Television had only two available destinations, it seemed: in one direction, public service, in the other, advertising.

In the late 1960s, a new set of issues was to swamp this debate. Television establishments were seen to have emerged as new conglomerations of social power; they required to be scrutinised and rendered accountable to society as if they were surrogate governments, centres of unelective power. The Select Committee on Nationalised Industries examined the I. B. A., for instance, and concluded that it was not behaving entirely responsibly with its power. It was as if the old question of culture had been settled by some great concordat between the intelligentsia and the entertainment industry, but the terms of the deal had never been made public. This feeling was, and is, very widespread, especially among politicians, and has led to the reorganisation of a whole series of broadcasting systems – indeed, the setting up of our own Annan Committee in 1974 can itself be traced to this anxiety.

The emphasis shifted from broadcasting policies to broadcasting structures. The broadcasting institutions seemed to lie across the nations like mediaeval abbeys ripe for some great act of dissolution; they had somehow, behind our backs, manipulating their powerful engines of societal contact, acquired more power than they needed; they entertained, but they also were setting the agenda of political discussion; they held sway over the rise and fall of political personalities; they closed their gates and refused access to those they deemed to be nuisances or irrelevant to their politically centralist conception of society; they were sweeping away the moral beliefs of centuries without society's prior consent. In Germany and Austria, the politicians used the situation to carve up broadcasting administration between them. In Italy, a political spoils system simply encompassed broadcasting with little challenge until the R. A. I. monopoly collapsed after a constitutional challenge; in France, the civil servants, utterly ignorant of the ways of the media, held all the key positions.

There has now been a reaction, under a new banner – pluralism. The entire broadcasting system of France was swept away in 1974 and reorganised on pluralist lines; in federal countries, the issue was posed as one of sharing powers between central and provincial authorities, and the latter began to win; in

Germany, the constitutional court had already frustrated the attempts of the Bonn government to start up commercial television. The people of Bavaria actually supported the cause of broadcasting pluralism in a popular referendum. The Swiss have also voted on a complex set of broadcasting referenda questions, and opposed the attempts of their central government to take a hand in broadcasting control. The Italians have broken into (but not up) the monopoly of the R. A. I. New Zealand and Sweden, among other countries, have gone in for bouts of pluralism in designing new two-channel systems. The access movement has spread throughout the Western world, scoring successes in most places, and gradually creating the notion that there might exist some kind of natural right to broadcast as well as to receive. The greater the victories of pluralism, the more intractable became the underlying problem of who was to pay for the medium.

The issue of finance has always lurked about the discussion of broadcasting, but it was concealed in the prosperity of the 1960s, as television was turning into a major industry. Inevitably, as soon as television became an important part of industry, it became impossible to seal it off from all the problems and pressures of which industrial management consists. If it was to be protected against the pressures and insecurities of economic life, then advertising was an unsafe source of cash. If it was to be protected against political interference, the licence fee was a risky financial basis.

The fact of the matter, however, is that most systems are funded by the licence fee, a few – the richest – by advertising, one or two by both, and a large number by licence fee supplemented with an admixture of controlled advertising restricted to certain hours. The era of inflation dawned at a time when television-set ownership had reached the point of saturation in most developed countries; more money was needed at the moment when natural growth had ceased. Broadcasters have begun to realise that an absolutely fundamental change has taken place in their relationship with governments and society, and the shortness of cash is both the cause and the effect. The finance crisis raised, in acute form, all the old issues which had been felt to be partly settled – or at least fully aired.

The licence fee is fundamentally a tax; in the growth period of broadcasting, it looks a little like a payment by pioneers in set-buying. The broadcasters feel they are supplying a service to that section of the society who have chosen to become viewers and listeners. After saturation, however, television, as it supplants other media of information and entertainment, becomes a necessity of life, and the licence fee begins to look much more like a road fund licence than a dog licence – a universal, equal (therefore regressive) and highly politicised source of finance. Until 1960, the licence fee looked like part of a transaction between supplier and client; after 1960, it turned into a poll tax. Even though it represents only a small part of what people pay for television (the larger part going to the manufacturer or renter of receivers), it is the part which lies directly in the path of governments.

The Japanese have attempted to give the fee a different aura by allowing the national broadcasting organisation to collect the money for itself; there, there is a kind of legal fiction by which everyone assumes – and no one, so far, has challenged it in a court of law – that there is a contract between the N. H. K. and every individual who buys a television set. But even in Japan, there are extremely grave fears about what might happen if the licence fee has to be increased by a substantial amount as a result of inflation. The Japanese have been protected against this looming reality by the sheer size of their population.

The erosion of the original concept of the licence fee is most apparent in small countries. In countries like Holland or Ireland, there has never been a serious possibility of making a full service of programmes and distributing the signal throughout the difficult terrain simply on a licence fee. In the last decade, all small countries have already been obliged to allow large doses of advertising, the proportion growing since the great crisis of 1973. In France and Holland, the total revenues permitted to be raised by this means have been limited to 25 per cent of the licence fee, but there has been enormous pressure generated, simply as a result of manufacturers wanting more advertising time, and because of the extremely high rates generated by the monopoly position of the supplier and the restricted supply of the total advertising time on offer. In any case, the licence fee in small countries has ceased to offer any possibility of growth; Switzerland, Ireland, even Canada, have resigned themselves to the fact that any country with a population much smaller than that of an immediate neighbour can provide its people with a free service or two just by letting nature take its course, and importing the neighbours' signals. Ireland attempted to construct a second channel for itself, partly by extracting material from the three (five including those of Northern Ireland) United Kingdom channels which are currently received throughout its eastern seaboard, but do not reach the Irish of the west coast.

But eking out this scanty media existence by taking in the waste signals from abroad only goes part of the way. At some point along the line, the governments of middle size as well as small countries have to decide whether they can continue mulcting their populations of ever higher sums of money, in ever more difficult financial conditions, for television services which not all the people want to watch all of the time, and which some of them find it hard to pay for. Shortness of cash, with no opportunity to go out and find more, renders any institution open to countless pressures. In the case of television, it reopens all the old questions: the proximity of government to the electronic media is made painfully and constantly apparent, the temptation to grab larger sections of the audience in competition with commercial rivals – as in Britain – becomes harder to resist in the effort to improve the public acceptance of the entitlement of the licence-fee recipient to increased funds.

The pressure grows simultaneously for new sources of finance to be found, especially in the form of direct government grants, something which has always been resisted in Britain, but which begins, to many, to seem plausible as the lesser of various evils. The problem with a broadcasting organisation which receives direct government funding is that it loses its incentive to maintain its audience. In Canada, for example, the C. B. C. – which operates on a direct grant from Ottawa – has retained only about 15 per cent of the audience in face of competition from domestic and foreign (U. S.) commercial rivals. Many of the ideals of universalism which go with public service broadcasting tend to be whittled away under the new financial pressures which are exerted in the era of saturation coverage.

Ever since the fee was first introduced, a series of arguments relating to its efficiency, expensiveness to collect, sensitivity to government, have been advanced. What, however, is often ignored is the fact that, in broadcasting, no one has so far invented a system of payment in any country which enables a direct transaction to take place between receiver and provider. It is not like any other service or merchandise. The receiver does not choose what he wants to get; the provider makes decisions about what to supply according to socially approved, not client-based, criteria. In so-called commercial systems, the viewers do not, as the owners of commercial stations sometimes try to claim, choose the programmes; money is raised by selling the audience – a by-product of television – to advertisers. The size of the audience is related to various factors, including mainly the time of day and the programme content of competing channels; the price charged has much to do with the state of the economy, and only a little with the supply and demand for the material transmitted. In any case, in Britain and other countries where there is only one commercial channel, the supplier of audiences to advertisers is in a monopoly situation. In other words, all existing television is paid for by indirect means, in various types of non-transactional funding. Television is financed, not paid for. Each method of finance carries with it certain risks – moral, practical, fiscal, political – some of which are worth taking in some societies, but not in others. It all depends on the nature and state and stability of the society concerned. No method of funding is sacred, let alone good. All are worse.

The problem therefore arises of deciding on what basis one should think about the finance of broadcasting in societies like our own, in times like the ones we live in. Radio and television are very odd products indeed. Bakers and shoemakers do not run through the streets 'broadcasting' their wares to all and sundry, attempting to collect sums of money from the passers-by afterwards, irrespective of how many loaves and shoes each has picked up. We have, however, learned certain enduring facts or lessons about the business. First, that untrammelled competition leads eventually to a lowering of what most of us would agree to call 'standards', especially if the competitors are fighting for the same limited, unalterable sum of money while trying to gain the attention of the same audience – a deplorable, and currently inexorable, fact of life. Secondly, that there exist various quite different methods of raising revenue, which can be roughly grouped into two: advertising in various forms and under various controls, and the licence fee, collected and supervised in slightly different ways.

This suggests a principle: where media compete for the same audience at the same times (for example competing television channels) they should draw upon different kinds of finance, so that they are not drawn, through fiscal pressures, into worse forms of competition than those generated by programming itself. There is a complementary principle: where media compete for different audiences at different times of day (for example radio versus television, or radio versus, in time to come, teletext), they may draw on the same basic source of finance. Local services drawing on local advertising are not directly competing for the same money as national or regional commercial stations. There seems, therefore, to be a sort of rationale of pluralism in broadcasting finance which is parallel to pluralism in content.

Both major forms of finance are riddled with faults. Advertising is extremely volatile, leaping up and sinking with each twist of the trade cycle. Licence fee rises have to be prised from the grasp of unwilling governments at the most politically inconvenient moments. There is a total level of service sustainable by the licence fee in a given society which is exceeded – as perhaps it is in Britain at present – at great peril. The Germans are currently using an important new device for eking out the licence fee by removing collection from the post office, and putting the task of collection into the hands of their own computer-based organisation; this might save them several percentage points of the total sum, though it is too soon yet to know. What is vital is to ensure that no extension of broadcasting – such as local television, the fourth channel, teletext – is made to operate on existing sources of finance. The problems of broadcasting finance can be traced to the very roots of the system, and there seem to be no stroke-of-the-pen answers, only a patient manipulation of existing circumstances in the pursuit of a plural solution.

Chapter 5

Social Accountability
and Television*

During the great I. T. V. franchise reallocation of 1967, Lord
Hill, Chairman of the I. B. A., after a tiring day spent judging the
contest of impossible promises between rival consortia, is said to
have remarked in a dead-pan aside to an attendant journalist:
'The wonderful thing about it is that none of them wants the
thing for the money.' British broadcasting often gives the
impression of consisting of a number of highly determined groups
of people, all kneeling in ostentatious prayer before the shrine of
public interest. Never more so than in the last two years as the
evidence to Annan has piled up, much of it published. Nearly all
of it consists of public interest arguments for the granting,
extension or confirmation of private or institutional prerogatives.
For Lord Annan the task must be rather like looking for the 'best
buy' in an oriental bazaar.

We have a strange system of broadcasting in which all the
various elements can quite justifiably claim to be the guardian of
the public interest. First come the politicians who make and re-
make the institutions; they have been elected and as they

* Originally delivered as a paper to the Royal Television Society in London,
summer 1976.

repeatedly remind the broadcasters, they are the only people in the broadcasting process who have actually been chosen by the public. Next come the Board of Governors of the B. B. C. and the Members of the I. B. A. L. – they have been chosen by the Prime Minister or his predecessors to supervise the whole of broadcasting in the light of the public interest. Then there are the senior officials of the broadcasting organisations whose job it is to maintain balance, to spend public money with discretion, to ensure that the programme-makers do not endanger the organisation by self-willed disservice to the viewer. Next, the broadcasting professions, last ragged remnants of the autonomous bourgeois artists of the last century, the writers and journalists, directors and producers, photographers and designers, who, by freely exercising their skills and intellects, are supposed to be keeping unpolluted the wells of public information. Finally there is a new element entrenched though without statutory involvement in broadcasting, the critics and academic students of the media – they too are trying to infiltrate into the broadcasting set-up a notion of an independent public interest. All of these groups require freedom from restraint in order to perform their public duty; each of them tends to regard all the others as mere self-seeking vested interests.

It seems that there now exists a range of considerations in broadcasting which, by their nature, lie outside the existing institutional structure. I don't mean just complaints and grievances, nor the measurement of audience and audience reaction, nor the effects of programme content. I believe that there are important ways of looking at the media, television most urgently, which can only be done from outside. All the existing discussion, academic or journalistic, of the media circulates around the stewardship of the B. B. C. and I. B. A. and the Post Office; and it is in the tactical interest of those bodies that this should be so. However, we are today involved, as soon as we begin to look at the issues arising from broadcasting and the various impending technical extensions of it, in a most important intellectual phenomenon indeed, one which defies existing academic boundaries as much as it defies institutional ones. We are confronted with a new subject in fact, a new branch of the humanities, as well as a new set of policy issues. I want to say a bit about both of these.

If you listen to a group of telecommunications engineers

discussing their own problems in the 1970s, it is like listening to the followers of a Columbus or a Magellan discussing their voyages. Telecommunications is entering a new found land, as vast as any known one. Yet the kind of decisions involved, which are being taken willy-nilly, within existing companies, ministries, corporations, have to be taken at a longer range in time than the life of Parliaments, or the career patterns of individual civil servants or engineers. No one who takes any of these decisions stays in the same post long enough to carry the can. No committee even can stay in business long enough to absorb the information necessary to make an appropriate set of suggestions. What is required is some form of continuous assessment of the broadcasting process in the full context of modern telecommunications. Developments in the field of micro-waves, semi-conductors, the manufacture of optic fibres, waveguides open up a vista of tremendous potential, yet altering decade by decade and dependent for the courses taken on perceptions of society's needs. The existence, the supervision and the financing of the prevailing institutions of broadcasting at any movement in time are among the questions which require permanent review. It is easy to say simply that there needs to be some kind of permanent Annan Committee. The kind of continuous assessment needed does indeed in my view, necessitates some new kind of institution but it also necessitates a different intellectual context for the examination of the media. The media questions I mean are not merely futuristic ones in which the answers are Jules Verne type guesses cunningly disguised as arithmetic; they involve backward-glancing as much as crystal-gazing.

A communication medium is a set of technical possibilities, their physical manifestation evolving under the impact of actual usage. The imaginative demands made upon the resources of television have led to major technical changes. The techniques of wireless telegraphy of the 1890s turned into the mass medium of radio of the 1920s as military perceptions of its uses gave way to civilian ones. The British Post Office seized upon Marconi's invention because it offered a chance to create a system of communication immune to foreign or enemy interference. The invention turned into a mass entertainment medium when American businessmen saw the chance of using it as a kind of musical box which could reach remote audiences, a simple evolution from the already successful phonograph. Media are congeries of equipment resulting from a complexity of social needs interacting with theoretical developments.

The very first periodic journals of news emerged in London in the early seventeenth century – to take a much older example of a medium – when an improved postal service from Europe, an enlarged London population, a vast continental war and the establishment of the retail shop interacted with the development by William Jensen Blaew of an improved printing press in which the platen moved on greased rollers, thereby doubling the capacity of the average printing house. The weekly newsbooks which emerged from this development provoked a terrific public outcry against the effects of news on the public. Learned men wrote pamphlets and poems about the structural constraints on content, about the lack of impartiality and accuracy in the writers of news, about the sudden and arbitrary power of the publishers. Looking back with three centuries of hindsight, one can see that it was the medium which was the *effect* of various social trends. The alleged transgressions of the newsbooks provided an institutional target for a debate about the state of society. An intensification of legal controls on the press merely created a larger, more bureaucratic institution for later critics to attack. The study of the media should be a study of all the processes on which they depend; it is a multi-disciplinary study which defies the current subject demarcations of academia.

Media sociologists of the last decade have all treated the media as if the historic order of influence went: autonomous technical development → content → effect on audience. I believe the order should go: perception of a public → technical innovation → institutionalisation of the invention → development of special content → further perception of audience needs, and so on. Media are in constant transformation and flux. We are temporarily passing through a phase which is labelled 'mass media'.

I think a useful historical analogy for our situation is that of the 1850s in regard to paper. Rag-based paper had for decades cost a penny halfpenny a pound; the structure of the press revolved partly around that fact. Suddenly the price started to spiral upwards in the early 1850s, with the expansion of the American provincial press. The international price of rags had gone mad. Although it had been known since 1800 that paper could be made directly from vegetable substances, it was this rag crisis which brought about an acceleration of the development of a paper based on Silesian spruce and other plants. The price of paper dropped after a decade or so to a farthing a pound and cheap books and papers became plentiful. The cheap reprint movement began, the New Journalism of the 1880s sprang up, followed by the halfpenny daily press of the late 1890s. Mass education was accelerated by the advent of cheap textbooks. But the non-literary changes were perhaps as important: cheap wrapping paper brought about a consumer revolution, a transformation in retailing and therefore in the manufacturing of cheap branded goods. The changes in social life – ranging from transport and town-planning to shopping and postal services – which the present telecommunications revolution is likely to bring about are of a comparable order. Between 1801 and 1853 virtually nothing had been done to bring down the price of paper because existing institutions found the prevailing system convenient, the paper merchants and the government unconsciously conniving at the retention of the taxes on paper which helped to maintain a mutually beneficial media system. We need today, perhaps what was needed then, some kind of intellectual machinery in which our vastly more complicated communication issues can be thought through.

One important complicating factor is that some lines of development are abandoned often for decades before being taken up again. The telephone, for instance, started to develop as a medium of general rather than just person-to-person communication, in the last part of the nineteenth century. In a few cities there were round-the-clock news services, in Paris and London there was the theatrephone device by which you could listen to the dialogue live from theatres in London and Paris; there were concerts and sermons delivered by wire both to the home and to grouped audiences in public halls. But the telephone got stuck as a person-to-person device. Even today it reaches only half of the homes in Britain. By 1980 it will reach 80 per cent of homes and a new mass communication device by wire will become possible again; the trunk and switching capacity required to increase the figure from 50 to 80 per cent will bring about an increase in national bandwidth sufficient to run all sorts of additional services, dependent on the wire. The technical

distinction between telegraphy with wires and telegraphy without wires – on which the whole institutionalisation of radio and
television has been based – will gradually come to an end, or at
least remain a matter of geographical convenience much more
than a defining characteristic of the media concerned. In various
other ways, too, the distinction between mass and individual
communication will become blurred. Suppose you could send
out information services from a selected domestic telecommunications device into hundreds or thousands of selected homes
simultaneously, would that be broadcasting? or telephoning?
Sending out written material in words through the air has been
deemed to be a form of broadcasting, and the B. B. C. and I. B. A.
are being allowed to go ahead with Ceefax and Oracle, although
these are clearly competitive in the long run with radio and
television. Should this old line of development via the wire and
the telephone be encouraged precisely because it helps to usher
out the era of mass media, or should it be discouraged in order to
prolong the useful life of the institutions which have occupied the
electromagnetic spectrum for fifty years on the grounds of an
alleged scarcity of wavelengths?

I think, therefore, that I have started to define an area of study,
concerned with the evolution and impact of media: it is technical,
economic, institutional, professional and philosophical: it involves questions of political science and law, copyright and
industry; it has epistemological aspects and iconographical. It is a
long way from standard media sociology which has enticed the
study of media into a series of grand cul-de-sacs, one of which
might be labelled 'statistics', another 'methodology' and a third
'more research of the same kind needed'. The media are a
partially autonomous, partially dependent, strand of human
society, which require their own public conversant with the issues
involved, situated somewhere between the media professionals
and the general viewing public.

I believe I have also started to outline an area of policy concern
which encompasses and widens the traditional range of matters
with which scrutineers of the media normally concern themselves. Several schemes currently lie upon the table for institutions which would render the broadcasting system more
clearly accountable to the public. They all contain valuable
elements and I would guess that some new institution for

reviewing the broadcasting system as a whole will emerge within a few years. There is a difficult set of double-binds which have to be avoided in starting such a body: on the one hand if it has executive powers it will become a sort of editor-in-chief of all broadcasting which would destroy the independence of the broadcasting bodies themselves; on the other it must be more than a remote busy-body organisation which can be asphyxiated by the warm embrace of the broadcasting institutions. It has to have certain powers, especially in order to obtain information; it has to be statuory in order to be authoritative; its responsibility should be to the Minister but not over any other institution. One plan for such a body, a National Broadcasting Centre, has been devised by Jay Blumler at the T. V. Research Centre in Leeds, with my help, and I shall try to explain the bare outlines of our plan because I think we have tried to address ourselves to some of the problems with which I have been dealing tonight.

The Centre would have a number of day-to-day responsibilities currently discharged by our broadcasting system, such as taking on the task of counting the audience and measuring appreciation. It would also have a complaints division though this would not in the main use quasi-judicial procedures like the B. B. C. Complaints Commission (which would be closed down). It would have a governing body set up like the other broadcasting institutions although some of its members would be delegated from the B. B. C., the I. B. A., the unions and perhaps other relevant bodies. It would receive payment for its audience research activities and the government would pay it (perhaps out of the Television Levy, if anything is left in that fund after the fourth channel and the film industry have dipped into it) an equal sum with which to conduct its other activities.

The third section of the Centre would be concerned with the scrutiny of the whole of the broadcasting system. It would commission, largely from outside groups and individuals, a series of studies of media issues as these arouse. It would move from topic to topic over the years. It would study, for instance, audience comprehension of news and current affairs and the institutional processes which influence programme content. It would examine more regularly the financial state of the existing broadcasting institutions and recommend the raising of the licence fee or the Levy or on new forms of revenue. It would examine those internal issues which are often referred to in the press but never on the basis of complete and authoritative information, such as the role of co-production or covert sponsorship of programmes. It would, most importantly of all, look at the technical questions, cable, Ceefax, Viewdata, in the light of all the historic and economic issues on which they impinge. It would, in short, provide the kind of data which Government enquiries would benefit from.

Perhaps its most important responsibility would be to be open to public suggestion as to the kind of topic it should tackle, which could lie in the moral/philosophical area as well as the technical and economic. It could hold public hearings and discussions where these are appropriate and desired on what one might call the Mary Whitehouse range of topics. It would command only the power of its own eloquence, but it would be there to be listened to, not obeyed, but not simply dismissible by the broadcasting bodies. It is similar in certain respects to the Audio-Visual Institute in the new French broadcasting set-up and in other respects to the Canadian C. R. T. C. It is important that it does not appear to the broadcasters as a remote, nay-saying, punitive institution. Its activities should be fed into the public discussion of broadcasting; it should work through climate rather than sanction. It should enjoy lines of access to the broadcasting institutions at all levels, unlike the official Committees of the past which have had all their data processed by the hierarchies of B. B. C. and I. T. V. before it reaches them.

One question that remains is the fate of the traditional commission or official investigation in this proposed new method for reviewing broadcasting. Personally, I think the periodic grand review still has a place, once every twenty years or so, not as a long reviewing procedure, but as a short sharp enquiry of a few months' duration to recommend on specific legislation. Much of its evidence would come in future from the new Centre as well as from the principal interested parties.

Lord Northcliffe once said that the wider the franchise the more powerful the newspaper and the less powerful the politician. He had noticed an important communications phenomenon, that the larger the audience the more influential are the controllers of the flow of information. In the last few decades we have placed the most important media of our time, as well as a host of other important social and industrial functions, inside large quasi-feudal bureaucratic fiefdoms, centralised bodies run on hierarchial principles. There are very interesting and powerful reasons for the prevalence of this neo-feudalism in late twentieth-century society. The state-supervised bureaucracy is the characteristic institution of our period, as much as the family firm a hundred years ago. To the politician the great broadcasting institutions, in Britain and elsewhere, have become overmighty subjects, candidates therefore for the axe. I don't believe that simply chopping their heads off would achieve very much because the same phenomenon would quickly crop up again, with ten heads in place of one or two. A semi-formal machinery between society and broadcasting is, in my view, the piece currently missing in the jigsaw of broadcasting organisation.

Chapter 6

The German Television Producer and the Problem of 'Internal Democracy'*

I

The purpose of this paper is to examine a familiar problem, that of the dilemma of rights between the producer and the broadcasting organisation. I take one set of events which occurred in one western broadcasting system in the early part of the 1970s as an exemplar of a general problem; like all studies of one situation intended for consumption in other national settings, it faces problems of valid comparison.

There are reasons why Western Germany, despite the obvious differences from U.K. in its broadcasting structure, is a good and valid laboratory for study: Germany is a self-consciously democratic country, with a new national constitution still being tested in certain fundamentals by the pressures of political history; it is a country where there is a deep-rooted national belief in documentation, in the explicit deliberation of complex issues and in the

* Originally a research paper requested by the Annan Committee and commissioned by the International Institute of Communication, London. It appears in the *Report of the Committee on the Future of Broadcasting*, Appendices E-1, Cmnd. 6753-1, August 1977.

driving of dilemmas to their logical practical extremes. It is still looking for its sustaining national compromise, in many respects, and certainly the broadcasting medium with its 'balkanised' *Land*-based structures has provided an interesting area for testing the stability of new German institutions.

There is, as the Annan Committee and all its predecessors have become quickly aware, a power concentration at the root of the broadcasting medium. Most of the inquiries which take place in many countries from period to period have been occasioned by the evolution in a new form of this central and ineradicable vexation. In the early years of broadcasting systems the discussion about this concentration of authority tends to centre on the fundamental powers of politicians *vis-à-vis* broadcasting officials, on the division of interests· and powers between state-appointed governors and the 'professionals' working within a career-system. But as broadcasting becomes more sophisticated, more variegated, specialised, as layer upon layer of professionalism develops, especially within the television sector of broadcasting, so the central dilemma inherent in the power concentration moves towards the programme-makers. In societies which place heavy emphasis, in the prevailing public philosophy, on freedom of expression, on creative dignity, on the right to know and the right to speak and the other host of shifting, conflicting and imponderable rights, the producer inevitably becomes aware of the various double-binds in which he is placed: he is an employee but a creative worker, answerable to his own skill and conscience; he gradually elevates himself in his own scale of importance as his genre gains public recognition. At the same time he finds himself in a public firing line because his power (grown greater through the development of his skills) is unelective and apparently autonomous and unaccountable (in both senses of the word). He seeks shelter behind the massive doors of the very institution which has deprived him of his individual freedom in the cause of its own security on a higher political level. From time to time the creative worker within television – in any system, including occasionally those in Eastern Europe – will experience great upheavals of conscience leading to passionate conflict with broadcasting and other authorities. Such conflicts are latent within the very institutional structures of the medium.

Of course, from time to time, the supervisors of a given system will speak as if their problem has been solved. Sir William Haley, in a celebrated paper,[1] called the problem we are discussing 'The Central Problem of Broadcasting' and spoke as if the B. B. C. had, through its delicately balanced and finely tuned internal arrangements, dealt with the matter for good and all. He would probably agree that his analysis should not have been read as prophecy. The 'central problem' of broadcasting will sometimes seem to disappear as it is swamped in some larger and more urgent problem of freedom. In the 1920s the producer was less prone to the vexations it occasions because he was himself more thoroughly socialised by the central machinery, more cut off from the intellectual and social conflicts of his time – he was himself, it now seems, a part of the machinery by which broadcasting was withheld from general participation; he was, in a sense, part of the apparatus of order. In the 1960s, in Britain and Germany, but not in France, the producer was carried along by the growing tide of intellectual freedom in the surrounding culture – his task was to catch up with what was already happening. The 'central problem' shifted its location towards a tension between the whole organised medium and society. At the end of the 1960s the tide was out and on the beach one saw the jagged rocks of the unresolved problem of the producer; in Germany, as we shall see, the period from 1970 until 1974 was one in which the broadcasting institutions were beset by frustrated producers demanding their own special rights and freedoms in contradistinction to those newly won by the Administrative Councils of the institutions and by the politicians themselves. More recently the tide has moved in again, this time confronting the producer with the problem of this simple right of employment. Economic depression has buried the 'Redakteurausschüssebewegung' – the movement for producers' councils – it has not removed the fundamental problem to which that movement was addressed.

This paper will offer no solutions. It is intended to act as an emblem of the issue, not pretending that the problem is capable of solution in any broadcasting constitution, merely urging that it must form one cornerstone of any reform of any system, or of any rationale of a continuing system.

There exists in Germany a debate about the rights and duties of editorial staff going back to the period of reconstruction following the First World War. It was in the 1920s, a period when newspaper owners were at the height of their influence throughout Europe that journalists started to question the extent of the moral authority of newspaper ownership *per se*. Thus when the German ·broadcasting journalist˙ rehearses the familiar arguments which encircle him (whether the obligation towards 'objectivity' cancels out his individual rights of expression) he has fifty years of literature and legislation to draw upon.

It was in 1920 that the professional association of German journalists (*Reichsverband der Deutschen Presse*) placed in its constitution the avowed aim to bring about a new press law which would protect press freedom 'in the pursuit of its public mission'. A draft collective agreement was drawn up by the same organisation (though never enacted) which began by declaring that 'the content of a newspaper is exclusively the domain of the editorial staff'. The agreement went on to state that 'The Editor is not the Proprietor's representative but represents the global interests of the newspaper in relation to the Proprietor as well as relation to the editorial staff.' The union wanted to give the owner the right to publish his own views in his own paper only when signed with his own name: in other respects the views of the editor were to be those of the paper.

Two years later the Employers' Association of the German Newspaper Trade set up a joint organisation with the journalists (the *Reichsarbeitsgemeinschaft*) which was supposed to draw up a new press law 'in keeping with the times'. In 1923 this new body drew up a new collective agreement (in draft) which recommended the formation of editorial staff committees, elected under the law governing works councils, but when, in a further twelve months, a new draft law was actually offered to the public, the proprietors rejected it. The 1924 law would have provided editors with firm legal rights. 'Since the press has by its nature the mission and duty to defend the public interest, the Editor must not be hindered in his rightful defence thereof.' The proprietor was to be barred from issuing specific instructions to the editor. A fine of ten thousand marks could be imposed on anyone inciting

an editor to disregard his duties. The Ministry of the Interior
published the draft law at the end of 1924 under the title 'A Law
governing the rights and duties of Chief Editors of periodicals'; it
separated the spheres of owner and editor by instructing the
editor, to serve the public interest and adjuring the owner to
'determine the general political, economic and cultural policy
and line of the publication' only by writing to the editor. Clause 5
of this contentious and never-enacted law caused further opposition among the owners: 'Within the framework of the defined
general political, economic and cultural line of the publication,
the formulation and representation of its spiritual content is the
concern of the Chief Editor. He has the professional responsibility
for the content of the publication, regardless of whether he has
also undertaken responsibilities in accordance with the press
law.'

Although the spirited opposition of the employers finally killed
the legislation, parts of the draft were included in the general
Labour Law of 1926. The proprietor was not to 'violate the
conscience of the Editor', but to guarantee the latter's freedom to
determine the content of the publication in accordance with the
generally accepted line of the paper. 'The Editor is duty bound to
have the global interests and the tradition of the publication at
heart. Trusting co-operation between Proprietor and Editor
implies consultation in good time, particularly in difficult cases
. . .' The German journalists still pressed for a specific press law
to replace the much vaguer contract of employment contained in
the 1926 Labour Law, but the owners expressed themselves
content. As late as April 1933 the Journalists' Association were
proposing new drafts of a press law, which gave the owner the
right to define a general line, while firmly placing the editor in
the position of defending the public interest. 'Editors and
proprietors neglect their professional duty if they mix public and
private interests in a manner likely to deceive public opinion.' In
October 1933, however, a Nazi press law swept the discussion of
the previous decade into limbo, by making the State the sole
'Master of the Paper' (*Herr des Journals*) interpreting the 'public
mission' in its own way.

When the Federal German state was establishing itself in the
1950s, the discussion about the sharing of responsibilities between
owner and editor in the new German society started up again.

The Ministry of the Interior in 1952 published the draft of a Federal Press Law which emphasised again the public mission of the press but consolidated this by insisting that truth and accuracy were the basis of the newspaper's duty. 'The press may only publish what corresponds to the truth. It must not vitiate news by leaving out important facts or in any other way.' The owner was the man who set the general line, while the editor had total freedom of decision in regard to editorial content. The new Union of Journalists started composing counter-drafts, but these never achieved wide acceptance until an important conference which was held in 1962 in Cologne which finally ratified a statement of 'Guiding Principles regarding Internal Press Freedom'.

> The journalist fulfils a public mission. Therefore he has the right and the obligation to report on all events of public interest in words and pictures truthfully and to comment or criticise in accordance with his own convictions, within the framework of the basic attitudes of his newspaper. The journalist must not be forced to write anything that contravenes his own convictions. He must not be penalised in any way on account of the editorial line he has taken . . . The fulfilment of the public mission of the press requires legal guarantees. The responsibility and the editorial freedom of decision of the Editor must be stated as basic principles in a press law and protected against inadmissible intervention, particularly against pressure and corruption. The protection of professional secrets by all those working in the press must be legalised more precisely than it is in existing law. The Conference of German Journalists considers that the realisation of these demands is a precondition for the existence and development of free democracy.

The proprietors of the German press continued to resist any scheme to give legal backing to any statement which delimited the duties of owner and editor. The Union of Journalists had already given up the policy of working for a joint policy or collective agreement between journalists and owners which would have made reference to a sharing of duties, but when, in 1969, a new collective contract on salaries was drawn up, the Union again tried to insert a clause relating to a delimitation of

powers. The proprietors totally rejected this, their attitude
having hardened over the years. The newspaper editors, in their
collective agreement with the proprietors of 1968, accepted a
clause which merely said that 'the Editor must abide by the
guidelines for the fundamental attitude of the newspaper'.

During the 1960s, however, a wholly new strain of thought had
started to develop, one which infected the universities rather
earlier and more spectacularly than the press, the notion of a
more generalised liberation of the individual from the institutions
and within the institutions which had grown up since the Second
World War. A working group on press freedom was formed in
1968 which urged a new formal press law and offered a new draft
of a 'Law to Protect the Free Formation of Opinion'. It separated
the prescriptions for 'external' and 'internal' freedom. On the
outside the press was to be protected against excessive concentrations of ownership, on the inside by preventing too
hierarchic a relationship between proprietor and editor. The
Arbeitskreis wanted legal action against the limitation of competition between newspapers and simultaneously a prohibition
against instructions passing from the owner to any employee on
the editorial side. 'Particularly prohibited', runs this draft, 'are
individual instructions regarding the nature, content and length
of items and the demand that certain sentences or paragraphs be
cut, changed or included, or to publish or not to publish specific
news items.' The group, however, saw the contradiction between
the rights of property of the newspaper owner and their own
demands for internal freedom. The owner had the right to
protect his property to the extent of making all the senior
appointments and only at the level of owner could the basic co-
ordination between the editorial pages and the advertising pages
take place. Yet private ownership of the press was the only means
by which the press could remain separate from the state. The
world of German journalism began to wrestle with this fundamental set of problems and in one paper after another attempts
were made to create sets of 'statutes' which enshrined the rights
and the commitments of the editorial staff. It was not long before
journalists working in radio and television establishments began
to see how certain of the same problems affected their media,
even though these were not privately owned but operated under
laws which governed their 'public mission' and their whole

approach to public affairs.

One by one, starting with *Stern* and *Mannheimer Morgen*, German publications started to adopt *Redaktionsstatuten*, lists of rules under which the positions of owners and journalists were to be regulated. The term was later changed to *Redakteurstatuten* (that is, the position of the individual journalist) to emphasise the individual nature of these rights and obligations and their relevance to the autonomy of the journalist.

III

Freedom for newspapers, both internal and external, is a matter of private rights, guaranteed ultimately by the laws protecting private property; in the context of broadcasting it is matter of public legislation and public authority. In the context of post-war reconstruction, West German society was very clearly confronted with this inherent paradox and in building up its radio and television institutions made a set of careful decisions concerning the *locus* of editorial power.

The broadcasting institutions emerged from the power of the *Land* administrations and were governed by nominees of *Land* politicians, but the chief executive in every one of the organisation proliferating in the late 1940s was a single individual, an Intendant (=Director General) upon whom the various responsibilities set out in the law rested. The law setting up *Hessischer Rundfunk* (2 October 1948) for instance, stated: 'The Director General . . . will compose programmes in accordance with the laws.' In the later statute governing Z. D. F. (1961) Clause 22 states: 'The Director General is responsible for the totality of the programmes.' But the individual Director General was loaded with duties under the same set of laws, duties which he was obliged to carry out under the supervision of increasingly politicised Administrative Councils and Broadcasting Councils. The W. D. R. statute of 1954, for instance, says:

> W. D. R. must take prevailing general, scientific and cultural attitudes into consideration. The moral and religious convictions of the population must be respected. The ethnic composition of the area serviced must be taken into account.

News information must be comprehensive, independent and objective. W. D. R. must actively promote international understanding, advocate peace and social justice, defend democratic liberties and be committed only to truth. It must not serve any one particular political party or group, any particular community of interest, any one religion or *Weltanschauung* [Clause 4].

The Z. D. F. *Staatsvertrag* (=State Contract) provides the Intendant with the now celebrated almost Sisyphean task: 'The programmes of the station should provide viewers throughout Germany with an objective grasp of world events and in particular´ with a comprehensive view of German reality. The programmes should above all promote the reunification of Germany in peace and freedom and understanding between peoples' (Clause 2).

No newspaper editor has ever been appointed with so complex and so far-reaching and yet intangible an instruction. These clauses were never allowed to live a life of quiet and obscure piety; from the beginning they were used as painful comparisons for the realities of mass audience television. Time and again the Federal Constitutional Court found itself trying to grapple with cases which involved judgements of programme content in terms of these high-minded legal provisions. One major Area of consideration was whether every individual working within a broadcasting enterprise carried on his shoulders these exacting rules, whether the Director General was merely responsible for their comprehensive long-term fulfilment.

From the late 1950s the Directors General of German broadcasting found themselves between two millstones. Above them lay a set of increasingly political and partisan Administrative Councils, whose members were chosen according to the 'Proporz' or spoils principle and usually from the *Land* Parliaments. Each group of politicians wished to consolidate its influence in the sphere of broadcasting by choosing or manipulating the choice of senior personnel, including the Director General, the Chief *Redakteur*, the Head of Programmes and sometimes more junior positions in the news and political departments. At lower levels, there were demands for participation' in editorial control from journalistic and production employees who sometimes based their claim for power not upon their own sectional interest alone, but in order to 'restore' the *Staatsvertrag*, or preserve the basic constitutional laws. The rights of employees and their opportunities of participation were contained of course in the normal labour legislation of the state and were enshrined in the *Personalrat* or plant consultative body. For the journalists faced with the politicisation of the controlling bodies, and sometimes pursuing their own political predilections, there seemed to be an argument for some sort of special privileged assembly in which producers could have a say in overall policy. From the perspective of the Directors General, any special power given to the producers might itself be a breach of the labour laws (which give equal rights to all employees) but would almost certainly be challenged as itself being a breach of the broadcasting laws. No Director General, whether S. P. D., C. D. U. or neutral (this last increasingly rare), wished to run the risk of having his editorial duties, already extremely difficult to carry out, subject to the veto of some hundreds of journalists.

Under this set of double pressures, some Directors General tried to interpret their tasks very liberally: in one case (W. D. R.) the Director General listened to the new organisations which had sprung up among the staff while refusing to grant them official recognition. In other stations a much tougher line was taken. A vigorous, part-public, part-private debate broke out among the stations. The situation was complicated by the fact that all of them contributed by joint agreement in making the programmes for a single channel, and the departure of any one of them from an agreed approach could have led to the break-up of the unity of programme-planning. From time to time there were threats from the Director General in one *Land* that he would refuse to transmit in his area a given programme from another station which allegedly breached the rules of objectivity.

Throughout the decade of the 1960s, therefore, the German station officials were walking on very thin ice. Not too far in the background the newspapers were going through a vigorous debate about internal democracy, where editors were free to make whatever concessions were necessary to maintain the financial viability and harmony of their enterprises. Broadcasting was very soundly financed, with licence fee money and a certain amount of advertising, and was being recognised as an increasingly important medium of political and social communication.

German television was therefore in a kind of moral state of siege; but those who were guarding the central fortress were increasingly hirelings, as it were, of some outside ideological tendency. Before every meeting of every Administrative Council and *Rundfunk* – and *Fernsehrat* each political party began to hold a 'para-meeting' of all its supporters among the employees of the station concerned; these have become known as the *Freundenkreise* or 'circles of friends' who provide sources of institutional espionage for the party politicians, information to be used as ammunition in the real upcoming meeting of the Council or Committee concerned. The *Freundenkreise* discuss individual programmes after transmission and various internal problems relating to programme content; the para-meeting, which tries to follow the agenda of the meeting which it is shadowing, is called together by a local party chieftain in the station whose task it is to help his political faction gain what advantage it can in the coming month or quarter. Producers sometimes try to guarantee their programme budgets or ensure that their ideas for pro- grammes are later accepted by making sure that they have friends batting for them at the *Freundenkreise*. The system became more fully institutionalised during the period when the 'Proporz' system became most firmly entrenched in German broadcasting, between 1965 and 1970. One (non-political) Z. D. F. official likens the situation to that of a later Roman Emperor who has summoned the aid of a German barbarian chief who then decides to stay on in Rome: the Emperor is a little surprised but com- pletely helpless. Thus the producer finds himself stuck with a 'protector' who was intended only to help him through one small crisis.

This then was the background to the start of the wave of activity known as the *Statutenbewegung* (= the movement for producers' charters or codes) which began in 1970. In almost every station a movement sprang up to demand that statutes guaranteeing 'internal professional democracy' be accepted by the Director General, and the *Verwaltungsrat* (= Administrative Council). A general meeting was held of all who qualified as *Redakteur* including all freelance producers who derived the majority of their income from the station concerned. The management has frequently disputed whether these general meetings actually did represent the whole of the categories of staff concerned. These meetings then elected a *Redakteurausschuss* (that is, a producers' committee, abbreviated to R. A.) which attempted to acquire rights of negotiation over programme policy and senior staff appointments with the management. In one station, Südwestfunk, the Director General managed to stifle the movement in its very early stages by relinquishing certain rights to the *Personalrat*; having given away rights to a (statutory) body representing the entire staff he was unable to take them back again in order to give them to a narrower body. This device was not used elsewhere, although the major argument used by management against the R. A.s was that what they demanded infringed the rights of the *Personalrat*. However, the *Personalrat* is not supposed to be active in the area of *Tendenz* (= policy-making) and therefore a further set of complicating arguments exist involving the propriety of certain topics on the *Personalrats* agendas.

In December 1972 a large meeting was held at Ronneburg at which the R. A.s attempted to establish themselves as a federation having called together R. A.s from thirteen stations of West Germany and Berlin as well as the German Overseas Broadcasting Organisation. Only eight stations were, in the event, represented, many of the R. A.s wanting to avoid too intense a confrontation with their local managements. In each *Land* broadcasting institution events followed a different course. In N. D. R. (Hamburg) the Director General granted certain forms of access to the management which left the local R. A. feeling that it had won recognition. The Directors General of other stations had written to their colleague in Hamburg imploring him not to give way. The result was a convenient ambiguity (over whether recognition had occurred) which at least survived the enthusiastic period of the movement. In Berlin, at S. F. B., the management worked out a different constitutional device. The Director General set up, within the aegis of the *Personalrat*, a number of special *Berufsgruppenausschüsse* (= professional group committees) which were to concern themselves with the discussion of special problems which were relevant to each separate professional group within the staff. The producers formed one of these natural groupings and could therefore, within this framework, discuss problems relating to their profession (that is programme content and programme policy) as part of the work of the *Personalrat*. Most of the actual topics discussed by these meetings and the R. A.s referred to programme 'rows', alleged acts of capitulation to pressure by management, or censorship of parts of programmes.

The main issue presented to the management by the R. A.s was whether an employee working as a journalist or producer should be obliged to make or transmit a programme the tendency of which contrasted with his own views. In other words, the R. A.s were claiming in effect that in the era of 'Proporz' (the system by which many senior appointments were handed out on the basis of party affiliation) impartiality and/or objectivity no longer existed (some argued of course that it never had anyway): and therefore that the conscience of the programme maker could now justifiably take precedence over his duties as a servant of the broadcasting constitution of his station. As one communications lawyer in Germany pointed out, the R. A.s were wanting a situation in which only the Director General would be obliged to supervise programmes with which he disagreed – all others responsible for programmes would be free to follow their consciences. In most stations a compromise was worked out whereby producers were given formal permission to remove their credits from the end of a programme which displeased them, as a result of interference with its content from above.

The trade unions never embraced the R. A. movement, although they were obliged under the pressure of events to involve themselves in the problems of producers' rights. The Deutsche Gewerkschaftbund (D. G. B.) formally declared that it wanted no change which endangered the unity of representation of employees in broadcasting. The R. F. F. U. (union representing workers in broadcasting) together with the D. G. B. came to adopt a policy demanding 'parity of participation' on the Administrative Council between 'internal' and 'external' representatives: the Broadcasting Council (the senior body containing, in most *Länder*, politicians of all parties) would nominate half of the members of the Administrative Council and the unions and the employees would nominate the other half. The R. F. F. U. and the D. G. B. have, however, never agreed on the process by which union and employee representatives should be chosen whether by the union or the workers within the *Personalrat*.

From 1971 the political parties themselves started to adopt new policies for formal reform of the role of the producer within German broadcasting. The S. P. D. called several special meetings of experts to help formulate their policy and the F. D. P. set up a special investigation. A number of conflicting and rather complicated plans for change therefore lie on the table, all of them tending towards greater 'democratisation' of the existing system. The unions and the F. D. P. all want to limit the power of the Director General and indeed want to replace him with an editorial group of five senior directors and the unions want to add to this a new *Arbeitsdirektor* chosen in consultation with the *staff* representatives of the Administrative Council. F. D. P., S. P. D. and unions all agree that minimum rights of editorial participation should be enshrined in law and that producers should in all cases enjoy direct rights of communication with the Administrative Council. The central power of the Director General would therefore, in any of the existing sets of reform proposals, tend to wither away. Some of the existing plans involve giving the editorial workers the right to veto senior appointments (with a minimum two-thirds majority for the veto). All the parties have been involved in the discussions for reform, including the C. D. U. C. S. U., although this party has no specific programme of reform.

The fragmentation of power within German broadcasting has been more potential than real; structures have in fact greatly changed, despite the conflicting demands for change. The rise and the more recent waning of the *Statutenbewegung* should be seen in the context of the rise and fall of 'liberation politics' in the period from 1969 to 1973; many of the active participants in the movement were students of the generation 1966-9 who had secured jobs in broadcasting and had not yet exhausted their radical energies. But part of the impetus of the movement, which is far from dead in the late 1970s, although quiescent, came from a recognition that a declining press and a broadcasting system under financial pressure were narrowing the opportunities for political dialogue in German society. The appetite of politicians for power over broadcasting, once aroused and directed towards the higher institutions of broadcasting, had set off a complex chain reaction of demands followed by dismissals of the legitimacy of existing institutions, and this must take many years to diminish. The German broadcasting system had been located outside Federal politics but inside devoluted *Land* politics, where the spoils of political power are jealously guarded and fought over. Broadcasting was not so delicate a flower that it could not survive the attempted interference of the parties, but it found that the constitution had given it no buffer between its professional sphere and the legitimate political sphere except in the Director Generalship, which was itself vulnerable in many *Länder* to direct politicisation. Once the chief executive's power had fallen to political patronage, a chain reaction of demoralisation was set off within the organisation in which the special professional ideology of impartiality and objectivity was quickly asphyxiated.

Many German broadcasters have said that what was (and is) needed is a powerful Director General arising in an important station who, whether he was a political appointee or not, would have the strength to force the political parties backwards. Some expect a figure of this kind to arise in Z. D. F. in a year or two. If the sanctity of one Director Generalship could be re-established in a powerful location it might be possible for a new movement demanding a purer and revitalised attitude of detachment to spring up.

It is possible to over-dramatise the effects of a temporary politicisation of broadcast journalism; it does not necessarily result in the output turning to propaganda overnight, despite the attempts, from inside the organisation and outside, to exert influence on programme content. The most powerful and stable safeguard is the professional training of the journalists concerned. In Z. D. F., for example, Mr Rudolf, the Editor of News, is a supporter of the C. D. U., which helped to secure the job for him. His second-in-command, Mr Schattler is S. P. D., and their more junior associate is from the F. D. P. The three plan the major news programme of the Second German Channel amicably together every day. 'I'm a journalist first, an employee of a public television service second and a CDU member third', declares Rudolf. 'We are all in discussion all day and our decisions are made together in the light of our experience of news.' Each of them knows when a decision is being made which is political in inspiration and is not frightened to tell his colleagues when he feels this to be so. 'We don't have to go through the *pretence* saying we don't 'like' a programme, when we really have a political consideration in our minds', says Mr Schattler. The political affiliations and predilections of editors are therefore very exposed when they do come to interfere with a programme decision; there are fewer opportunities, some would claim, for political pressures to be covertly exercised. But few broadcasters in Germany would argue that the 'Proporz' system has been an *a priori* bonus for radio and television; at best it has been a political expedient which has failed in its primary objectives. It if could be wished away without the wisher losing his job, then it would disappear overnight.

IV

German broadcasting has depended for many years upon an enormous (and fairly prosperous) army of freelance producers, directors, writers and journalists. It has been estimated that up to 100,000 people have lived or partly depended upon freelance earnings in German radio and television. Technically a 'free-lance' was anyone whose contract specified a 'fee' rather than a salary, although several thousands of such people operated (by working in several stations simultaneously) on a more or less regular basis. Broadcasting work is geographically spread widely in Germany, providing multitudinous opportunities. Many of the freelance producers have always been treated as if they were regular employees for whom no established post existed. Much of the flexibility and dynamism of German broadcasting has resulted from the widespread and well-established use of the freelance system. In the period of inflation and economic strain which began in the early seventies the German freelance began to find that his standard of living was was under threat. The salaries of regular employees had risen every considerably but the successful freelance whose total annual earnings had often exceeded those of his staff colleagues doing similar work now found that he was slipping back. The purchasing power of freelance earnings was perceptibly falling. Within the broadcasting professions the freelancers began to become more militant; as the discussion about 'producers' rights' developed it became apparent that the freelance, now working against market forces, was more vulnerable to institutional pressures than the staff man.

The whole issue of the security of employment of freelancers became inseparable from the problem of freedom of expression for creative workers in broadcasting.

In August 1976 the case of Ute Diehl, a freelance producer who had been working regularly for Hessischer Rundfunk on educational programmes, was brought before the courts. Her services had been suddenly terminated, as an economy. She established that she was not in fact a freelance; the law decided that, using the criteria of personal economic dependence, her obligation to work office hours and the involvement of a specific place of work, the nature of her employment was not freelance at all. An avalanche of lawsuits followed all over Germany from freelance producers who had been working regularly (though not necessarily full-time) for a given station. W. D. R. and N. D. R., two of the most important television establishments in Germany (one might say in Europe) found themselves particularly vulnerable. Other stations had suspected the legal situation for some time and had been deliberately making their freelancers work irregularly and haphazardly. At N. D. R. and W. D. R. a high proportion of the freelancers found themselves eligible to sue for firm and secure employment. The situation of the freelance, so the law now ran, was very similar to that of the casual dockworker in the ports; regular employment conferred a high degree of legal security.

One prominent freelance, Harun Farocki (see Note on Sources below), has described the German freelance producer as 'the last remnant of the autonomous bourgeois artist'; radio and television had existed for many years by convincing large numbers of hardworking but mediocre employees that, in working without security, they were somehow 'artists'. That is what attracted them to the life of insecurity. In fact only a tiny minority of creative people in broadcasting were genuine 'artists' for whom complete detachment from an institution was essential. Under the pressure of the great inflation of 1973-5 the German freelance system discovered its weakest point and started to crumble.

The stations on the whole decided to face the situation quietly, waiting for the freelancers to sue for secure employment one by one. For the rest of 1975, many stations decided to offer no more freelance contracts at all, in an effort to establish legally that many freelancers were genuinely casual and unattached workers. Freelance work would begin again in 1976.

The archetypical case was that brought by a trombone player in one of the broadcasting stations' orchestras; he was a very bad trombonist and the station had fired him after many years of service as a holiday relief instrumentalist. He explained to the court that he had always been an incompetent trombonist, but had obtained several months' work per year nevertheless. He won his case and has now to be employed permanently for the same number of months in each year as he has been employed 'freelance' in the past. The R. F. F. U. had long pursued a policy of transferring as many regular employees as possible to staff status. The stations now, however, have found themselves confronted concentratedly with the logical culmination of their policies of many years.

The movement for producers' right has therefore found itself swamped by this issue of the freelancer which has diverted producers' anxieties and tended to conceal without either resolving or eradicating the problems to which the producer's work force had been addressing itself in the period 1969-72.

Sources

Most of the information (and opinions) comes from conversations with officials of broadcasting institutions in Germany and German broadcasters. The specific references are often from newspapers and magazines which are not easily accessible outside Germany. However, the *Statutenbewegung* has generated a considerable literature of its own, much of it repetitious and ephemeral. What follows are the titles of works which contain most of the *loci classici* of the discussion and main texts.

One of the best guides to the ideological conflict among media researchers and professionals in Germany is a collection of essays edited by *Ulrich Paetzold* and *Hendrik Schmidt*, *Solidarität gegen Abhängigkeit: Auf dem Weg Zur Mediengewerkschaft* (Darmstadt: Luchterhand Verlag, 1973).

Most of the actual documents listing the demands of print and broadcast journalists for internal rights in the first period of the movement are contained in a collection edited by *Ansgar Skriver*,

Schreiben und schreiben lassen – Innere Pressefreiheit Redaktionsstatute
(Müller Verlag, Karlsruhe, 1970). This book also contains a
good deal of background historical material. The historical
documents quoted are referred to in *Marie Matthies, Journalisten in
eigener Sache. Zur Geschichte des Reichsverbandes der Deutschen Presse*
(Berlin: Colloquium Verlag, 1969).

The most up-to-date account of the state of play of existing
policy among the German parties and unions is given in an
unpublished paper by *Hendrik Schmidt* delivered to the Rundfunk
Commission of the German S. P. D. in July 1975. He is also the
author of *Kommunikationspolitische Alternativen?* (Berlin: Volker-
Speiss, 1972). The problems of the freelance workers are well
described in one of several contributions to *Filmkritik* by *Harun
Farocki: 'Notwendige Abwechslung und Vielfalt'* (August, 1975) pp.
360–69.

One of the many activist – ideologists of the movement, Otto
Wilfert has circulated a useful paper entitled *Innere Pressefreiheit in
Funk und Fernsehen – Der praktische Versuch, aus einer Zwischenbilanz
für die nächsten Jahre zu lernen* (undated). The R. F. F. U. trade
union has published two relevant documents, *Redakteurausschüsse
und Personalräte* (September, 1974) and *Neue Mitspracherechte für
Arbeitnehmer in Hörfunk und Fernsehen* (October, 1973).

The Redakteurausschus in Cologne has brought out an
informative (and argumentative) bulletin of its own entitled
R. A.–INFO, copies of which can still occasionally be located.
There are scores of internal documents emanating from broadcasting institutions all over Germany, but one of them, written by
the Intendant at Z. D. F. and dated Mainz, 1 December 1972 to
all 'Mitarbeiterinnen und Mitarbeiter' contains a very clear and
characteristic statement of the position of employees in German
broadcasting as seen from the perspective of existing management. Another valuable statement by management is a paper by
the Administration Director of W. D. R. (Cologne), Friedrich-
Wilhelm Freiherr v. Szell, *Meinungsfreiheit in Rundfunk und Presse
aus der Sicht der Verfassung*.

For general comments on the evolution of the movement from
1969 to the present day (including the new problem of the
freelance) one of the several magazines published by the German
churches on broadcasting affairs is greatly recommended, *Kirche
und Fernsehen* (published by the Protestant organisation E. P. D. in

Frankfurt). The *Frankfurter Heft*, a monthly magazine, has also published a number of useful texts on the question of 'Proporz' and 'Innere Pressefreiheit'. The discussion paper on broadcasting topics published by the Catholic Institute for Media Information *Funk–Korrespondenz* (Cologne) has followed very closely over the years the debate between the stations on 'programme guidelines' and is an important source for official statements and other 'Texts'.

One of the most valuable sources of statements and policies is the script of a television programme transmitted on 14 April 1973 by the Third Programme of W. D. R. (Cologne), *Pressefreiheit – für wen?* The *Frankfurter Rundschau* as well as the ecclesiastical papers referred to above have followed the employment problems of the freelance with detailed attention.

Chapter 7

Management and Creativity in Television*

It is often asserted that the special restraints which encompass broadcasting are the result of spectrum scarcity, of the fact that the medium is of its nature in short supply; society, runs the familiar argument, must be protected against the potential wilfulness of those who might use this means of expression for, as it were, personal ideological gain rather than the general public good. I have never completely understood this argument partly because broadcasting outlets have in this generation become far more plentiful than printed ones but mainly because the idea of separating expression from creativity, and thus of building a kind of Janus-faced ideology *into the medium itself* has always seemed to me to be a hopelessly idealistic endeavour. It has meant that the people at the heart of the medium, closest to the techniques, are obliged to relinquish the privileges and the responsibilities which exist alongside all other forms of creative and expressive activity.

I should prefer to re-run that argument in a slightly different way: radio and television are media in which gubernatorial and managerial activity is fed through the technology. The physical

* Originally delivered as a paper to the Manchester University Symposium on Broadcasting Policy, March 1977.

shortage of spectrum may or may not provide adequate historical justification for this. The controls which society exercises over these two media flow through the provision of technical facilities. Unlike the press and the cinema, broadcasting is not free within the restraints provided by law; broadcasting is subject to a complex, far-reaching set of controls which operate in a kind of mesh. There is a point at which government offers sections of spectrum in exchange for promises of editorial restraint, for obligations of geographical coverage and subject balance. There is a further level at which space within a schedule is made available for prescribed categories of material deemed to be suitable for viewing by a mass public at different times of day. There is a level at which film crews and studios are made available in exchange for detailed promises about the purpose and nature of programmes. All of the technical resources arrive weighed down with prescriptions.

There is no commercial transaction between provider and receiver in television to offer counter-pressures to the lines of physical control. Nowhere does the public undertake an act of consumer sovereignty. In commercial systems of broadcasting the transaction is between a secondary supplier and a secondary purchaser, leaving the programmes subject only to non-transactional bargaining between creative workers, management, governing authorities.

The social controls flow through the systems into the minds of creative workers. There is no area of social space separating out the different roles played by different individuals within the system. As Lord Windlesham[1] puts it:

> The writer or producer may believe . . . that he is responsible for *his* programme, and that once its main lines and its cost have been agreed its content is his affair. At the same time the B. B. C. Governors, members of the I. B. A., directors of a programme company, or executives within the organization, may regard it as something for which they have formal responsibility, and consequently as *their* programme . . . for neither group can afford to hand over all its responsibility to the other.

Note the use of the words 'neither group can afford to hand over all its responsibility'.

The system we have devised provides a large number of people, all of whom regard themselves as being involved in making television possible, with a variety of mutually abrasive roles. At each level the purpose of the system has a different *appearance* and a different set of bargains is demanded. All of these roles are positive in the sense that no one is trying to prevent a given programme happening: rather the reverse, within the system everyone is trying to make the programme happen. Power over the programme exists at every level. Bargains are made at every level and between every level, exchanges of pressure, as it were, compromises which render the effective discharge of roles easier. Precedents are established and then slowly eroded as different sets of circumstances arise. Increasingly the system is internationalising itself, under financial pressures, and the exchanges which occur involve a larger canvas of social inhibition and commercial opportunity.

We have a system of television which, if judged by the standards of other media and other periods, is over-managed. Producers tend to see the system (when a critical mood) as over-bureaucratised rather than over managed; what they *feel* is that the procedures concerning the deployment of resources and the establishment of schedules are over-long. That complaint may have substance. What they less often draw attention to is the way in which the system obliges them to play a constant series of roles, like pieces on a chess-board, some of which have more freedom of movement than others but all of which are obliged to stay in the same game. The much discussed 'Kensington House Document' (produced during the Annan Committee discussion by a group of B. B. C. documentary producers) summarises its criticisms of the present procedures of the B. B. C. by saying that 'the structure that controls, initiates, plans and finances programmes is over-elaborate, and should be simplified'. Perhaps it will be simplified; what the Kensington House group proposes is a regrouping of skills into smaller production units. They do not see the connections between the range of frustrations and the regulatory system as a whole. The Kensington House document assumes that the B. B. C. as a whole is totally free, that the restraints have grown up inside; that the bureaucratisation is in itself the evil to be eradicated rather than the result of the institution's efforts at self-protection against the outside. The pressure for access says the document, is a sympton, 'a desire that broadcast systems should be more versatile, and those who produce programmes should be in closer touch with an area and its people'. Is broadcast management of the same *genus* as industrial management; can the notion of reorganisation be applied with the same hopes? Broadcast management is the internal counterpart to the regulatory system, the means by which social controls filter through the provision of resources into the creative processes.

The B. B. C. Director General Sir Charles Curran has built up a case for the present departmental divisions between News and Current Affairs in the B. B. C. first upon technical factors.[2] 'I start by saying that the nature of the flow of news material – constant, relentless, with inbuilt editorial imperatives – dictates the organisation of separate units for news, and for current affairs.' He goes on to reinforce this with a consideration of the needs of scheduling: 'If there is a daily flow of material . . . there has to be a regular daily pattern of programme spaces into which the news will fit. There is no point in building up an enormous overhead of daily reporting and then to find oneself without sufficient outlets either to justify the original outlay or to satisfy the people who are doing the reporting.' Later he says that 'the shape and character of programmes has to be conditioned by the relative rates and volume of flow of material and the organisational forms which follow from that . . . In a single organisation like the B. B. C. there must therefore be a single approach to these matters. Nature abhors a vacuum and a unified organisation abhors inconsistency.' I would suggest that Sir Charles makes very clear the connection between the organisation's view of technical exigencies and its approach to kinds of programmes and the organisational means by which these must be obtained. These divisions and departments *imply* in themselves a kind of ideological outlook. 'The whole concept of our establishment depends upon our support of Parliamentary democracy . . . The news programmes are intended to provide the participants in democracy with the material which forms the ground of the variety of their opinions.' The internal structures flow as an inevitable consequence of the social role of the broadcasting institution; broadcasting is not separable from its institution or its role. There is no way into the package. As a *package* it is satisfactory. What it does not allow – and the managerial systems are the means by which this is prevented – is the seizure of resources for individual expressive purposes. Sir Charles of course was speaking specifically about news, but his general line of argument, loosened to be sure, would apply to Kensington House, the regions and the I. B. A. commercial system as a whole.

In the I. B. A. system, of course, the separation of powers is made more explicit. The Authority itself is regulatory rather than editorial though it has in recent years been at pains to assert and reassert that it *shares* editorial control, both positively and negatively, with the programme companies. It can enforce its view, should it develop one, that a given programme is doing too much of one thing or too little. It has over the years established ever-fuller implications of its duties under the 1954 and 1964 Acts. Indeed the whole logic of the strictures of the Pilkington Committee (1960) against British commercial television was that the I. B. A. should encroach more completely into the terrain of editorial management.[3] Both systems in Britain, though different from each other, have learnt that to discharge their regulatory responsibilities they must mingle administration with editorial control, and strike bargains with the producer which effectively remove from him the ultimate responsibilities of authorship of the product. The producer is a caste within an organisation, rather than a profession working directly upon a technology.

It is interesting how a similar set of realisations has been dawning on television producers and television observers throughout the continent. Television has become associated with certain repetitive forms of frustration against and also on the part of management. Each system produces its own version of the double and triple binds in which the process of programme-making is drifting. If you take even a country which has built its system upon the most extreme forms of pluralism, the Dutch, you find certain forms of accumulating resentment against the complex power concentration which has come to rest at the heart of the broadcasting process. In the Netherlands editorial control rests in the hands of a number of ideologically and confessionally diverse programme companies, each of which is creatively sovereign; in these the source of the tension is precisely the ideological orientation itself. The producer is not free in the Dutch system because he is there to support one of the registered 'pillars' of the pluralist system. There is of course a much wider degree of public involvement in broadcasting but that does not lead to more creative freedom nor does it lead in itself to a reduction in the extent of managerial involvement in the product. The Dutch system is much freer in many ways, but it has not discovered how to turn the producer into an author.

One topic to which the sociological literature of broadcasting makes frequent reference is the separation of selves, of identities which takes place within broadcasting work. There is a gap between what a person is and the purposes to which he allows himself, in the course of his working arrangements, to be assigned. The producer takes on a series of roles which are, as it were, invented for him by the broadcasting body, which collectively become his career. At different points along the line between enrolment and resignation he finds himself considering the gaps and overlaps between his own identity and those roles which he has played out, in the course of producing different programmes or working in different departments. Given the constraints within which broadcasting operates it is inevitable that this series of inward confrontations should be stronger in the various professions of broadcasting than in the academic or newspaper worlds. Looking back towards the earliest days of the B. B. C. one can see, in autobiographies and diaries, how this phenomenon began to grow as the sheer social power of radio and then television began to be felt in the world outside and to filter back into building. It became ever more important for the editorial processes of broadcasting to be founded upon a set of ritual acts on the part of the programme-makers, which amounted to an abnegation of self, a total refusal to allow the claims of conscience, of preference, even of personal interest to come before the objective requirements of the task. Professionalism in broadcasting in fact came to mean the ability to do just that, to repress all but the physical, intellectual and increasingly the emotional skills which responsible broadcasting production demanded. This tension became most apparent with the development of the film director as the most important single figure within the world of factual programmes. To read Mrs Goldie's book of memoirs[4] is to see into the anguish inherent in this bifurcation of self: the very criteria of success and failure become confused in the process. We read 'That Was the Week That Was' was removed from the air in abject disgrace because its producers could not be made to see where the Corporation's (and society's) laws were drawn. Working within the pressures against being oneself in one's programmes is itself the training school of professionalism. The task is to observe the skills developing around one and apply them to the raw material of a world which passes through the producer's hands but which he must not openly manipulate. The television management in the early 1960s for a moment found that it had isolated the virus of power itself; to touch it was perilous. Dealing with it consisted in producing procedures acceptable to politicians and meaningful to broadcasters in their role as public servants.

This has been precisely the problem which has beset German broadcasting management for the last six or seven years. In the German system with its fourteen separate entities, a double system of Broadcasting Council and Administrative Council filters the pressures from the provincial Parliaments into and out of the business of programme-making. Between the outer structures and inner management there sits the lonely figure of the Intendant, who, acting quite alone, has to reconcile all pressures above and below. The greater the pressure of the politicians above him to control programme content or ensure that internal power is fairly divided up among adherents of their various parties, the greater the pressure from the producers for more individual editorial autonomy. The long saga of the producers' rights movement (see Chapter 6) has left a residue of greater individual intellectual leeway for producers, but this movement gathered momentum partly because politicians clamoured for more direct control of the institutions within the A. R. D. and Z. D. F. systems, and the producers abandoned the obligations of neutrality while watching management being pushed in one political direction or another. The Intendantship was all that stood between the two sides. But in Germany there exists a very large freelance segment of broadcasting, consisting of people who have built up temporary working relationships with all of the diverse elements within the German radio and television set-up. It was this vast army of detached workers who constantly kept alive the idea of the producer as an autonomous intellectual, a much more numerous group than their counterparts within British broadcasting. The severe financial problems German television in recent years have greatly depressed the position of the freelance producer and all the other unattached technicians and artists in German television. But more than the financial position, the sheer demands placed upon the system by the needs of management, to resist, evade and co-operate with the political forces, have meant that German television is taking a very similar road to our own, towards managerialism as a solution to the problem of creativity within a socialised medium. It is at best an interim solution, the temporary nature of which is apparent from the very frustrations which it breeds.

Perhaps the most interesting of the efforts to deal with the problem of creativity and management is in the new French broadcasting system created by the law of August 1974. The system addresses itself of course to the specific problem of French society, the difficulty of achieving through consensual politics a sufficient basis for building secure and independent broadcasting structures. None the less there is much to be learned from certain elements within the new French structure. First of all, the producers, when the French call réalisateurs (producers are rather different creatures and so are rédacteurs) are all freelance, apart from those who work in news. They are free to work for any of the five programme-making groups in French television: the three channels, plus the French Production Society (which makes the more complex and expensive programmes on behalf of all the channels) and the National Audio-Visual Institute, which does research, holds the archives and makes programmes of its own about the media and related problems. A réalisateur is accepted as a member of the profession of programme-maker after his name goes on a list the composition of which is decided by a committee consisting half of television management and half of trade union representatives; there are firm objective criteria by which an individual may qualify – so many hours of work transmitted, so many productions working as an apprentice, etc. The profession is therefore a loosely regulated one and its overall size can be limited to ensure that the market does not become flooded. However, the programme maker is basically freelance and cannot be guaranteed work or pay if his ideas are not accepted. He has a market consisting of five major purchasers, plus, of course, dozens of medium-sized production companies who also feed programmes into the French, and other broadcasting systems. There are many difficulties with the system.

However, in conditions which had made it impossible for a broadcasting system on the conventional European pattern to operate in France in the 1960s and early 1970s, the French have found a way of operating a managed but competitive broadcasting system in which the programme-maker operates as a free intellectual.

Everything has its drawbacks, as Sam Weller would say. If all programme-makers require is an utterly secure position until retirement then you have managerialism plus creeping bureaucracy leading I suspect to creative stagnation. Together with that goes a form of anomie which some find debilitating and distressing. The long-term symptoms are atrophying schedules and a decline in innovation. The second choice is institutional compartmentalism perhaps along Dutch-type confessional lines which tends to have all the socialist producers working in one small company and all the conservative producers in another, all working in a kind of plural harmony. That has enormous creative advantages but can be intellectually constricting, especially in a small country. The third is regional federalism when it becomes utterly impossible to keep politicians' meddlesome hands to themselves; the producer can acquire sometimes more power within this system if he happens to be willing to spend his time in politics as well as television; the German system is certainly more open than our own in Britain, more people know more about what is going on and there are so many more places in which developments are occurring, in a country without an effective capital. When cash is plentiful the producer is in a good position to sell his ideas to one of many programme controllers. But he lives in an atmosphere generated by politics; politics is everywhere, in the choice of a researcher, of a subject, of an interviewee. There is, however, my last example where the producer makes all the vital existential choices; he works alone in a system in which the freelance in not a fringe luxury, a professional excrescence but where broadcasting is built around the freelance programme-maker, and helps him to make his choices, but the system is also repressive and sometimes arbitrary, leaving the producer to take the brunt of the risk entailed in broadcasting. He is ultimately unprotected as an individual against the tyranny of audience vogues, against the whims of programme controllers. But he addresses himself directly to his society; he speaks in his own voice; he is as good as his programmes; and he must always have another profession to turn to if things turn sour.

Personally I would borrow heavily from the French system if asked to design the broadcasting system of a developed country entirely from scratch. Unfortunately the condition of scratch does not exist and I would opt for a gentle grafting of a freelance sector onto our existing system. In that way one could help to mitigate the faults of over-management, perhaps without throwing away the stability, the learning from collective experience and indeed, the kind of diversity which *can* be contained within the British system. Its great weakness lies in what Tom Burns calls the 'expropriation of commitment',[5] that diminution of the ego which makes an act of self-expression less meaningful than it should be. There is something to be gained from a broadcasting system in which you resign after *every* programme.

Chapter 8

A Maturing Telocracy – Observations on the Television Coverage of the British General Elections of 1974*

A general election campaign ought to provide the ideal testing ground for theories of media influence: an election is a political set piece with skilled performers, an organised audience ready to take concerted and measurable actions at a given moment. The evidence for the 'who', the 'what', and the 'to whom' is virtually public from the start. But elections in practice have been notoriously difficult areas for media study: the lessons from one electoral situation are difficult to transfer to another; the periods between elections are normally long enough for the theories, conceptions and methodologies to shift significantly and the researchers to move on to other fields; the great techniques of propaganda itself are, many of them, inapplicable to the short period of time in which electoral battles reach their peak. 'A campaign is the simplest, most imperfect form of modern

* From *Changing Campaign Techniques: Elections and Values in Contemporary Democracies*, edited by Louis Maisel; reprinted by permission of the publisher, Sage Publications, Inc. Copyright © 1976.

propaganda', wrote Jacques Ellul, 'the objective is insufficient, the methods are incomplete, the duration is brief, pre-propaganda is absent, and the campaign propagandist never has all the media at his disposal . . . the one case in which the measurement of effects is comparatively easy . . . is also by far the least significant.'[1] The difficulty has perhaps been that researchers have tended to separate the content of propaganda from the events and the audience concerned; we examine constrains upon the media themselves as if these were separate phenomena from the effects of the media upon the public; an examination of the forms and methods of electoral television, as it is developing in Britain, would suggest that the constraints (of impartiality, say, or the exclusion of particular groups or parties or issues from coverage) are also constraints upon the ability of the audience to perceive an event in a particular way. The *expectation* of impartiality as a prescribed constraint within broadcast content might itself affect the audience's willingness to vote or to participate in the electoral process. An audience cannot be influenced by a medium which is visibly constrained; it can be entertained and informed, but it is less likely to be persuaded if it is constantly reminded that the forms in which the communication occurs are somehow prearranged precisely to prevent the audience feeling the full impact. British general elections have been haunted by the constant spectre of information withheld. 'We are not being given the facts', say many voters to pollsters, although information is pouring at them through print and electronic media in unprecedented quantity. It could be that the programme formats have created or reinforced a kind of cognitive reticence, which defies measurement.

It seems necessary to this observer to adjust our mental pictures of political communication to take into account the dominant nature of the genres within which political pro-grammes are beamed at the audience, genres which are supposed to act as simulated models of 'real' political activity. The phone-in show, for example, gives the impression of direct enquiry or inquisition by a doubtful voter of a political candidate; but it is simultaneously one segment of a prepared pattern of pro-grammes in which a broadcasting authority, operating under licence and in the light of precedent and policy is attempting to provide no advantage to any party other than that which news events (that is, political 'history') necessitate. The discussion programme or debate, which is presumed to present a balanced presentation of arguments, carries with it an aura of having been transported from the real scene of political battle into the studio. It is a *version* of the political debate being carried on spontaneously elsewhere.

Television has acquired the additional function of being the register of which historic events are significant, and the process of event → news coverage → critical assessment → point scored → voter influence begins to feed upon itself. The original 'event', which may be a speech or the announcement of a statistic will be monitored and timed in its announcement to feed into the pattern of other events, to prevent risk of an accusation of bias; the events are selected partly to fit into the needs of the genres within which coverage is to be slotted. Of course, great pains are taken to separate news bulletins from the strict application of the rubric of impartiality; comment is deliberately balanced while news is supposed to follow its own non-balanced set of 'values', but the total machinery of broadcasting has now become so important to electoral activity that that distinction tends to be obliterated under the sheer weight of the overall necessity to balance. An 'unbalanced' item in a news bulletin takes on the feeling of a major piece of editorialising during the tense weeks of an electoral campaign, even though it is formally permitted within the broadcasting rules.

In the relatively small quantity of literature which the two British general election campaigns of 1974 have hitherto generated, two views emerge, views, in fact, which re-emphasise the trends of what has been said in studies of previous elections ever since the mid-1960s. The first asserts that television dominated the election to the point at which it has become impossible to say that any election existed at all outside its televisual manifestation. 'The General Election Campaign as the creation of organised parties is made to exist by them in ways dictated by the presence of the mass media in general and television in particular.'[2] Senior party leaders organise their walkabouts to get the best coverage in the early evening bulletins on all three channels. The content of the big set-piece speeches at public halls in the evenings is designed partly to catch headlines the following morning, but mainly to get live coverage in the mid-evening news bulletins and the later discussion programmes on television. The morning press conferences given by all three parties are designed to get pithy statements into the early afternoon radio news programmes and the afternoon papers. The audience, therefore, experiences its election largely through the mediation of television, and the flow of debate and argument is made to fit the contours of programme scheduling.

The second discussion to emerge is whether the collectivity of constraints which affect broadcasters' activity 'sanitises' the content of the programmes and angles the whole election to the needs of those groups already dominating political life.

> Rather than employing the medium to cast a journalistic eye over the political questions of the election, studios and facilities were effectively given over to the propagation of the ideas and feelings of the three main parties.[3]

The constraints in this argument are twofold: there are those which emanate from the organisational hierarchy, the broadcasting authorities, the party leaders, and to some extent the electoral law itself, and there are others which arise from the professionalised assumption that the audience finds politics boring and that their needs and interests can be satisfied only through the sacrifice of adequate reflection of political issues.

An older line of research, into the effect upon voting of the mass media coverage of a campaign, is gradually gaining less attention than the modern and more subtle issues of social control through constraints upon content. Most modern discussion about propaganda has emphasised that campaigning is itself the least effective because it is the shortest-term means of influencing opinion. Opposing arguments neutralise each other: the population is indifferent to the material offered; none of the really powerful techniques of modern mass propaganda can be effective in a few short weeks.[4] The first full-scale study of television's influence on a British general election reached the conclusion, consistent with that of similar studies in American elections, that the previously held presumptions of the persuasiveness of television were gross exaggerations.[5] Throughout the 1960s the view prevailed that election campaigning on television was helping to improve the level of general political education in the country but not to influence attitudes. 'Television may inform or reinforce attitudes, but it rarely converts', was the view of one of the Nuffield College electoral studies.[6] Later and more elaborate studies of television effects in elections have tended to explode even more of the common assumptions which have been held: for instance, examination of the 1966 election indicated that television is far less of a personalising medium than has been thought. 'Impressions of politicians are no more susceptible to media influence than are attitudes towards the parties'.[7] The findings of the same study tended toward the abolition of other prevailing notions too: television did not tend to force the election more towards national at the expense of local issues than would have been the case anyway, nor does it tend itself to 'moderate the tone of political argument;' that process has been the result of the growth of a more affluent voter learning to appreciate practical rather than ideological argument. Nor even was there convincing evidence that television had helped to raise voting turnout, although there did appear to be in broadcast coverage a positive aid to the rise of third parties in a traditional two – party situation.[8] (Certainly, in the context of the partial fragmentation of the party system in the general elections of 1974 the allocation of broadcasting time to the new spectrum of small parties was felt to be of crucial importance.)

What has happened, broadly speaking, in the study of media influence on elections since the first 'television election' of 1959 is that a series of wide-ranging assumptions of media power have been refined into a series of supposed special tendencies latent within broadcast coverage; these, in turn, have been dethroned as the political circumstances of one election after the other have exploded one theory after another. We are left with all the old hypodermic theses in ruins, and in place of them what we have acquired is a view that television professionals merely reinforce the prevailing set of political relationship and, in the interests of viewer appeal, emphasise conflict among policies and politicians. The media, it is argued, have come to define the campaign more than the contending parties themselves. One observation of the whole trend of mass media coverage of elections in the postwar period argues that the media 'struck the balance between issues and personalities, seeking continually to impose a differentiation on the parties, in the interest, presumably, of clarifying the choices open to the electorate. They sought also, doubtless for the same reasons, to avoid a "quiet" campaign.'[9] Some observers have tried to argue a much more vigorous case, alleging the complete trivialisation of politics by the media; television has been responsible for the virtual elimination of cognitive activity by the voter.

> We have already indicated that the classical Jeffersonian image of the voter – the voter who is capable of making purely rational judgements based upon the (factual) political information he seeks out and receives – is simply a quaint hyperbole in the light of present social-science evidence . . . Politics on television affords voters a sense of participation in the dramatic political events of their time without the work that is involved in understanding the serious abstractions involved.[10]

Television, so goes this argument, has changed the patterns of political campaign activity, the habits of the thoughtful voter, trivialising the political process at every level.

What we are seeing is a unitary concept of television being applied as a necessary and sufficient cause of whatever changes have in practice occurred in the conduct of electoral and other political activity. The very nature of the tendencies within the political scientists' arguments between the 1960s and the 1970s indicates a consistent willingness to label television as the cause of a series of ever-changing circumstances. The development of political television since 1959 has enabled more and more elements in the campaign in the 'real' World to be reflected on the screen; that, in itself, reflects the increasing willingness of the various actors within the arena of politics to permit the access of television. It also reflects the increasing versatility of television in developing formats and professionalism which exploit the increasing opportunities. As more of the activity is tailored to the needs of broadcasting, it is inevitable that more of the actual changes in the conduct of politics will be ascribed causatively to the medium through which they are reflected. In one sense this process of argument is quite logical; in another it becomes increasingly tautological. In an era of prosperity, an election will inevitably appear to involve the auctioning of material goods more than the debating of serious historical questions. In periods of major economic and social tension, third and fourth parties will tend to emerge, or fragmentations will occur within existing parties; all these processes will be increasingly apparent from watching television. Whether, in any real sense, the medium can be properly seen as the historic 'cause' is doubtful.

That is not to say that television is a crystal mirror passively reflecting the circumstances of history. Television encompasses a series of institutions operating a series of technologies which transmit heavily processed and predetermined images within a series of genres, which range from advertising to news bulletins. Broadcasting will tend to portray different images of political activity – from occasion to occasion – within different dominant genres. Since television, as we shall see, has acquired the taste of *mobilising* the society to vote as well as that of presenting the electoral options, then it has to turn ceaselessly from genre to genre in order to keep the material interesting and therefore politically effective. The broadcasters exercise a sufficient range of professional options to be blamed for the effects of political activity as portrayed on the screen, but within politically prescribed constraints so tight as to make their medium a secondary one. The initiatives within the world of political communication have to come from elsewhere – from newspaper journalists, from politicians, from community leaders. Yet the broadcasters must devise formulae which unite two contrary impulses, of independent thought and of independent arbitrage of an objective struggle. As one major figure in British television, Sydney Bernstein, said in a *Times* article in 1961:

> The two streams of British journalism – the journalism of protest and the journalism of authority – meet uneasily in television today. It is one thing for a newspaper to canvass a variety of opinions in its features and editorials over the year. It is another thing to impose upon an editor the responsibility of producing every feature and every editorial in such a way that exactly balances the conflicting opinions of every situation.[11]

In many respects the British electoral system has slipped painlessly into the era of television. We are now a case of advanced telocracy. Electoral contests in Britain are relatively brief three-week affairs preceded by a period of speculation as to the date likely to be chosen by the reigning Prime Minister. Television, restlessly searching for novelty and for the dramatic, builds up the audience's interest in the forthcoming spectacle and then throws enormous resources into the coverage of the brief campaign. In British politics the basic cast of characters is quite small; a brace of party leaders, already known but perhaps not fully tested in advance of the big match, pitch into the fray, one or more of them knowing that his political life as well as his party's chances of office may well be at stake in the struggle. Although our constitutional life is not what has come to be labelled presidential in style, our electoral life does necessitate the projection of a few people to the mass electorate.

In the actual conduct of national electoral warfare, day-by-day television has entrenched as much as changed many of the traditional practices. It has enabled senior politicians to go on the stump and yet be seen night after night by the whole electorate as well as those in a particular region of the country. Senior party men and women, always with their eye on the clock, must organise their key statements around the anticipated requirements of newspaper editions, long-distance trains, and the engineering of front-page layouts, and they find it sometimes easier to cope with the needs of television politics. They emphasise, of course, the difficulties when asked to comment on the impact of television on their professional lives as politicians, but at least they know that once their skills are acquired, the timings of television are predictable, precise and zealously fair between sides. Communicating with a mass electorate entirely through the press and the platform involves pitting one's wits against a wall of doctrinal hostility on the part of at least some of the newspapers. With television (and radio) at least the politicians enjoys *rights* as well as undergoes risks. There is, among the various added frustrations, the appalling problem, in live performances, that one political gaffe or one piece of unfairness on the part of the broadcasters can bring terrible penalties, when the whole of the rest of the media can seize upon it and exploit it for days. But in the rapidly flowing three-week campaign the skilled politician also has the opportunity to exploit the instantaneity of television for himself.

I emphasise the convenience of the television campaign to the politician in the British context not merely because this is sometimes overlooked but because we are beginning to see certain changes in the public acceptance of political (and especially electoral) activity on the screen. The two general elections of 1974 might well, when looked back on with the hindsight of a decade, prove to be some kind of turning point. The first of these elections took place on a day in late February – a time of year when television viewing is usually fairly high and the long winter evenings conducive to long hours of continuous passive reception. In any case, the sheer volume of political broadcasting was greater than in any previous election. Between the dissolution of Parliament and the day of polling, the two B. B. C. television channels projected eleven and a half hours of coverage of actual politicians, excluding the fourteen programmes which are transmitted on all three channels simultaneously and are under the editorial control of the parties themselves rather than the broadcasters.[12] (In Britain, where no political paid advertising is allowed by law, the broadcasting authorities by agreement between themselves and those parties contesting a modicum of seats, allocate various periods of time between the parties in which they can transmit their own programmes of propaganda. At these times no other competitive broadcasting is allowed on any channel, leaving the politicians, for a brief period, with a wholly captive audience.) Each evening on B. B. C.-1 there was a one-hour block of news and politics between 9 and 10 p.m. On B. B. C.-2 a forty-minute discussion programme was presented at 11 p.m. Five other major current affairs programmes, which normally deal with the whole range of public matters, presented special editions dealing with the election during that brief campaign period. Three editions of the weekly 'Panorama' (fifty minutes in length) were devoted to the British economy, and two editions of 'The Money Programme' looked at the problems of food and other prices and at questions of industry. There were also three editions of a programme entitled 'Election Forum', long periods of programme time in which the three party leaders, each in a programme of his own, answered questions submitted by viewers. (On radio nearly one hour every morning was being dedicated to an innovation in British election broadcasting – direct telephoned questions from listeners.) Some of the party election broadcasts, in addition to other election programmes, were transmitted regionally rather than nationally, to give opportunities for local issues to be dealt with by politicians contesting seats in those regions; these gave an opportunity for Welsh and Scottish nationalist parties, for instance, as well as the right-wing extremist National Front party, to have their own broadcasting time, although the Communist party, which had fielded the necessary fifty candidates to qualify for television time in the 1970 general election, failed, in February 1974, to put up the necessary modicum of candidates. Altogether, in February 1974, the total amount of B. B. C. television time devoted to the election was a third higher than in the previous general election.[13]

On the Independent (commercial) channel a similar pattern of increased attention to politics was apparent. During the campaign period, there were three and a half hours of party election broadcasts, plus sixteen hours of national news coverage by I. T. N. (the special national news unit which operates within the basically regional structure of the British Independent system), plus eight and a half hours of nationally disseminated programmes dealing with discussion and comment on political topics. In addition to all of this there were fifty-two hours of regional material broadcast by the regional companies which compose the Independent system. It was clear that British broadcasting was not playing down the 'snap' election called by Prime Minister Edward Heath in the complex political circumstances of winter 1974.

There had been tense circumstances which had given rise to the election and to the one which followed it in the autumn of the same year. In February 1974 Britain passed through the most serious and the most tiresome of its many financial–industrial crises in the postwar period. A long-drawn-out national miners' strike was depriving the country of coal supplies necessary to maintain industrial activity; the international crisis in energy was simultaneously beginning to bite deep. The government under Edward Heath refused to concede the pay claim of the miners and the entire country was put on a sort of war footing; television closed down at 10 p.m.; the whole of the working population was put on a three-day week; an atmosphere of appalling gloom was made suddenly to envelop a population which still, despite all the trappings of national emergency, was failing to take its economic disasters seriously. Television ran a governmental 'Switch Off Something' campaign, and we all dutifully looked for some convenient appliance to turn down. We shivered patriotically while waiting for the posturing to cease. The climax was an announcement that Edward Heath was to call a general election as the result of which he hoped to achieve a reaffirmation of his leadership from the people so clear that the miners would capitulate and accept a lower pay increase and the government's policy of sternly controlled wage rises would be saved.

What happened at the end of a very brief and intense electoral campaign was that Edward Heath lost office and Harold Wilson, former Prime Minister and Opposition Leader, returned to office, but without an overall plurality of votes in Parliament behind him, which betokened an inevitable repeat election within a brief period. In October 1974 that election was held, and the country gave Wilson a tiny overall majority in Parliament, sufficient to govern, but insufficient to claim any total mandate. One quarter of the electorate had voted for parties other than Labour or Conservative, a proportion unprecedented in modern postwar politics. Parliament henceforth was to contain a cluster of small parties, nationalists of various half-submerged Celtic nations, the odd independent, a minibusful of Liberals.

The tenseness of the general political atmosphere during the miner's strike had encouraged most commentators to predict an explosive election campaign. Class conflict of the kind experienced in the prewar period was thought to be about to return. Violence was even expected by many. In the event, the first election campaign of 1974 was fought in gentlemanly fashion, the claims and counter-claims of the politicians being far less shrill than political circumstances had led the public to expect. Only Enoch Powell, the maverick Conservative right-winger, became a major source of inter-party tension when he recommended the public to vote Labour, on the ground that the election had been called on a false basis and that a Labour victory would ensure the departure of Edward Heath and the establishment of a government more likely to take Britain out of the Common Market. The only television programme to cause an important rumpus during the campaign was one (an edition of 'Panorama') dealing with the Common Market in which Mr Powell was intended to play an important part; even in this case the row blew over when the B. B. C. agreed to use, not a live appearance by Mr Powell, but a recorded extract of a speech previously made by him on the Common Market issue.[14] Both Labour and Liberal parties made protests during the campaign at various aspects of the coverage but not of a very strident nature. It was a quiet campaign which seemed all the quieter for the atmosphere of extreme drama in which it had been precipitated. Perhaps it was not surprising that the B. B. C. began to receive complaints that television was overdoing its coverage.[15] Night after night the audience looked in to prolonged periods of political discussion and reporting, waiting in vain for the gladiatorial combat between Heath and Wilson, between class and class, between unions and public interest, which various influential 'experts' had promised.

The B. B. C. conducted an Audience Research inquiry shortly after the election which showed that a large proportion of the electorate thought that television had concentrated too much on the campaign. Even among that category of the sample who were 'enthusiastic' in their political interest, one third thought television coverage excessive. Among those who described themselves as 'apathetic' toward politics, nearly 90 per cent held this view. [16] It was inevitable that in the next election, imminent because of the indecisive nature of the February one, the broadcasting authorities would reduce the total coverage for fear that, by boring the audience, the broadcasters might inadvertently be doing a disservice to the democratic system.[17] In the event, the total coverage was reduced by about a quarter, and much of the time that was devoted to political material was no longer concentrated in peak hours; in particular the one-hour band of news and comment between 9 p.m. and 10 p.m. was abandoned by the B. B. C. and divided into separate parts, as had been the pattern in many of the general elections of the previous decade.

One Conservative politician, who is himself a writer on media questions and a broadcaster, analysed in a speech delivered in the summer of 1974 some of the implications of excessive coverage of an election. Lord Windlesham invited his audience to consider whether this might induce 'cynicism' in the audience, whether the tone of political debate as presented to the public in hour after hour of political discussion in television studios might not bring discredit on the practice of politics. 'Is it necessary', he asked, 'that the conventions of political broadcasting should result in transposing to the media the confrontation style of politics which marks the proceedings on the floor of the House of Commons?'[18]

It is worth paying a great deal of attention to the question of 'overkill', of inducing boredom or cynicism, because it is through this fear that one can observe the role played by broadcasting in doing more than report, as if it were a whole series of newspapers, a quantity of political activities. In taking deliberate measure of its own excessive attention to political activity, the broadcasters, in a sense, are acknowledging a power different from that traditionally ascribed to the press. It is the power to shape a society and a power inescapably moulded by mass communications; it is the acceptance of a manipulative function in society, a realisation that the broadcasting environment of a society is an element in the political environment and has responsibilities to it, not merely to reflect it but to sustain it.[19] In the early months of 1975, as another event unique in British constitutional history drew near – a referendum on whether the country would retain its membership of the European Common Market – the broadcasters took a further deliberate decision not to overplay their coverage. The rules of impartiality, of strict minute-for-minute balance between major parties with due acknowledgement of the minor parties, was no longer a sufficient doctrine for broadcasting coverage of political campaigns; henceforth an additional consideration would become crucial – that of whether the total range of material offered to the public might be likely to deter them from playing their part as citizens, whether by implication it might even have the effect of making them turn aside from the electoral process toward other forms of political expression. Among the various social phenomena for which television is henceforth liable to be blamed is the sense of disillusionment within society with the overall political process. The broadcasting authorities in their commitment to impartiality in all its forms are coming to accept a more far-reaching responsibility, harder to guarantee: that of keeping a society wedded to its political structure. The coverage of major political events, therefore, such as general elections or a referendum, is by implication expected to do more than maintain unbiased news values but in fact to act as cosmetic artist to the political system. 'If I read the signs aright', said the chairman of the B. B. C. in a speech at Leeds University in which he summarised the B. B. C.'s experience of the two elections, 'I believe the greatest risk we all face is that the public cries a plague on both your houses and proceeds to abstain from voting.'[20] Looking forward to the referendum campaign of 1975 he saw that television, by presenting 'too much wrangling', could produce dangers.

> We in the B. B. C. – and our colleagues in the I. B. A. – have a major responsibility here. I am in no doubt that we overdid things a bit in the February election . . . We took note of the fact, and in October I believe we got the emphasis more nearly right. But now we look like having a third major election-type campaign within eighteen months, and a campaign moreover restricted to the one topic. The risk of overdoing things is a very serious one, and we shall, I expect, set, or endeavour to set a slower tempo and a lower key than we have done for ordinary elections.[21]

Almost unnoticed, the B. B. C. was accepting the job of official guardian of democracy, a role which other senior broadcasters had been proclaiming in various degrees of enthusiasm since the attempt began, in the 1970s, to recover from the alleged breakdown of consensus in the previous decade.[22]

Electoral broadcasting is caught in a double bind: in fulfilling a journalistic role it has to confront those in public life with the views of the broad mass of the governed – to put the questions, as all interviewers incessantly repeat, 'which the average man would like to ask if he had the opportunity'. However, as a medium which is obliged to operate within rules of impartiality of an extreme nature (especially during election campaigns), it finds itself reflecting the great centre block of national opinion at the expense of the fringe views and therefore finds itself responsible for a bias against certain forms of political initiative. Since a broadcasting organisation must orchestrate its overall approach to a major political event, it finds itself creating a simulated model of the political process which it is supposed to be displaying. The forms of programme which it devises and the genres within which it conducts its political communication are produced both by the rules of balance and the desire to present the election to the public. The election is presumed to have some independent historic existence; it is a contest within its own traditional rules and customs, and these are transferred to television through television's own acquired responsibilities and norms. The two have on the whole fitted well together, but, as television has tended to obliterate the original form of the hustings and the practices of the platform and the press, it has had to accept this new responsibility, that of providing the *basic* structure by which politicians communicate with people. Today, if the fears of the broadcasters in the aftermath of the February election are to be taken as evidence, it has to guarantee the satisfactory mobilisation of the public, it has to guarantee the *effects* of its forms upon political life, even though these have grown up primarily in the attempt merely to mirror traditional electoral genres.

A great deal can be learned about the political content of a society by examining the structures and forms of programmes in which political material is transmitted. British television, like English literature, is particularly rich in forms or kinds, and the audience is felt to be highly sensitive to changes in structure. The basic fact about the relationship between the audience and the medium of broadcasting is that the former in a sense chooses the genre but not the content. The purchaser of a newspaper has at least the opportunity, in certain cases, of looking at the banner headline before he buys the paper. The reader of novels can read the reviews. The television audience is made to associate certain times of the week with certain strands of programming and he learns to choose the series, the slot, or the generic title. In the case of political television, every genre represents or encompasses a sector of the overall political process; it provides an image of what politics is, while allowing the political debate to move on one stage.

We have already referred to the role of the party election broadcast, which is presented to the viewer as a propaganda form, like the pamphlet or squib of the past. It is not a programme which itself contains controversy, but it is intended to be received as a shaft of polemic; the parties adopt different forms for these programmes from election to election, ranging from the strip-cartoon approach, adopted by the Labour party in 1959, to the extremely serious and carefully argued 10- or 15-minute speech by the party leader which many such programmes have consisted of in recent years. The objective, in the latter type of programmes, is to make the party leader as weighty as possible, to make him appear a real leader, serious, worthy of attention, treating his audience as adults. The audience is informed before and after every one of these broadcasts that the programme is a party broadcast and therefore outside the editorial control of the broadcasters themselves.

In complete contrast is the case of the constituency report. In these, which are normally sections of news bulletins or of one of the major regular weekly current affairs programmes, a reporter tours a given constituency and interviews all the candidates and emphasises the special issues of controversy or political circumstances which might influence the result of the campaign in that particular place. The rules about appearances in such programme are extremely complicated and are controlled by the provisions of the Representation of the People Act (1969) and the Independent Broadcasting Authority Act (1973). A candidate is considered to be taking part in a programme if he 'actively and consciously participates'. If he is seen in a piece of film as a result of deliberate arrangement, then all the rules of balance have to apply: he may only take part if all the other candidates take part or if they agree that one of their number may appear without them. If one candidate refuses to appear, the others may do so, and the views of the absent candidate will be presented in some other way (over a still picture or in a reported statement by himself or his agent); however, in such a case, no debate is allowed between the other candidates actually taking part. A candidate in a particular constituency may, of course, take part in any other type of programme, including a party election broadcast, but he may in no circumstances refer to the name of his constituency without infringing the rules of balance.[23] The reporter acts as interviewer and attempts to describe impartially the circumstances of the constituency concerned; he may sum up but obviously must do so in such a way as to enable the viewer to reach his own conclusions. Reporters who have strong personal styles take good care to keep them firmly under control at election times when politicians are seldom shy of crying foul. Harrison describes some of these reports in the October election as 'unhelpfully inhibited'. 'Campaign Special', the B. B. C.'s nightly television programme which provided large amounts of election news (in both elections), was the main vehicle for such constituency reports. The reporters are allowed to exercise their usual imagination and their verbal ability but within the very firm structures which the rules of appearances of candidates have created. The constituency report is like a sonnet, a form with extremely rigid rules of form and shape which exudes always a highly predictable sentiment: the voters of X-land or Y-land must make up their minds between three, four or five candidates, some of whom are politically and intellectually marginal but are taking part in a solemn political ritual. The image of the 'real' election provided by the constituency report, as a form, is quite false; the viewer knows it is false, but, like the audience of the Elizabethan sonnet, he becomes a connoisseur of the form, knowing that the content is utterly predictable and, as it were, irrelevant.

The creation of programme formulas is influenced more by inhibition toward politics than creativeness, and several of the most familiar formats can be traced back through the years to various ordinances or negative declarations by the politicians. For instance, ever since a programme called 'The Last Debate' in the 1959 election, politicians at election times have refused to face live audiences; neither side has been willing to run the risk of facing an audience the composition of which might be fixed by a competing party or its supporters. The subject has been one of recurrent contention. In most general elections an attempt has been made by the broadcasters to coax the politicians from this collective coyness, but so far in vain. Only if the audience members are handpicked by the party organisations and tickets given out in carefully worked out proportions, will the party leaders participate. When that formula is employed, the results are not only dull but occasionally offensive: each party group in the audience feels it has to support its side and shout down or laugh down the efforts of the others to deal with questions. The spectacle of the democracy provided is a caricature of free discussion – a slanging match – and is apt to confirm the uncommitted viewer in his distrust of the political process.

In the 1964 election the B. B. C. managed to take one important step toward confrontation between politician and public. A series of programme called 'Election Forum' were started in which the leader of each party was invited in turn to spend forty minutes or more answering questions sent in by viewers: the first time that this format was employed, over 30,000 postcards arrived and a small team of (professional) interviewers made a selection and put a series of often highly testing and provocative questions to the three main party leaders. Although this formula would seem hardly different from a press conference situation in which a panel questions a single individual, in practice the flavour of viewers' questions turns out to be quite different from that normally provided by professional inter- viewers even though the viewers' questions are actually chosen and put by a group of professionals; the viewer is sometimes more direct, not afraid to put the naive question, nor to put it again and even again. 'Election Forum' became a central format in the elections of 1966 and 1970, but in the February election of 1974 the brief space of time available between the announcement of the election and the transmission of the programme meant that the questions had to be put in the studio by a panel.

In 1974, however, further important steps were taken toward bringing voters and politicians together before the cameras: one of these was the introduction of the election phone-in, which was used in a long one-hour programme every morning on radio but also in several television programmes. Sometimes the viewer putting the question was invited to a studio in some other part of the country; sometimes an ordinary telephone handset was used in the studio. It was not difficult to notice an increased freshness in the questioning and in the answering. British television interviewing has been dominated for over a decade by a small group of extremely skilled professionals, and the composition of this band has changed only slowly throughout that time. Nor indeed have the politicians changed so greatly; the result is the sense of an increasingly skilled group of insiders all involved in playing the same game. The introduction of the telephone has created several new genres in political broadcasting and has helped to break down the deep-rooted inhibitions of the politicians towards meeting live voters.

None the less, the attempt to persuade the politicians to give up their objections to live audiences has continued. The B. B. C. advisory council report of the February election explained that

> the main parties would only agree to allow their spokesmen to appear when the public were chosen on a fixed ratio of party political allegiance. The same consideration applied to in- terviews outside the studio. The difficulty of deciding in each case which particular political interest was represented by

each individual had an inhibiting effect on prospective items of this type[24]

In the course of 'Campaign Special' in the October election, an ingenious and partly successful effort was made to evade this problem. A series of short films was made about a single constituency in the north of England, Keighley, which has always chosen its Member of Parliament by a knife-edge of votes, an evenly divided community which has won the election over the whole nation. The Keighley programmes were made by a team who spent the whole election in the town and singled out a group of undecided voters, returning to them frequently during the campaign to see which way their minds were turning and to analyse the influences which ultimately persuaded them to decide their vote. In the last of this series of programmes all the candidates for the Keighley constituency were persuaded to face a selection of the voters, an unusual event.

In the Independent system the broadcasters had taken a slightly tougher attitude toward the politicians on the question of crowds. The I. B. A. itself decided to inform the Committee on Political Broadcasting (the semi-official group of politicians and broadcasting officials who plan the allocation of party air time and arrange other matters of joint importance affecting broadcasting and politics) that it would, in the February election, allow programmes in which politicians faced voters and their questions. The Independent system consists of a group of regional companies (fourteen of them) each of which operates with a very large degree of commercial and creative independence under the supervision of the I. B. A. Several of the companies, working under the general protection of the I. B. A.'s statement, did manage to create successful programme formats involving live audiences. Scottish Television presented two one-hour debates, involving representatives of five parties speaking to audiences of several hundred voters. Thames T. V. (one of the London companies) managed to get one such programme on the air, but was then faced with an embargo by the politicians on any further experiments with live voters. Yorkshire Television planned a series of nine such programmes but found that it had to use retired politicians because the actual candidates in the election refused to face live questioning from voters. Thames T. V. then managed to get five more programmes on the air with live and participating audiences, although these were of the specially selected variety rather than the spontaneous (the panel did eventually contain a modicum of uncommitted as well as loyal party-chosen voters). An embargo by politicians can thus prevent the evolution of programme formats according to the predelictions of the broadcasters; in fact, the image of the overall electoral activity presented by television can be and frequently is profoundly affected by the constraints imposed by the political establishment itself. The whole problem of the politicians and the crowds is merely one of a long series of now traditional inhibitions which in one sense hamper, and in another actually encourage, the development of political genres in broadcasting.

In the Independent system, there is one company, Granada T. V., which has, since its founding in the 1950s, attempted to act in the forefront of the evolution of television politics. It was the first company to cover an election at all (in February 1958), when in the famous Rochdale by-election it managed to force the candidates to take part in a television discussion based on questions put by a panel of journalists.[25] In the 1959 general election it broke new ground by giving television time to every single candidate of every party fighting an election in every constituency in its region.[26] In the February 1974 election it mounted a series of seven television programmes, each on a different subject (prices, energy crisis, housing, government, Common Market, poverty and the election itself), in which large audiences of electors took part and put questions to a panel of experts. The chairman of the programmes ruled out of order all questions of a partisan nature, in an effort to move the discussion to the plane of factual analysis and keep it there. The project was called the 'Granada 500'; the audiences were drawn from a large sample of voters from one town, Preston in Lancashire, which has an age distribution roughly similar to that of Britain as a whole. The voting intentions of the sample were checked at the beginning of the campaign, and the idea of the producers was to feed the sample with large quantities of clear, factual political information and then check the actual effect on their voting by following up the sample after voting day. Another sample, taken from the same town of Preston, but not allowed to participate in the television project, would serve as a control group. The operation proved to be extremely complicated to organise; the sample had to be kept fed with printed factual information throughout the campaign and had to be transported from place to place as the series of programmes progressed. The project naturally became a major subject of conversation and comment within that part of northern England in which Granada's programmes are seen.

In the last stages of the campaign the producers tried to get the candidates in the area to attend one of the 'Granada 500' live sessions to answer questions and debate. All but one candidate agreed, but the dissenting candidate refused to waive his rights of representation and thereby allow the public debate to take place under the 1969 Representation of the People Act. Granada was forced to concede defeat, while promising to keep the struggle for live-audience questioning going until the next election.[27]

In examining the influence of any form of mass entertainment, one must accept the centrality of the genre. It is the genre which links the two ends of the communication process by means of a series of strands and influences which pass through the society as a whole. To guarantee an audience, the communicator must offer an overt or implied promise, and, since the material may be unfamiliar to the audience, the vessel in which it is served must be recognisable. The creation of genres, however, involves the whole cultural tradition of a society; it has to be founded on elements which are known in advance not to be 'boring'. Television, more than any other medium, is obsessively concerned with the problem of confronting the impending boredom of the audience; and, in dealing with politics, it is trying to grapple with the transmission to a mass audience of a part of the political culture which, without television, could not be part of mass culture at all. The concept of boredom therefore is the dominant element in a political broadcaster's view of his audience. His genres are the product of the dual desire to avoid boring the audience while carrying the burden of the preservation of the political culture. The audience is therefore loaded with information which is difficult to separate from comment, although the canons of traditional journalism command that this be done; and at the same time the audience is presented with image after image of the electoral process, in terms of argument or confrontation or the questioning of experts or as a mass decision-making process by the multitude. All of these images are in a sense wrong, or partial. Each new genre in political broadcasting attempts to capture one of those images and force it home, thereby sustaining the validity of the political system while trying out a simulation of one of the supposed central processes of democracy.

Chapter 9

Television Coverage of Northern Ireland*

Ever since the problems of the unhappy province of Northern Ireland returned to the front pages of British and foreign newspapers in the middle of 1969, they have presented a fascinating challenge to the prevailing notions of what constitutes a proper degree of control of the content of the broadcasting media. Broadcasting is the only instrument of social communication that is wedded inextricably to an *ideology* as well as a function of its own. That ideology is variously described as neutrality, objectivity, fairness; it invades the whole of the work of the broadcaster and is the basis of the whole system by which broadcasting is licensed, controlled and made publicly accountable in Great Britain. In Northern Ireland, however, we have a province in which a large section of the population has for many decades been deprived of various rights considered normal in the rest of Great Britain; and while the ideology of broadcasting operates in a manner designed to prevent the medium becoming a *maker* of events, as well as a reflector of them, it can only operate

* This article first appeared in *Index*, vol. 1, no. 2 (1972). It was later published in the Irish magazine *This Week*.

in that neutral way when the receiving society as a whole accepts a common set of standards. Where those standards are not accepted this neutral ideology is subjected to stress and broadcasting necessarily tends to become an *agent* of events.

In Northern Ireland, to raise the question of equality of opportunity in jobs, education and council housing before the growth of the civil rights movement was to be inflammatory. One of the means whereby the province was held together was silence on the part of the media. For radio and television to report on its internal affairs using the normal ethical and social terms of reference of the rest of Britain in the 1950s and 1960s was considered a breach of broadcasting's neutrality. A profound silence prevailed for several decades, until the processes of political change made Northern Ireland once more a centre of news. At that point, pressmen, reporters and producers from every part of the globe poured into the province, bringing their own assumptions and prejudices to bear upon the problems they saw there. Spanish reporters came and saw the afflictions of fellow Catholics. Soviet reporters came and saw the final spasms of British military imperialism. French marxist pressmen saw a liberation movement enacted before their eyes. Maoists came and saw the birth of a European Cuba. But for British broadcasters and journalists the anguish of Ulster lay outside these categories: it lay in the revelation of the existence of inequities and oppression within these islands of a kind unthinkable in any other part of the country and sanctioned by a kind of helpless feeling of inevitability. The existence of those conditions, it was widely felt, was somehow partly the fault of a long period of cowardice by all the media towards Northern Ireland. Because the social wrongs toward Protestant and Catholic alike were the partial product of silence, the media were by definition partly responsible.

The tensions between broadcasting and authority were thus to a great extent part of an argument about what kind of instrument broadcasting was and should become. Given its privileged status, could it act as a primary medium of information, or should it always remain one step behind the other media and therefore behind its own technical and intellectual competence? Should it always be a reflector and deliberately step back from being an influencer or causer of events? The answer of the broadcasting

authorities was clear: radio and television were to reflect and not
to provoke. The answer of (some of) the broadcasters was the
reverse. The 'real' meaning of the censorship argument in regard
to Northern Ireland was thus a struggle between old and new
attitudes towards television journalism.

It is very difficult to discern in the discussion anything
resembling a traditional argument about 'censorship' or even
'self-censorship' as those terms are usually understood. For one
thing, it is difficult to decide which is the self that is conducting
the censorship. Is it the reporter, or the producer, or the
departmental head, or the Director General, or the Chairman of
the Board of Governors of the B. B. C. or of the Independent
Television Authority? Where truly does the editorial centre of
broadcasting lie? The B. B. C. has a quick and easy answer: it lies
with the institutional authorities who in the course of the weary
months of crisis gradually asserted themselves in actual daily
practice as well as in title as 'editors' of the programme content.
But how far away from the straight reporting process can you get
and yet remain truly an editor? In 1968 it was not felt that
Broadcasting House could realistically keep hour to hour contact
with and control over news. In 1972 that control is a reality. It is a
reality thrust upon broadcasting by its political critics and by the
fears of senior officials that without the show and then the reality of
central control, power over broadcasting would be taken away
and placed in the hands of a Broadcasting Council or some other
instrument of political intrusion. Undoubtedly in the Northern
Ireland crisis the whole independence of broadcasting was (and
is still) at stake. At the same time I believe that the sequence of
events leading to this profound change in the structure of British
broadcasting was, however unfortunate, inevitable. The point is
that beneath events perceived on the surface there lies a pattern.
In the detail of all the public rows over specific programmes, a
series of dilemmas repeatedly crops up. First, the question of
whether the reporting of an event will cause a counter-event,
whether by describing a gathering crowd of Catholics at a given
street one is going to encourage a crowd of angry Protestants to
gather as well; secondly, how to report the activities of illegal and
ever more frequently armed organisations; thirdly, how to
'balance' discussions and reports in political terms in a society
with so many political factions; and fourthly, to what extent to

make programmes which seem in themselves to be usurping certain of the functions of government. To some extent all broadcasting is conducted against a backdrop of the anticipated reaction of the audience: the whole debate about violence in television programmes involves a steady consideration of the likely immediate effect of a given piece of programme content. In Northern Ireland the producer and the broadcasting manager are confronted with a mass audience whose characteristics of arousability and immediate involvement are known. He can quickly see the results of any judgement he has made in the reaction of members of the audience on the streets as well as by letter and telephone. There is probably no part of the world today where the audience is as much involved with the content of television programmes as in Northern Ireland, where the discussion about the effects of broadcasting is not at all an abstract matter. What is objective or impartial in British (that is, English, Scottish, Welsh) terms is not necessarily so in Irish terms; there is no shared frame of reference on the question of Ireland, no generally agreed centre of intellectual or political gravity. A glance at the history of broadcasting in Ireland will show how carefully over the years the problem was dealt with by avoidance and retreat.

*   *   *

Inevitably, broadcasting in Northern Ireland tended to be heavily influenced by the special political problems of the province. While the civil war within the Irish Free State in the early 1920s prevented Marconi (with the intended help of the *Daily Express*) from developing a radio station, developments were able to take place more easily in the North. The first station on Irish soil was called B. E. 2, it first took the air from the converted linen warehouse in Belfast in September 1924. The Government of Northern Ireland possessed the right to stop transmissions if the public interest required it. Listeners south of the Border, at least those with the most advanced kinds of apparatus, were able to listen in. But all the news came from a locally owned news agency and the only political statements allowed were those delivered by major local politicians. All events south of the Border were studiously ignored; even the results of matches played by the Gaelic Athletic Association were refused air time. (As if replying in kind, Dublin radio in its early days refused to broadcast the results of Association Football matches.) In 1926 Gerald Beadle became station manager (later he became Director of B. B. C. Television) and battled with the province's nerve-wracking sectarian problems. His drama department was attacked for its use of 'southern' accents in some of its plays; his decision to celebrate St Patrick's Day brought a storm of Unionist protest; his policy was to act as if the Border was an Atlantic Coast. None the less the B. B. C. produced a flourishing musical culture and created a small school of Ulster dramatists.

It was the mid-1930s which produced the major crisis in broadcasting–governmental relationships. The riots of 1935 brought demands that the B. B. C. be taken over completely by Stormont, so that it could be used to send out daily ripostes to the propaganda of Radio Eireann which broadcast from Dublin and was uninhibited about reporting Belfast events. Under G. L. Marshall the Director of B. B. C. Northern Irerland (as it had become) there was a move towards a kind of liberalisation: a debate was broadcast between Queen's University Belfast and the two university colleges of Dublin. But northern Unionist opinion made itself vigorously felt to oppose any development of a normal friendly station-to-station relationship, just as opinion south of the Border similarly served to inhibit Radio Eireann. On the whole, however, the Unionist establishment felt content with the role of the B. B. C. which steered clear of coverage of extremist Unionist sentiment as much as of opposition sentiment. No election broadcasts took place at all before the Second World War. The annual 12 July demonstrations of the Orange Order were not reported. Marshall's policy, continued until his retirement well after the war; was to keep an iron grip on all local news and allow nothing to go out which suggested that anything in Northern Ireland could or would ever change. The B. B. C.,apart perhaps from its enterprising drama department, spoke in the tones of the Ulster establishment and worked in their interests. Also, foreshadowing the problems of a later day, Marshall demanded and was given the right to be consulted by all departments of the B. B. C. on any matter relating to Ireland in any way. Thus, the chief in Belfast came to act as a kind of censor over the whole of the B. B. C.'s output from London both in its domestic and overseas services, and naturally this tended to give a Unionist tinge to everything that came out. Similarly, the Controller Northern Ireland was deemed to have the right to prevent any communication between the Overseas Service and Radio Eireann except through his office and with his knowledge. But this, as it turned out, was to prove self-defeating, for it was the Overseas Service which first rebelled against the system, because it obstructed easy contact with Dublin.

Meanwhile London occasionally tried to moderate Marshall's policies, especially during the Second World War when, with the Republic remaining neutral, the Ministry of information was anxious for Irish listeners to hear the presentation of a British point of view. The Ministry wanted the B. B. C. to build up its relationship with Eire, and the B. B. C. responded by starting, with the approval of Radio Eireann, a regular 'Irish Half-Hour'. Simultaneously it started an 'Ulster Half Hour' which was soon dropped. It was a strange irony that dictated a wartime situation in which a London government wanted the B. B. C. deliberately to foster a sense of Irish nationhood while the Belfast government continued to browbeat the B. B. C.'s local officials into maintaining the restrictions of the 1920s and 1930s.

After the war considerable measures of liberalisation appeared. The Roman Catholic Church sent a representative to the religious advisory committee. A regional advisory council was set up with fairly broad representation. Gaelic games were reported at last, and so were demonstrations on 12 July, live and on the spot. But events south of the Border were still ignored, and nothing was heard on Marshall's airwaves which hinted at discontent or injustice in Northern Irish society. But when he retired in the late 1940s political comment became slightly more realistic. There were talks on Ulster history and a Catholic nationalist was allowed to take part in weekly discussions on local affairs. Not until the 1960s, however, were programmes permitted which dealt with Irish history as a whole. Strangely enough, the new regional advisory council of the B. B. C. was one of the extremely rare places where Catholic nationalist and Protestant unionist opinion were able to come together anywhere in the province.

Television came to Belfast in time for the Coronation to be seen

throughout the province, and in the late 1950s a certain amount
of locally produced programming began to appear. That was the
time of an earlier bout of I. R. A. activity; and the streets of
Belfast gave B. B. C. cameramen their first experience in covering
street violence, that speciality of the Belfast news scene. Lord
Brookeborough, Prime Minister at Stormont, who paid scru-
pulous and tireless attention to the work of B. B. C. news, took
part in a number of spectacular contests over various items of
television content, in some of which he was successful. Amid a
blaze of publicity the second of two programmes with Siobhan
McKenna was dropped in which, unscripted, she declared to Ed
Murrow that some of the I. R. A. internees in the Republic, who
had been released despite British opposition, were 'young
idealists'. Lord Brookeborough intervened personally in this
affair, as a result of which the B. B. C. withdrew the programme
and suffered an internal convulsion of protest for its pains. Later,
Brookeborough intervened to cause the disappearance of an item
about the Border, presented by Alan Whicker, from the schedules
of 'Tonight'. He also protested at the showing of a film about
rural electrification in the Republic on the grounds that viewers
might be misled into thinking it referred to Northern Ireland. He
did not shrink from the dramatic phone call to Broadcasting
House – today a regular feature of our political life. And it was
this backstairs obscurantism of Unionist politicians that tended
to deflect criticism from the person of the B. B. C.'s senior official
on the spot. In the late 1960s, however, the carpet under which so
much dust had been shovelled was suddenly tugged away:
attempted suppression ceased to be a valid technique for
Unionists. Television news-collecting created new facts of life for
the politicians of Belfast. Until 1965 it had been possible to
prevent reporters from London from ever setting foot in the
province at all. After 1968, such a course became totally
unthinkable.

*   *   *

The basic problem for the broadcasting authorities, as we have
seen, was to prevent the coverage on radio or television of
political or social events from being itself the cause of further
events. The B. B. C. (together with broadcasting authorities the

world over), has always been shy of committing any act that can be construed as outright interference in the world it is observing. But in a province as tightly controlled as Northern Ireland, living in a sense an artificial political life based on the suppression of a series of social forces by means of manipulated boundaries and police powers, it was difficult to provide any kind of broadcast coverage (in an organisation committed to objectivity) which failed to arouse tempers and invoke the ever-latent spirit of civil commotion. Broadcasting in such a context is inevitably an agent of political action; the very facts under observation could only continue in existence if they remained unreported. The very fact of the unity of Northern Ireland and Great Britain should have necessitated comparison in any reporting of the situation. The paradox of Northern Ireland's pretensions to be British while trying to live apart, however, made it impossible for any coverage to be done according to the usual B. B. C. standards that would yet satisfy the needs of a Unionist society as interpreted through the local office of the B. B. C.

But perhaps the most important new fact of the late 1950s was the coming into existence of commercial television in Belfast. When, late in 1958, the I. T. A. announced that bids for a Northern Ireland franchise were invited, two groups based in the province contended: the first was headed by the Duke of Abercorn and represented interests in local cinemas and *The Northern Whig* newspaper, the second was headed by the Earl of Antrim and involved the Belfast *Newsletter* as well as a wide spectrum of other local interests. The latter won the contest and became the basis of U. T. V., Ulster Television, under the management of Brum Henderson, whose brother runs the virulently Unionist *Newsletter*, as well as The Century Press, which prints a number of government papers including the Stormont Hansard. He is also chairman of the Ulster Unionist Party's publicity committee and is believed to be a great force in the counsels of his party.

Nevertheless, commercial television is a great equaliser of men: there is no point in setting out to sell goods if you cut yourself off editorially from a third of your potential public. Ulster Television accordingly earned itself, to the surprise of many pessimists, a good reputation for its fairness in coverage: it did, however, have to be nagged and cajoled at times into venturing into public affairs coverage on any important scale. U. T. V. quickly gained 65 per cent of the audience, although it originates only six hours of material a week within the province. It fought to get all sections of the population to turn to its programmes. It started its own newsroom a decade ago and presented a local magazine which, true to the principles of the Television Act, provided impartial and balanced coverage of local affairs.

The B. B. C. responded in kind. The political atmosphere of Northern Ireland television began to change substantially. Processes which were occurring throughout Britain as a result of the growth of commercial competition were inevitably felt in Northern Ireland in an accentuated form. When the civil rights movement began in 1968, broadcasting in Northern Ireland was already reformed. After Marshall the most prominent senior figure in Northern Ireland broadcasting was probably Henry MacMullan who built up the role of the Head of Programmes. He was, many thought, a liberalised version of Marshall. In 1966, however, a new professional newsman, Waldo Maguire, took over the Controller's chair at the height of the Greene era at Portland Place. Maguire was a native Ulsterman who, although he was to earn considerably greater opprobrium at home and derision abroad than the previous holders of his post, ill deserved such abuse. He set about the task of running his bureau in the manner to which he had become accustomed in the newsroom at Alexandra Palace: reporters from London were welcomed and helped to do their work; dissenters of all kinds were allowed to take part in programmes; local talent, Protestant and Catholic alike was encouraged.

But the Controller's power over content remained. Maguire was still expected to exercise the right of enforced consultation with all programme-makers from London. Technically he had the power to insist on being told the details of every programme project dealing with Ireland, north and south. Increasingly, as the political crisis deepened, reporters from news and current affairs, sound and vision, working out of London were expected to work from his office under a high degree of supervision. His seniority in the organisation of the B. B. C. is extremely high: to appear over his head the reporter of producer must get the ear of the Director General or his constant aide, the Editor of News and

Current Affairs (E. N. C. A.). Theoretically *editorial authority* does not reside with Controller Northern Ireland, but through the programme producer and his departmental head with Broadcasting House, although the Controller has the right for his views on every aspect of the programme content to be heard by the producer. But a further problem intruded: in the era of Greene it was decreed that as far as possible the content of the B. B. C.'s programmes should be identical in Britain and in Northern Ireland – the transmitters were not to divide their content as far as the province's crisis was concerned. If something was to be said about Northern Ireland in England then it could be said to the population of Northern Ireland to their faces. At the same time the Controller of B. B. C. Northern Ireland did have editorial authority over anything that went out through his own local transmitter up on Divis Mountain. Thus Maguire, while he could not forbid a producer to put out a given interview, could insist on shutting off his transmitter and putting out a different programme if the producer continued with his plan. Meanwhile, the Director General had also instructed producers to do nothing that would provoke Maguire into the need, or supposed need, for such an action. It was a case of 'Catch 22'. On only one occasion was a decision made to allow B. B. C. Northern Ireland to opt out of a major programme dealing with the crisis: that was when in 1970 'Panorama' presented a report which contained a widow crying for vengeance for her dead husband, shot by terrorists. It was decided that the report might provoke further bloodshed and Belfast 'opted out' of that one edition.

In U. T. V., meanwhile, the situation had developed differently and was far less interesting than during the early days. It was an independent company, which had to work in close consultation with the locally resident official of the I. T. A. With his approval, it could opt out of the regular current affairs programmes. It often urged him to do this and succeeded on six or seven occasions. It also presented far less coverage of the situation, *in toto*, than the B. B. C. Perhaps that was part of the reason why it was subject to so little local attack. At the same time *The Newsletter*, blood relation to the commercial television company, took to protesting against B. B. C. coverage almost incessantly. Year after year it conducted a campaign of attack on the B. B. C. and the wretched figure of Maguire, wanting to be

liberal, highly excitable, warm, well-informed and, like the
B. B. C. as a whole, prone at times to retreat into extreme
caution. He was similarly abused and condemned by extremists
from all sides, especially the more militant Unionist elements,
and like other prominent figures in Northern Ireland who have
tried to follow a policy of fairness within a polarised population,
was vilified and intimidated beyond all endurance. The attack
came from all sides, within the B. B. C. and within the province,
and it was progressively extended to the senior staff to whom his
powers were delegated within the office at Belfast.

*   *   *

By the end of 1971 the situation had become chaotic and on 31
December an anonymous B. B. C. reporter described it in the
New Statesman as follows: 'Any current affairs editor who wants
to do an item on Northern Ireland now has to submit the idea
both to the News Editor in Belfast and the Editors of Current
Affairs for television or radio in London. On approval, the items
are recorded and then once again submitted for inspection to
London and Belfast, and frequently as well to the Editor of News
and Current Affairs for final approbation.' This complicated
system began to operate in a way which many reporters and
producers found humiliating (although others found it wise and
unrestrictive in practice).

It was accused of leading to the B. B. C.'s failure to report
allegations about the torture of internees (which ultimately led to
the Wilberforce Tribunal) until after the *Sunday Times* had
reported them. It was accused too of leading to various forms of
bias within reported stories, such as the occasion when, in a
report of a tarring and feathering incident in Londonderry, all
reference was omitted to the fact that no woman could be found
to condemn the incident. One programme was allegedly required to ignore a meeting of the Alternative Parliament after the
opposition withdrawal from Stormont.

The anonymous reporter in the *New Statesman* argued that
these and similar incidents constituted a degeneration of the
B. B. C.'s refusal to allow I. R. A. terrorism the right of outright
advocacy on the air into informal support for the army against
the whole Catholic minority. A more likely explanation, how-

ever, is that these decisions were the result of broadcasting's desire to be 'secondhand', to report nothing really big that had not already been reported elsewhere. One aspect of 'cautious' broadcasting is that news editors feel easier reporting a report, rather than taking the initiative in reporting a new phase or an incident of especially controversial significance. That really is the essence of the dilemma that gradually defined itself during the months of greatest tension when I. R. A. violence really began to mount: should broadcasting go out on a limb and behave like an independent and self-confident reporting instrument or should it hang back and refrain from taking any significant initiative? This tension emerged as a dispute between two groups as to what manner of role radio and television should play within the media.

As the dispute increased in intensity, it was not merely the hapless Maguire who was under attack; the entire management of the B. B. C. found itself ceaselessly and personally under fire from the beginning of the crisis in 1969, and especially after January 1971, when the Provisional Wing of the I. R. A. took spectacular control of the situation at the Ballymurphy flats and found itself in direct conflict with the Army. Whenever an institution is being criticised from two sides it is always a simple matter to turn the argument to its own advantage. John Crawley, special assistant to the Director General, told a conference of Conservative women in December 1971 that 'some reporters and producers and junior editors in radio and television . . . are apprehensive or uneasy about the strictness of the control we are applying'. In a letter to Mr Maudling on 19 November Lord Hill had defended the reporting staff against the allegation of pro-Catholic bias: 'The charges are that the B. B. C. reporters and editors snipe at the Army, and are "soft" towards the I. R. A. The charges are untrue, and are deeply resented by our staff, many of whom do their work at great risk to themselves. The reality of the B.B.C.'s reporting of the Army's role is strikingly different from the picture painted by some of its critics.' But Desmond Taylor, the overall Editor of News and Current Affairs, justified the growing supervision of reporting work in Ireland on the grounds that it 'protected reporters and avoided mistakes of judgement'. 'I am just acting more like an editor and less like a bureaucrat' he said in the B. B. C.'s house magazine.

The rule that interviews with members of the I. R. A. (north or

south of the Border) had to be referred upwards through the
E. N. C. A. to the Director General in every instance before
being *sought*, let alone conducted or transmitted, was progressively enforced. At first it was part of an attempt to
orchestrate the B.B.C.'s coverage in a manner that would not
exacerbate the troubles of the province; it was presented as an act
of 'self-restraint' on the part of the B. B. C. After January 1971 the
system of reference upwards operated (more or less) as a means to
ban interviews with the I. R. A. altogether. Permission had
always to be sought and therefore was requested less and less
often – and when requested it was more and more frequently
refused. At first the B. B. C. was coy about the whole thing. One
reporter said his boss treated the rule as a kind of guilty secret. But
as events moved on and the pressure mounted, the rule was
openly paraded as an act of statesmanship. Lord Hill wrote to
Maudling, the Home Secretary: 'But, between the British
Army and the gunmen, the B. B. C. is not and cannot be
impartial.' (It was not under the rubric of impartiality that access
to the I. R. A. was required by reporters, but rather out of the
need to reach primary sources in the course of collecting
information.) As the dual supervision between Belfast and
Broadcasting House continued, power gradually moved away
from the former towards the latter, and as it did so, and as
editorial supervision therefore moved away from the eye of the
storm, it liberalised. In respect to the coverage of Northern
Ireland itself, the growth of the power of E. N. C. A. in Portland
Place was editorially liberating. The trouble was that the process
meant that E. N. C. A., through the Irish crisis, had developed a
controlling influence which would be used in future across the
board in respect to a rapidly increasing area of subject matter.

It is important to emphasise that not all reporters felt the
broadcasting authority's restrictions to be stifling. When a wave
of indignation at 'covert censorship' spread through various
sections of the public and commercial systems, the ordinary
B. B. C. newsmen were largely puzzled by it. In the reporting of
straight news the restrictions were not troublesome; battles,
shootings and burnings could all be frankly and factually
described. Key figures in events could be interviewed. Public
press conferences by I. R. A. men, even self-confessed gunmen,
could be filmed and transmitted. The apparatus of internal

censorship did not interfere with the normal course of interviewing major political figures and 'Panorama' staff, for instance, did not to any great extent feel that their functions were becoming difficult to discharge. It was 'World at One', 'World in Action' and '24 Hours' which found the new situation cramping. As one of this group of reporters recently put it to me: 'There exists between us and B. B. C. Belfast a fundamental difference about the nature, purpose and style of current affairs broadcasting which cannot be bridged by amendments to scripts, however much effort and goodwill is expended on such an exercise.'

One significant incident, which has frequently been referred to in the press since, arose from a '24 Hours' report on changing sentiment within the Ulster Unionist Party, shortly before the resignation of Mr Chichester-Clark as Prime Minister in Northern Ireland in February 1971. The report included film of a number of party meetings at which Chichester-Clark was roundly condemned, and in which Paisleyite sentiment within the party was shown to be widespread and unconcealed. The gist of the report was that Northern Ireland could well find itself in search of a new Prime Minister within a very short space of time. The report was not shown on the persistent advice of the Belfast Controller, pending a series of changes, including most importantly some indication of the feelings of 'moderate opinion' within the Ulster Unionist Party. The whole point of the report was that moderate opinion was evaporating, and the later addition of an interview with a 'moderate' saying precisely that did not reconcile Belfast to the notion of transmitting the report. As the days passed the event predicted actually occurred, and the report was rendered valueless.

B. B. C. Belfast appeared to have begun, in its fear of the consequences of failure by the Ulster Unionist moderates to hold onto power, to slip into the shoes of moderate Ulster Unionism itself. Maguire and some of his staff seemed to fear that the B. B. C., by pointing to behind-the-scenes pressure on Chichester-Clark at that moment, would help to bring about the very collapse of his power it was predicting. But by neglecting to point out to a British auidence the kind of pressures that existed within the province at the moment the B. B. C. made it, if anything, B. B. C. for Chichester-Clark to bring home to Maudling why the processes of reform were proving so difficult.

Once broadcasting tries, for reasons however liberal, to lighten the burdens of government, it steps upon a slippery slope that ends with fear and reality becoming progressively indistinguishable.

*   *   *

Within the world of independent television an astonishingly similar pattern of events was asserting itself. While the B. B. C. had in its complex internal processes of consultation been trying to work out a way to serve the purposes of journalism without interfering in the active work of government, or, for that matter, in the active work of opposition, the I. T. A. almost unconsciously was in the midst of a similar voyage.

The I. T. A. has always felt that its distinctively loose structure, devoid of any outright editorial control at the centre, makes it less vulnerable to attack and more democratic at the same time. The role of the regional officer of the I. T. A., for instance, is a hazy one, varying from region to region, and in Northern Ireland the regional officer has been involved not merely in an exercise of restraint, but in encouraging the local company U. T. V. to be, if anything, more daring. But in an initial panic reaction to the political crisis in the summer of 1969, U. T. V. decided to limit its reporting of the situation to hard news and not to go out of its way to solicit comment. It decided also that its reporters and cameramen should, if they found themselves in danger, remove themselves immediately from the scene. Finally, it decided (in contrast to the B. B. C.) not to allow any activists or extremists to take part in studio discussions in the studios of U. T. V. for fear of provoking direct attacks on U. T. V. buildings and property. The I. T. A. was also involved in setting these conditions for the operation of U. T. V., but relaxed them in August 1969. At the same time the I. T. A. cautioned Independent Television News that the dividing line between information and incitement was difficult to draw, but should at all times be a subject of concern. 'Balance' in reporting did not necessarily result in calming events and could in fact cause a double provocation.

Simultaneously the I. T. A. began to scrutinise programmes, especially 'World in Action' and 'This Week', with a view to determining whether each edition should be shown in Northern

Ireland. Community leaders joined a delegation to the I. T. A. asking it to ensure that its programmes avoided anything likely to exacerbate the situation or lead to public disorder. The Television Act forbids any programme which 'incites to public disorder' and the I. T. A.'s interpretation of this in the context of the crisis then led to a series of decisions to allow U. T. V. to opt out of programmes, sometimes without their being viewed at all a finished state. Later, as the situation deteriorated, the rule of the I. T. A.'s consultations with the programme companies increased considerably: I. T. A. officials, national and local, began to apply exactly the same criteria to the work of I. T. N. and the programme companies as high officials at Broadcasting House. Although U. T. V. could more easily than B. B. C. Belfast choose not to show a given programme within the province, it became I. T. A. policy not to encourage this. Programme-makers within the independent system were thus hoist with the same petard as those in the B. B. C.: they had to make programmes that could be seen as through uncompromising reporting in England, Scotland and Wales while not provoking politically involved groups within the province itself. The story of the recent 'South of the Border' affair illustrates just how far the I. T. A. has moved since 1969 in developing a central editorial policy strikingly parallel with that of the B. B. C.

There had been a history of mild conflict between Granada's 'World in Action' team and the I. T. A. beforehand – in the B. B. C. it would have been seen as 'creative conflict', but within the independent system it led to a slowly degenerating relationship based upon a series of minor cuts in programmes, delayed transmissions, accusations of bias, soured bouts of 'consultation'. In mid-September 1971 the I. T. A. made its view known that the withholding of a network transmission of a programme dealing with Ulster 'was in some sense a public admission of failure'. Granada meanwhile indicated that it wanted to prepare a programme which would show the pressures present in the Republic Ireland as a result of the crisis in the north. In consultation with the I. T. A.'s staff, Granada proceeded to shoot film for the programme using the October Sinn Fein convention in Dublin as its starting point. The programme was to examine the I. R. A. in Ireland from a critical standpoint, and to include interviews with Dublin politicians hostile to the I. R. A. The Managing Director of Ulster Television informed the I. T. A. that the showing of such a programme anywhere in the United Kingdom would be deplorable in that it would simply give publicity to I. R. A. extremists. The I. T. A. decided that the programme would be unacceptable for transmission and informed Granada accordingly. At the point the programme ·consisted only of uncompiled and unedited rushes. The Authority had held only a brief discussion on the matter lasting for a few minutes, before making its decision.

This unwonted quickness of decision gave rise to allegations that the I. T. A. had been 'got at' by government ministers. Certainly no formal instruction in regard to the programme had been issued by Maudling (which of course he has the power to do), but equally certainly the government was anxious that the I. R. A. should not be presented on any of the domestic media in a favourable light.

There followed an exchange of statements between Granada and the I. T. A. on the issue of whether the I. T. A. had given authority for the company for continue working on the programme. By early November, however, on its own initiative, Granada had in fact finished the programme and asked the I. T. A. to view it. The I. T. A., through its Director General, had been at pains to point out that its objection was to the subject matter fundamentally and not to the treatment. Nevertheless, on 16 November members of the I. T. A. watched the completed programme and decided that it was lacking in the necessary balance. Their reason was that none of the governments concerned in the Irish question, in Dublin, Belfast or London, was represented in the programme and that this gave the offensive impression that the I. R. A. and the Provisionals were 'a properly established political party in a democratic community'. Simultaneously the I. T. A. vigorously rejected allegations made in the press at the time that it was being subjected to political pressure and had decided to 'ban' any kind of coverage of the problems of Northern Irish affairs at all, while Granada proceeded to show the press 'South of the Border' and received comment that was generally favourable to itself and hostile to the I. T. A. decision (although *The Guardian* expressed the view that the programme also suffered from a number of weaknesses). The whole affair brought to a head the deteriorating relationship between Granada and the I. T. A. and led the latter to charge that Granada's 'World in Action' series showed a decided political bias and was guilty of partial reporting.

The rumpus that followed marked a turning point in the history of Independent Television with consequences that have not yet been fully digested. What is certain, however, is that when members of the I. T. A. came to look back on the affair a month or two later, in early 1972, it was clear to all of them that the authority had travelled a good distance in the course of the Northern Ireland crisis. First there was the fact that the I. T. A. was sharing editorial control with the companies, in a positive as well as a negative way, and was exercising power over the choice of subject matter as well as its treatment. Second, according to one member of the authority, it had made a decision in effect not 'to make the task of government more difficult' in any programme over which it exercised its new-found editorial control. Granada had offended by giving prominence to men who were public outlaws: it had confused 'balance' within the context of Republic politics with 'balance' within the only context that mattered, i.e. that of British politics. By now, moreover, the I. T. A. had also made up its mind more clearly on the whole question of incitement to violence and 'opting out'. Although it had traditionally made a distinction between transmitting a programme within the area in which violence was potentially to be provoked, and its transmission elsewhere, now the need to show the same material throughout the country was conceived as so overwhelming that *all programmes* had to be fit to show in Northern Ireland. At the same time the Director General continued to emphasise that the I. T. A., despite the highly publicised visit of its Chairman to the Home Secretary, was in no way being subjected to governmental pressures.

There has not previously been so explicit a revelation of the relationship between the I. T. A. and the programme-makers, or between a British broadcasting authority and the government, as occurred during those troubled days. The Irish question within commercial television, as within the B. B. C., had caused a solidification of relationships and the delineation of a set of tensions which are likely to develop in the next decade. No actual changes in power are involved; the B. B. C. retains all editorial authority, in a legal sense, at its highest level, and so does the

I. T. A. What has happened in the course of the Irish troubles is that the structures of control have digested the actual nature of the professional decisions that are made in the course of programme-making and have caught up with them. Broadcasting House and the staff of the Independent Television Authority have understood how programmes are made, and are confidently taking over various reins which they had previously left slack.

*　　*　　*

After the banning of the 'World in Action' film, 'South of the Border' by the I. T. A., a public meeting was hastily arranged to protest against the ban and the alleged growing 'censorship' in Ulster reporting. Although its organisation had been hasty, several hundred reporters and producers turned up at the I. C. A. in London, some of them from very far afield. The gathering included representatives of all the media involved in reporting the Northern Ireland scene – with one exception: no broadcasting 'official' was there. Protests flowed freely. One radio reporter alleged that a free and accurate representation of events on radio was being prevented. Several television reporters described their daily frustrations. But no picture emerged of a phenomenon corresponding to a classic definition of 'censorship'. Rather what the television and radio reporters were saying was that they wished to operate the machinery of broadcasting as if it were the press, free of any special requirement of 'impartiality' or 'objectivity'. The tension emerging between the broadcasters and their employers was a tension between an old feeling about broadcasting and a new one, between the view that broadcasting should invariably create and transmit a simulated, balanced model of the prevailing political scene and the view that broadcasting should now exist as a reporting tool pure and simple. The doctrine of impartiality had forced on broadcasting organisations a social role that now made them extremely vulnerable. Since objectivity did not flow naturally out of the material being presented, it had to be imposed by hierarchy.

*　　*　　*

During the decade or so since television reached technological maturity and saturation distribution within society, British politics has operated under a set of rules which have been widely agreed and seldom put to any strain since the Suez crisis. There has not been any serious disagreement about what constitutes 'fairness'. The troubles of Northern Ireland have made 'fairness' difficult to interpret, or rather have brought about a situation in which 'fairness' in a traditional sense has itself involved interference. It has proved impossible to report on Northern Ireland as if it were South Vietnam, because to do so *within Britain* and on television involves interfering with the course of events themselves. With the abolition of Stormont it has become easier again to return to 'fairness', because the events of the province have been placed within the context of the British political scene, and because the Ulster Unionist politicians have begun to look like a faction themselves, like men trying to alter a *status quo* rather than men trying to defend one. The rules about interviewing the I. R. A. have not been relaxed but their interpretation has been liberalised: a reporter feels now that when necessary it is worth asking for permission to include an I. R. A. man because it is far more likely to be granted. But the apparatus of supervision within the B. B. C. is well oiled and will not be dismantled in the foreseeable future. It took many years to wrest editorial power from Broadcasting House to Television Centre and Lime Grove in the days when television was first hit by commercial competition and started to build up the reservoirs of talent necessary for the struggle. It has taken the Irish crisis for that balance of power to swing back again. Broadcasting House (that is, E. N. C. A. and the Director General) once again 'edits' the content of programmes on a day-to-day basis, from concept to transmission. The whole mood of broadcasting is changing under this transformation.

The power of Broadcasting House when used to orchestrate the content of two television channels and five radio wavelengths to the tune of a single institutional policy is awesome indeed. It is a power which has necessarily to be wielded responsibly. But that, in a sense, is the trouble. Broadcasting in Britain now waits in practice upon the judgement of a couple of men, fallible, under constant harassment and no doubt overworked. What does 'responsibility' constitute in the context of the miners' strike? How is the 'national interest' to be defined in the context of mounting industrial trouble in order that broadcast reporting of the latter should not rock the boat? There is growing anxiety in certain sections of the broadcasting world about the role of the authorities in regard to recent strikes. To hold enormous centralised editorial power is to incur an obligation towards caution. Rather than decreasing the pressure on broadcasting it is likely to increase it. The greater the expectation on the part of the audience of total impartiality (balance within every programme) the greater is the impact of television, and the greater the subsequent tensions. The religion of objectivity makes the whole medium excessively exposed to the discontents of various social groups. It is also the most chimerical of religious beliefs and the hardest to put into practice.

The paradox in the British system of broadcasting is that the organisations are powerful in self-defence as well as irresistible in their periodic fits of caution. In the case of 'A Question of Ulster', the B. B. C. programme in which three distinguished men sat on a kind of 'tribunal' and questioned a group of people representing the whole spectrum of Irish politics, the B. B. C. was able to ignore a concerted attempt by Home Secretary Maudling and the Prime Minister of Ulster, Brian Faulkner, to get a perfectly straightforward, predictable and untroublesome programme off the air. The sheer power generated by the size of the B. B. C. was sufficient to thwart government pressures of that kind, which in this case were aimed at persuading intending participants to withdraw. And as it came about, both Stormont and Downing Street were left without live representation in the discussion, which was marked by its atmosphere of all-round restraint. Of course the Home Secretary's fear was that the open and comprehensive nature of the programme would tend to usurp the function of government in bringing the various elements in Northern Ireland together: but ministers constantly fail to appreciate the difference between television and reality: a television programme is a representation, it is not the real thing.

But there is a further lesson to be absorbed from television's 'Irish crisis'. All programme formats are in essence formulae for handling events and explaining them. Once you define a programme format you create a tool which is likely to implant its own image on the events it is trying to represent. There are things which cannot be contained within 'Panorama', certain perspectives fail to become visible in that particular context among that particular group of reporters and presenters. Similarly 'World in Action' contains a different set of opportunities and concomitant limitations. News is itself a formula, a format, into which some phenomena fit and some don't, some expectations can be realised and others cannot. What has happened in some respects in Northern Ireland is that reporting on television quickly ran out of formulae; the 'Panorama' or '24 Hours' 'story' which depends on the depiction of events around a theme chosen by the reporter, around a personality or a paradox or an issue, was simply unable to contain the kind of material which the situation was accumulating in a way which could satisfy the B. B. C.'s own special needs. To explain the events of Ulster using anything more than the straight day-to-day techniques of news reporting, you have to go back to the beginning of the story each time, or you have to ensure that each partisan group involved in a particular situation was studiedly represented. The 'film story' as a formula simply cannot cope with the amount of detail involved.

On a number of occasions the major current affairs programmes went back to 'the beginning', to 1969, to 1916, to 1912, or to 1688, to explain fairly and accurately the origins of a particular issue. But to do that properly involves a colossal amount of intellectual and technical work, even to cram the material into a programme of an hour's or two hours' length. That work has been done, frequently and adequately. But it cannot be done every day and the issues and events week by week cannot always be placed in a vessel of that nature. The whole set of formulae by which current affairs programmes have lived in this country since the foundation in 1957 of 'Tonight' and the extension of daily and weekly journalism into television is under strain as a result of Northern Ireland's crisis.

No one could call the manifestations of this strain 'censorship', not when viewed from outside the broadcasting organisation as a whole. But inside, in a context in which the reporter sees his duty as coinciding with and competitive with that of the print journalist, and at a time when the techniques available actually enable him to provide a service of this kind, the impending and existing restraints *feel* like censorship, or a demand for self-censorship. The question therefore is how broadcast journalism is to be controlled in future. There is little likelihood that the authorities are going to relax their control soon, especially when it is being partially exercised to ward off worse threatened forms of control from outside (a Broadcasting Council, the splitting of the B. B. C. into separate groups, etc.), which are being pressed for in certain quarters.

In my view the only viable path ahead is another slow and irksome one, involving the growth of professional organisations among programme-makers and 'media workers' in general. These could create their own counter-pressures and their own counter-precedents. In Germany there has for two years now been a considerable growth in organisation among producers to combat the increasing interference of politicians directly in the internal affairs of the programme companies. In France too the trade unions within television have taken an increasing interest in questions involving programme content as well as pay and conditions. So many of the day-to-day problems are difficult to resolve by argument; they are questions of mood and emotion. But at some stage the increasing centralisation of power in our broadcasting organisations is bound to invoke countervailing force to balance it.

Chapter 10

Community Conflict and the Media*

Whenever I am asked to speak or listen to others speak on a topic which contains one of those now familiar equations between the 'media' and something else, I experience a sudden shudder of anticipatory gloom. It is the gloom with which one might be condemned to roll a large boulder up a steep hill, in the certainty that it will roll downwards as soon as the summit is within reach. In trying to discover a precise or even meaningful connection between the media and smoking, or violence, or hygiene or drug-taking or the increasing incidence of sunspots, we are at the outset nearly always involved in a methodological error: we are trying to build discussion about human values around a mathematical metaphor. To study the influence of something on something else one is, implicitly, promising to find a numerical answer to question which cannot have a fair answer at all; we *want* to be able to say that a mysterious factor X in television programmes causes the viewers to behave in certain way; we half-consciously hope we will isolate the virus of violence from the totality of media content, and thereby cure society of a hitherto un-

---

* Originally delivered as a paper to a conference on Ireland and the media held at the Corrymeela Community, Northern Ireland in the spring of 1975.

diagnosed disease. But personally I doubt whether a media sociologist will ever get the Nobel Prize for Science, though I pray that one of them will one day deserve the Nobel Prize for Peace.

Yet at this inference we have set ourselves one of those quasi-scientific problems; we are to talk about the connection between community conflict and the media. A law of uncertainty supervenes in all attempts to examine connections between social phenomena: things that you can measure you simply cannot predict, and explanations once discovered can never be re-applied. You can find out very precisely the avowed voting *intentions* of an electorate, but you cannot predict the way they will vote. When the votes have been counted you certainly know more about the prevailing direction of politics but without being able to deduce which way the same people would vote six months later. Societies behave, it seems, according to the second law of thermodynamics; the apparent randomness of human behaviour and events increases through time. We can know the position of any one thing at any one moment, but not the direction in which it is going; or, we can detect the direction, but without being able to know where the object is. I hope I am not doing any great damage to thermodynamics in borrowing this concept of entropy. It is certainly a valuable cautionary device for presenting our topic. It is possible, to use the classic example of the last decade of the interaction of media and social conflict, that in the famous riots in Watts County, California, the use of live television cameras mounted in helicopters showing looting in the streets of one block encouraged the neighbours in the next block to engage in similar pillage; but one cannot deduce from this that the same thing would happen again in the same or any other place: the attitudes of the people would have evolved differently towards the idea of property, towards the police, towards the media. The very known history of what happened in Watts County altered the nature of later militancy in times of communal tension. Different leaders exist in the larger world, and different ideas are circulating in society. I am not merely saying that anything one tried to say in the way of prediction would have to be imprecise; I am saying more than that. I am saying that the intervening variables between one state of reality and the next are great enough to make nonsense of the process of prediction. It is all very well for pollsters to say that they have a margin of error of 3 per cent in both directions; that 6 per cent is more than enough to decide the outcome of any actual election. One might be able to say that in a particular situation a television programme which emphasised certain emotions actually brought about a riot or averted one; but you can deduce from that absolutely nothing at all about any other programme in any other situation. Personally, I am very encouraged by this conclusion; as a broadcaster I have always felt that decisions about programme content should be rooted in personal moral values rather than in sophisticated calculations about effects. It is hard enough to find out the truth and tell it, without trying to think of ways to modify or withhold it in order to bring about or to avert certain consequences. A consequence which appears to be averted may well assert itself immediately after the period of observation is over; by withholding information about the bellicose intentions of organisation A, one might prevent organisation B from arming itself, but they might do so as soon as one turned one's attention elsewhere or they might fail to believe one's reports about organisation A on a future occasion, thereby multiplying the prevailing dangers. One may make judgements about intentions without being able to trace clear results. The discussion about community conflict and the media, therefore, as I see it, is necessarily one about values, about the morals and ideals of communicators, about the constraints and ethical systems within which media operate or fail to operate. They work within immensely complicated sets of social interactions, which are so mutually reactive as to be incalculable. The after-effects of media coverage upon a situation, like the after-effects of any other piece of activity within the political continuum, multiply with time, not like the ripples in a pool but rather like the molecules in a gas, which move along increasingly random paths.

I am also very nervous about the phrase community conflict. Was the English Civil War a community conflict, I wonder? What about the first Arab – Israeli War? Or the seaside fights in the last decade between Mods and Rockers? The Notting Hill riots of 1958 certainly were, and so are the troubles in Cyprus. Must community conflict always imply that there are two different cultural or racial groups struggling within the same geographical or political entity? Is class war a form of community war? When larger issues superimpose themselves, as in Vietnam or Malaya, does the classification remain viable? I'm not certain of the way to answer any of these questions, but I know that a firm 'Yes' or 'No' to any one of them would necessarily alter anything one could say on the subject of the role of the media. In Belgium, two cohabiting communities are divided along linguistic lines with partial religious and social overtones; they have now found it necessary to divide their media and their universities along communal lines; each insists on total control of its own television and its own teaching; although both appear to want to stay inside Belgium, neither wishing for eventual union with France or Holland. Neither side, as far as I know, blamed the *media* for the conflicts of the 1960s in Belgium, because French- and Flemish-speakers knew they were fighting over actual interests; neither community expected fair journalistic coverage of the situation from the other, and it quickly became clear that the business of news collecting as well as the business of entertainment necesssitated completely divided control. R. T. B. would speak to and for French-speakers. B. R. T. would have the same relationship with Dutch-speakers. Both communities perfectly happily watch French or Dutch television across the frontiers – those services are outside the quarrel. The Belgians discovered, tragically but perhaps in a spirit of well-justified realism, that you cannot have political autonomy without separate media, especially news media. Autonomy of information is inextricable from autonomy in other spheres. The doctrines of journalistic impartiality and accuracy do not have the reality of applicable facts; they can be little more than pious intentions when a society suffers from real or believed divisions of interest.

The difference between the modern media and those of the past is that now mass newspapers and mass television speak as to an audience of the whole society. The economics, the administration, the policies of journalism are national rather than sectional. In England we still enjoy a very clear sense of shared news values – one can assume that the same headlines will be meaningful in Manchester, Stockton-on-Tees and Southampton, although in recent years it has become clear that on certain issues, especially relating to economics, there are widely different perspectives which cannot be reconciled within the same set of news priorities; but, as I say, in England, those differences are still marginal. In Northern Ireland, we have learned that there are quite separate sets of news values prevailing over a large area of topics. I don't just mean that there are different points of view – I mean that certain felt truths can only be stated by means of the suppression of other felt truths. In a society divided into parties and factions there can be, there has to be, an agreed set of news criteria; in a society divided into communities or confessional groups which do not wish to form or continue political union on the same terms, there can never be a shared set of news values, and in the context of modern media this means that the conflict in the political sphere spills over into or out from the media sphere. Imagine you were the news editor of, for instance, Israeli television, addressing an audience containing a number of very lively political factions but also a captured Arab community; you can, with difficulty, develop techniques of impartiality to provide news for all the former, but the news values of the latter have to be suppressed; if the Arabs were to run their own news service within the same organisation, they could only do so on the basis of their own values, which would only offend the majority Israeli audience. There can be communal media, in other words, but in such a situation no truly shared media, unless one side simply adopts the perspective of the other.

In a divided society there can be no real agreement about what constitutes news. Journalists like to believe that the judgement of news values is a mystery – a professional skill – and so it is, in a way; judging particular items of news in relation to others involves talent, skill and training; but the overall mesh of values into which such decisions fit is decided by forces which are broader than the profession of journalism. You have only to dip into the enormous treasury of journalistic literature in the English language to see how, at times, double standards have existed. The middle-class press of early Victorian Britain had a unified set of news priorities, but look at the illegal unstamped newspapers which circulated through the working class at the same time and you get an utterly different picture of what was happening; true, these versions were based on rival sets of news values operating within the same society, but one set of values was free and permitted, the other existed to serve a completely cordoned off, indeed illegal, news market. With the ending of the tax on papers in the mid-1850s, the old unstamped working-class press, lacking the necessary capital to participate in the great expansion of the press which then occurred, simply disappeared together with its whole journalistic approach, surviving only in the odd struggling radical Sunday paper like *Reynolds News*.

All societies contain suppressed sub-groups whose view of the central world may be different from the rest of the society and who therefore lose out in the struggle for journalistic consideration. As political realities change, so the concomitant media values change. Just compare the treatment of women in British newspapers, six years ago and now. News stories which involved women were at one time angled coyly, always emphasising the feminity of the subject; under the pressure of protest and as a result too of the general shift in public attitudes towards the acceptability of women in prominent jobs, it is now possible to read stories featuring women presented in a quite normal way. It is a question of fashion, but there is a powerful political tide which flows beneath fashion and influences both our attitudes and the realities of the society. Perhaps historians will be able to sort out or at least argue more clear-sightedly over the development of causes and effects. In the sphere of news values, one is looking at both cause and effect at the same time, one is looking at a kind of barometer registering the standing of an issue but also at a power which tends to influence events. Communicators provide, through repetition, our political symbols and imagery and they therefore perform the function of legitimising, as well as recording. The symbols of ignored or suppressed communities or classes within a society are themselves ignored and therefore suppressed. Politics and journalism are inseparable powers, overlapping battlefields, disputed pulpits. In current sociological writing one sometimes finds the term 'repressive communication' and I find it an apt one. The news media can in effect deprive a group or class of its place within the arena of discourse by giving it low or distorted priority editorially; to do otherwise would in effect be to perform the political act of liberation itself. The great controversies which some of us have witnessed over the presentation of news from Northern Ireland reflect, in a coded private world, the problem of registering political change as if it were merely verbal contextual change.

One implication of what I am saying is simply that where communities are divided politically, there *will be* dispute over what journalists report and the way they report it. There will also be some dispute about the values of mass entertainment. The carefully nurtured doctrines and practices of detachment and impartiality which are particularly important in broadcasting cannot survive in the context of communal conflict, if we are speaking of conflict between groups who wish to build the same society in fundamentally different ways. I am not saying that the media organisations cannot survive the conflict, but that they themselves cannot hope to remain outside the lines of fire.

As one talented journalist in the midst of the English Civil War of the 1640s was obliged to lament,

> I doe find that whosoever undertakes to write weekly news in this nature, undertakes to sail down a narrow channel, where all along the shore on each side are Rocks and Cliffs, that threaten him; and though for the present one side seems not so full of sands or Dangers as the other, and therefore many of us . . . do seeme to lean to that side most, yet who knows but that new tides may rise, and the rolling sands may remove to the other shore.[1]

The narrow channel of impartiality is a political convenience more than an intellectual ideal, and reality makes nonsense of it in difficult times. The problems of the media in the context of social conflicts are merely transmuted versions of those conflicts.

Northern Ireland has illustrated very clearly the problem of the inherent bias of news in recent years because its conflicts have had to be reported to a national audience which does not share an area of common historical allusion with the Irish. All reporting consists of taking events out of one context and describing them to people who live in another context; the rows which break out over reporting tend to arise from accusations of partiality, from allegations that the whole truth has not been presented. Occasionally too, disputes arise from allegations of complete untruth, but these are remarkably few and reporting from Northern Ireland has achieved an astonishing level of accuracy in purely factual terms compared with the reporting of any other conflict situation. But the historical context of each episode, well understood, though in different ways, throughout Ireland, is not *felt* in England or Scotland. News as a genre is founded on the criterion of new-ness – on the presentation of the 'freshest

advices' – and contains a profoundly important bias in its very
raison d'être, one that itself triggers off the kinds of distrusts which
have given rise to this conference. Every item of news is the
topmost bit of an iceberg of unspoken information; each fact in
our newspapers and bulletins contains with it the implications of
a whole theory of the situation; a general historical interpretation
is embedded in each item of information which may in itself be
'true' but utterly biased at the same time. To say that the acting
President of Cambodia fled from Phnom Penh with the retreat-
ing American Ambassador implies a whole historical theory of
the situation in Indo – China and cannot be understood or at least
is in practise not understood outside a very broad context of
historical knowledge. It can be accepted as a fact of news which
different people can absorb into different ideological contexts;
but many items of information cannot be thus absorbed and
remain both truth and lies at the same time.

We customarily blame the conditions within which journalists
work for the over-hurried assessment of disputed information; we
blame the impatient eyes of news cameras and the hungry
rumbling of printing presses, the insistent demand of the
audience for the hottest of uncheckable facts. I see the position of
the journalist in quite a different way. It seems that the journalist
is imprisoned in his genre – whether this is hard news for the
nightly bulletin or in-depth investigative sensation for the
Sundays or even the Penguin Special summarising a complex
situation at a particular point in time. It is the genre which
determines the methods of the journalist, and the genre is an
expression of values which lie deep in the society for whom the
news is being fashioned. The sonnet is not an epic and its
sentiments are different. The novel is not drama and its whole
structure of episode is different. News is not history and history is
not news.

I want to take a very simple example of a news medium, a
rather unusual one, perhaps, but one which might help to show
how deeply politicised a process news collecting is.

In a village not far from where I live, some men have spent the
last thirty years of their lives making a waist-high model of their
village; it contains every detail of every building constructed
exactly to scale, every lamp-post, every shop sign, every stone
and slate. Whenever a change occurs in the village they pride

themselves on the speed with which they build the change into the model. As you may imagine, the model attracts a great deal of attention and brings far more visitors to the village than the village does itself. In fact you can learn more from looking at the model than you can by walking along the real streets. In the real village there now hangs a large notice on the church appealing for funds to pay for restoration and, naturally, on the model the same sign now appears – except that the money collected in the miniature boxes on the model is given to the real church fund. Recently, to the anger of many villagers, an ancient and much-loved oak tree was cut down; it had stood for centuries in the middle of the village and the makers of the model are so angry with the decision to remove the tree that they have refused to make the change in their model.

Now it occurs to me that the makers of this model have done far more than produce a replica of their village environment – they have created a news medium and they are using their cardboard and glue as a means of reporting. Suppose some terrible threat to the village were to be announced, the building of a motorway right through it for instance, or suppose the church collapsed one night in a heap of rubble; they might well rush to their model and make the relevant alterations, but everyone who came to see it would experience that emotion which is produced by news. The simulacrum of the calamity would create a focus for all sorts of tensions. If there were some important internal controversy within the village about a proposed change, the exact appearance of the changes in the model would automatically become a source of controversy itself; if the model makers made the change appear attractive, those opposed to the change in the real village would presumably take umbrage and complain that their point of view was being distorted, propagandistically, partially, in a biased manner.

Any medium of reporting carries with it the potential for being something more than a source of information and entertainment; every formed mimesis of events in a real world involves gestures towards the centre of power and therefore of controversy. Every attempt to represent the continuum of reality in a medium of communication – whether it be in music or sculpture or history or the newspaper – necessitates a statement evaluating the thing or event represented or described. It invites others to comment on its truth to nature; it confers a certain legitimacy on the described event and does so in terms of its own version of it by rendering it recognisable to those not directly involved.

I keep using the word power, although I know it isn't exactly what I mean. The reporter does not commence his function with the precise aim of usurping governmental or any other functions; that usurpation occurs as a result of a complicated interaction between the event, the society or community in which it occurs, the authorities within the society and the primary audience of the medium involved. I don't think anyone yet has adequately described that interaction though it has been profoundly felt by sensitive reporters in all media at all periods. What we do know is that in recent decades the various technologies and professions which specialise in reporting have become major conditioners of our experience of the world, and just as the villagers of whom I was speaking now learn more about their village from the model than the reality, so we derive a larger proportion of our scanty knowledge of modern events from television and the press than from any other means. The many tensions which constitute the power-lines of the world are expressed in the simulacrum of the reality created by the media.

A news event is only a news event when it is reported. It is the machinery of reporting which transforms a piece of reality into news. Until then the event is an unseparated part of reality as a whole; and any part of reality is potentially an element in news. The newsworthiness of an event is a man-made, a socially constructed attribute ascribed to events. The circulation of information in modern societies depends upon the complex physical and intellectual machinery of professionalised journalism.

What I think has gone wrong with the news circulation of our society is that it has become over-concentrated, over-professionalised; too few views of the reality – biased though they all are – are allowed to circulate powerfully. In the streets and neighbourhoods of a modern city you can cross a road and pass through an enormous gap in social space. Go to Columbia University in New York and walk up three blocks. Go to Paddington and look across the Harrow Road. In the past there have been many more routes through which news has travelled than there are at present. There have been many more sources of news, many more sub-genres within the world of reporting and journalism than there are today. What we have come to label the problem of 'access to the media' is a major cultural problem of our time, though it may appear a marginal one. I do not think that many of the growing conflicts within society would be avoided if we simply created more news outlets in broadcasting and the press for non-professionals; the very seeming marginality of 'community' journalism demonstrates the nature of the problem. Our minds and judgements are dominated by vast news-making bodies, which impose centralised images of the society upon us. We are all caught in the same trap; the professionals try to keep their imagery of the society abreast of events, in step with some kind of general demand, and their influence grows and grows. Beneath their powerful criteria by which issues are formulated and judged, there are other pressures which suddenly burst forth in the streets, in journalism, in schools, in industry. It is useless to argue that the machinery which has now come to fashion our imagery of political life can or should be fundamentally changed overnight. One should distrust any remedies for the historical ills of society which are based upon organisational shifts in the media preceding other forms of change.

However, there are certain changes which I believe one should watch out for and encourage. One of these is a major shift in genres within the media. What Northern Ireland's affairs have demonstrated for the British, and Vietnam and Watergate for the Americans, is that the forms of journalism which are currently employed are no longer adequate, they have cracked up under the strains of the events they try to reflect. The domination of banner headline news in the press and the thirty-minute blockbuster news bulletin in television has worn out its usefulness. This structure has succeeded in keeping society always one step more ignorant of what is happening to it than it requires to be. The research which followed the British referendum on Common Market membership indicated that, despite the media's desperate efforts to inform the public during the campaign itself, most of the voter's had not absorbed the basic facts. News media, by their nature, operate at too late a stage in the cycle of information. There is a gap between the picture of the society's dilemmas which is given us and the permanent deep-rooted feeling we all have that the crucial facts are not being set before us. Look, for example, at the reporting of the affairs of Northern Ireland before 1969; a deep and long-conspired silence prevailed; the instruments of news and of current affairs, of feature-writing and of front-page news, had all failed to find a form in which the truth of life in Northern Ireland could be described. It wasn't news, it wasn't background, it wasn't feature, it was a tiresome piece of history that was very boring and wouldn't lie down. It didn't seem to *do* anything else. A century ago, much was suppressed within the British press, but there were far more forms and models within journalism in which reports could be presented of apparently out-of-the-way social problems. The trouble has been that, with the domination of harder and harder news, a subject only gains the attention of journalists after it has reached the front page; and to get on to the highly competitive front page involves the intense dramatisation of an issue. How we bring about relevant cultural changes *within* British journalism is a difficult, delicate and many-faceted subject; we need to work out a new relationship between hard news and other material. We need to recognise that major media must be allowed to operate with sectional news values. We have to realign the professionalism of the reporter towards the society, outwards from the centralised criteria of the major news organisations. We have, in fact, to democratise the news-making machinery of our society in a variety of ways, to serve a variety of communities, not to divide up the society but to make the elements mutually comprehensible and the different priorities of each mutually credible. That will not solve any problem and the central problem will continue to produce conflicts within the media themselves. We know the journalist is not an historian, nor is he a doctor, nor a priest. His skills have to be shared throughout the society, though precisely how that should happen would be an entirely different subject.

Part 2

The Press

Chapter 11

News Values and the Ethic of Journalism – a View of the Western Tradition*

I

The American musician of the Jazz Era, Fats Waller, was once asked by a woman admirer to explain what a sense of rhythm consisted in; 'Lady', he replied, 'if you don't know, you ain't got it.' If you ask the average British or American journalist what his sense of news consists in you are likely to get a similar answer: for the journalist his sense of what makes news today is the result of long conditioning and subtle training in the knowledge of his audience and medium. He is likely to rub his thumb against his first and second fingers holding his palm upwards and explain, as if having chosen the spices for some subtly flavoured sauce, that his instinct for arranging facts into news is partly professional

---

* Originally delivered as a paper at the University of Cracow, Poland, in July 1976 at a symposium of journalists and broadcasters drawn from Eastern and Western Europe who gathered to discuss progress in communications since the signing of the Helsinki agreement.

folklore, partly the house-style of his own newsroom and mainly personal genius.

In modern times, since the overall importance of the journalist's activities has come to be generally acknowledged, a corpus of academic material about journalism and its values has emerged, all of which tends to ascribe to the maker of news for his individual creativeness than the profession ascribes to itself. Media sociology has been concerned with tracking down a range of constraints under which news is produced. 'Mr Gates' is the sociologist's journalist, who selects his news according to a narrow set of prescribed principles, the gatekeeper of news whose 'values' are imposed by the surrounding institution and society. The academic students of news and newsmakers have created in fact a whole range of competing explanations for the way in which the news values of a particular newsroom have evolved. All of them tend to dethrone the journalist and replace his creativity with a group of inexorable pressures.

Edward Epstein in his *News from Nowhere*[1] offers us a series of operational and commercial criteria for the selection of news, which are internalised by the journalists. Bernard Cohen in *The Press and Foreign Policy*,[2] published some time ago, shows us a journalist imprisoned within a hierarchal set of criteria which constitute the genre of news and which tend systematically to prevent that genre operating as a mirror of the world. In England, in the last year or two, we have Jock Young's analysis[3] of his 'amplification' effect, which shows how the popular press in particular conjures great archetypes of public concern out of the air and influences government through the creation of folk heroes and folk devils, the 'facts' of news growing out of the socially provided preconceptions of the journalist. I have chosen random examples. No media sociologist enters the field without discovering his own model of the news situation; we can now choose from many available models.

All of these sociological models are stimulating to consider but it is also worth looking at the origins of a problem before trying to reach a definite explanation or diagnosis of it, and in the case of journalism, in Britain and those countries now in the 'West' which have a well-established news tradition, one can trace the present subject of our concern back through several centuries. In fact, there has been a vigorous debate about news and the power of the media generally, since the publication of the first periodic organs of news in the 1620s. Quite quickly after the establishment of the genre, there grew up two separate parallel debates – the first about how and why the journalist chooses one story rather than another, the second about the personal ethic within which he works. Both of these debates have tended to employ the same terminology through the centuries, the words gradually altering their meaning through successive formulations. What we inherit is a confusing collection of meanings.

Before and during the English Civil War of the seventeenth century, journalists were already having to justify themselves according to the rubric of 'impartiality', for instance, although that word has acquired a number of quite separate applications. Another topic has always been the relationship between foreign and domestic news; the allocation of priorities between these has been a subject of constant historic concern, especially perhaps in an island nation like Britain. Yet another has been the tension between journalistic 'freedom' and social 'responsibility', which brings out the inseparability of the question of news from the wider question of social order. In fact, it seems to me that when we study the evolving values of news in a given society we are examining a phenomenon which reveals the successive terms on which social order has been established, contested and re-solved.

It is no accident that we speak of news *values*; the value of something is decided in a market place among buyers and sellers, some of whom are richer than others. The 'values' of the journalist are established under constant pressures within the society he serves; there is a tension between his existence as a free or creative craftsman and the nexus within which he works. He has a certain autonomy; the constraints, however, are the subject of permanent and unavoidable contest. His so-called 'values' are the interim contracts he makes with his audience as readers and his audience as society. Sometimes news takes on the character of a manufactured product, protected against outside interference according to the rules which guarantee a perfect market; sometimes news is openly acknowledged to be the basis of ideology and therefore administered directly by the state; though the apparent location of news in western society has shifted, it has always rested close to the issue of social order and its formal constraints have been provided precisely in order to guarantee truth, accuracy, impartiality.

II

Much can be learned by looking at the evolution of the concept of journalistic impartiality century by century. It was the Thirty Years War and the Civil War in England which followed it, which provided the material for the first news publications. The early editors were often so nervous of the repercussions of publication of political and military material – even when their publications were officially licensed – that they constantly resorted to defending themselves in print. Some of the titles of their papers even begin with the phrase 'An Impartial Account' of something or other. But the impartiality for which they strove was not directed at an abstract approach to pure truth; it was an attempt to steer through the political factions which surrounded them. 'So much exceptions are taken by one or the other that we know not what to relate. . . . In time of this nature it's not good to hold Argument'[4] was how one editor of the 1640s described his task. One paper even apologised for not giving the result of the great battle of Naseby, because the generals on the Parliamentary side were divided into two main factions and the editor wanted, as he tells his readers, to make certain that he divided the honours of victory evenly between them, and that would have to wait for another edition. The ethic of the seventeenth-century press was not an ethic of exposure, but of presenting under official licence the most important facts of the day or week; but even then the journalist had to hold the ring between factions within the licensing government. He was in politics because he dealt with material before the formal world of politics had digested it and his refuge was a doctrine of impartiality.

If you jump across a century and open the newspapers of the 1750s or 1760s, a quite different phenomenon is apparent. Now the papers are not licensed; the government controls the press through the laws of seditious libel, through bribery, paying for editorial material and leaving other political groups to pay for theirs also. Papers are very plentiful and so are factions. With the end of the Divine Right basis of kingship, power ultimately rested on opinion. The poet, Crabbe, mocked the 'journals of the night' as he called them, for what he saw as their unrelieved corruption:

> Some champions for the rights that prop the crown,
> Some sturdy patriots sworn to pull them down;
> Some neutral powers, with secret forces fraught,
> Wishing for war, but willing to be brought.[5]

It was a press of almost pure and open 'access' as the 1970s would see it. There was no great difficulty in getting your own point of view presented and in bringing before the public the facts of news as you saw them. Crabbe goes on to mock Henry Sampson-Woodfall, the one editor of his time who insisted on printing political speeches from both sides; Crabbe implies that his virtue was without point. In this context, however, the journalist still had recourse to the defence of impartiality. It meant that in the welter of propaganda and lies he was calling attention to the accuracy of a particular statement. It meant that he had not been paid to write something. There was no source of hard fact in such a news system, no independent news agency on whose accuracy you could rely. When a particular writer claimed to be being impartial he was claiming to have acquainted himself with all the factionalist material and to have reduced it to certain firm propositions, unpaid.

A century later the notion of impartiality started to become far more central to journalistic practice. The scores of sheets had been reduced to a small number of middle-class papers, expensive because they carried a heavy tax on each copy; there was also a wide range of illegal and untaxed papers which tried to present the news from the standpoint of anti-establishment factions and lower social groups. The middle-class papers were competing for the attention of very powerful and very large audiences who were still searching for their social coherence. *The Times*, for decades the principal paper in terms of circulation and influence, changed its policy on substantial issues from year to year as its editors sought to identify the needs of their readers. *The Times* wanted to lead and instruct its readers but never stand too far ahead of them or too far behind them; it had to solidify their attitudes to political reform, the repeal of the Corn Laws, the freeing of trade, moral questions, education, the monarchy. Hazlitt, one of the great literary writers of the earlier part of the nineteenth century, used to attack the paper for its fickleness – it could not be *bought* because it was always chasing after its readers. Indeed, the French Ambassador in London had once to explain to Louis Napoleon, shortly before he became Emperor, that it was fruitless to try to bribe *The Times* out of its anti-Napoleonic policy, because its prosperity rested upon its readers who were now so numerous that money simply did not exist in large enough quantities for *The Times* to be bribed over their heads.[6] Market forces now invalidated the ethic of the bribe. In such a context, impartiality in news had acquired a new meaning and function.

The paper existed mainly for the purpose of persuading its readers and therefore persuading the government. It was a platform for a class. The readers bought the paper for its opinions and the editorial writers were the lynch-pins of the news organisation. The reporters and correspondents who supplied the news had the function of keeping the editor as well-informed as possible in order that his editorial line would be unassailable in later debate. The editors of *The Times* are constantly reminding their staff to send in detailed appraisals of every battle and foreign election, reserving their own personal comments until the end. The great engine of the newspaper was to be powered by facts and unpolluted information, some of which would be published, the rest of which would go to keep the editor well-informed in directing the papers' propaganda line. There was still, however, no firm doctrine of hard news, 'faits secs', as the French call it, on which to build the profession of journalism.

It was the electric telegraph and the wire agencies which, in their quest for a market consisting of many newspapers at once, provided the basis for the emergence of hard fact in news. For a long time *The Times*, for example, resisted the whole idea of allowing anyone outside its own directly controlled staff supplying it with editorial material. Eventually it relented. The quantities of news demanded by readers were too great for one newspaper staff to supply. The telegraph was just too expensive for all the available foreign material to be sent over for one paper's use. 'Telegrams are for facts', said Moberly Bell, Managing Editor of *The Times*, to his correspondents, 'background and comment must come by post'.[7]

In the heart of late-nineteenth-century news there grew a new phenomenon and a new ethic of news, the transmission of an isolated picture of what had happened, presented with the apparently complete impartiality of the wire service. The medium was now the message. Of course, the European agencies were all highly biased in a national sense. The Americans found Havas and Reuters presented them with material which American readers did not want to read. There was an ethnic bias running through all the agencies, but within each geo-political area the news agency created the idea of there being an irreducible core of pure fact. The newspaper's task was to take this fact and embroider it, adding comment, rearranging it, personalising it, twisting it perhaps into pure propaganda, but always at the basis there was *an event* which had been observed and primarily recorded with supposed completeness and accuracy. Competition between journalists and papers in the era after the telegraph was based upon the skilful editing and presentation of pre-existing material. When the popular mass press arrived at the end of the century, the papers competed not with their editorial columns, but in the skill with which they selected the main news for their headlines and encapsulated it in terms meaningful to the vast audience. The editor no longer used ideology as his basic raw material, but information; the ideology is buried one layer down inside the news. Propaganda was something you did *to* the news.

There are important philosophical roots of the phenomenon of 'hard' news. It represented the triumph of positivism. The mind of the reader was considered to be a *tabula rasa* upon which sensory data was recorded. Opinion was reached as a result of his judgement working its way through the successive accretions of information. Facts were sacred and comment free, as C. P. Scott of the *Manchester Guardian* used to say. In news, as in post-Darwinian science, careful observation could lead to the incontrovertible discovery of pure information. At least, that was the archetype which formed the basis of journalistic training, the complete bifurcation of fact and opinion.

III

The twentieth-century journalist, therefore, came to inherit two contrary sets of duties: on the one hand he was now the agent of opinion, the conscript soldier in the social battle of ideas, the employee of a free press living by controversy; on the other hand he had become tied to an ethic of pure fact, he was expected to put truth before everything else. He had acquired social responsibilities in the light of which his performance, as an employee of a newspaper owner, frequently became the object of attack. What previous centuries had found tolerable in the journalist, the twentieth century, its political faith resting upon the uncorrupted moral supremacy of the uneducated common man, rejected. The collector of news, in fact, was now working against a background of infulfillable expectations on the part of the society which have led to the whole business of news becoming a major flashpoint of controversy.

The First World War was accompanied by a terrible carnage of truth in reporting; newspapers throughout Europe and America were placed at the disposal of systematic propaganda. The newly established mass press in Britain became an engine of anti-German lies, professionally organised by men who had acquired a crude understanding of the science of mass psychology pioneered in previous decades. The mass press and its owners were at their most powerful politically. The chief owners of the popular press in Britain climbed directly into the world of politics; it was supposed that Northcliffe and Beaverbrook must have political ability if they could wield such great behind-the-scenes political power. Their performance belied expectation and on the whole the power of the press barons declined as the century wore on. They became pure businessmen, interested conspicuously in profits rather than political aggrandisement. In the 1920s, public opinion recoiled in horror at the recollection of the misuse of the press in the 1914 – 18 period, and in the reaction against what had happened, a new press ethic rapidly evolved. It owed much of its rapid establishment of itself to the arrival of broadcasting, which had at first eschewed news altogether on the grounds that this would lead the new medium into the difficult field of political controversy; however as radio grew up it became clear that it could fall back firmly upon the doctrines of hard fact and build up a news policy completely bereft of the traditional functions of news as part of controversy. With broadcasting's arrival as the new dominant medium, the primacy of the social responsibility of the newsman became general. From the 1930s onwards, therefore, the 'social responsibility' theory became the main ethic of the journalistic profession. The National Union of Journalists drew up a code of conduct, for example, which clearly put truthfulness even above obedience to an employer. In Germany the post-war Federal Constitution spelt out very firmly the 'social mission' of the press. In the United States, the Federal Communications Commission in the field of broadcasting and the Hutchins Commission on the press have both helped to establish in the information industries codes of conduct which place social duties well above the normal range of master-and-servant responsibilities. The Fairness Doctrine emerged as a neutralising force in broadcast journalism, which counteracted the journalistic ethic of the market. News was an industrial product, but with a difference.

In the eighteenth century the principle of 'freedom from prior censorship' was established through struggle though frequently observed for periods of time, but the nineteenth century transformed the *audience* of news to the point at which a new formulation of old dilemmas emerged. In our century we have begun to grapple with these new problems, which relate mainly to the *effects* of journalism upon the mass audience which has not come up to the expectations of the positivists. It is volatile, not rational, and as a result of this sort of disillusionment with the audience, the subject of news values, in our time, has been wrapped up in the realisation that media power overlaps with political power in its sheer reach over the enfranchised politicised mass audience. We are far from resolving this issue and are reaching a stage in which we can see that a clear conflict exists between the ownership system of newspapers (and in some cases of broadcasting too) and the responsibilities of the professional journalist. We have seen in France, Germany, Britain and Scandinavia, as well as America, the development of a movement for 'newsroom democracy' for some sort of professional control over or representation on the management boards of news enterprises. The argument used against this new-found cause is precisely that the journalist is unelected and exercises his political power arbitrarily. The owners, whether private persons or public bodies, by accepting on behalf of their organs of news, some sort of general social responsibility, are a better guarantee of non-propagandistic news than a democratic newsroom in which small political factions could usurp the policy-making function.

Until the Second World War the main tension in British journalism was between editors and owners, who daily fought out a subtle battle of wills, sometimes one side coming to dominate, sometimes the other. In the days before the new mass press, the editor had created a position for himself as the representative of a political grouping; if a paper was sold to an owner of a different political persuasion (even within the same political party) the editor would leave and move elsewhere. That happened very frequently indeed and prominent editors, like Sir Edward Cook and W. T. Stead and A. J. Gardiner, moved from paper to paper as wealthy Conservatives, Imperialist – Liberals and anti-Imperialist Liberals bought and sold their papers among themselves. With the establishment of a mass press competing with news, and news presentation, rather than with editorial comment, the editor tended to become a pure technician and played the role of close confidant of the owner, chief steward in his great household, like Arthur Christiansen to Lord Beaverbrook. Today, the editor has become far more important and is the object of major tensions within the world of journalism; he has much more political power in the British press than his immediate predecessors and the problem of how a story is to be selected and presented has become a source of conflict in some newspapers between journalists and editor. A number of newspapers and magazines have developed elective processes for choosing the editor, and this new 'democratism' is leading inevitably to important changes in the notion of what constitutes news and what the duties of the journalist consist in. What we are feeling today is the destruction of the bifurcation of fact and opinion.

IV

The positivist belief in a central core of hard fact is receding; we have discovered that ownership and control are the key influences upon the selection and arrangement of news and the right of ownership has lost the moral supremacy it once enjoyed. The market forces no longer content us as the sole basis for guaranteeing the freedom or impartiality of journalism. The generation of students of 1968, today firmly entrenched in the world of journalism throughout the west, has lost perhaps its revolutionary fire but has brought to the newsroom none the less a sharpened set of radical disbeliefs which are changing the basis of authority within the news enterprise, and with it fundamental assumptions about what the duties of the journalist consist in.

What we today accept as the central set of notions governing the conduct of journalism in the western world thus consists of the successive encrustations of ideas about the role in society of the mediators of information going back over centuries. Each country, or rather, each language, has acquired its own pattern of ideas which exist frequently in a state of tension with prevailing systems of newspaper ownership and government control. The evolution of the notion of impartiality has been very roughly stretched here, but it indicates some of the many traditions of journalism which are together fused into a non-coherent but recognisably autonomous western view. It contains the notion of total separation of press from government, analogous with the doctrine of the separation of powers; allied with that is the idea of the press as Fourth Estate, standing over against the civil power, a rival focus of social authority; it involves also the belief in the supremacy of the readers as this is expressed through market forces, and this makes it difficult in western countries for governments to own newspapers or control them, even where there are arguments for this to happen. This whole group of beliefs is infused with the idea that authority automatically militates against credibility: if someone says something which he is obliged to say, then it is probably untrue or biased.

There is a second main group of inherited assumptions which belong to the ancient crafts which make up journalism: there is the belief in the protection of the identity of sources which goes back to the days when the printer took legal responsibility for his material in respect of the laws against seditious libel: he could escape the law and imprisonment only if he offered to reveal the identity of the suppliers of material to his publications. The journalist acquired, therefore, this same *esprit de corps* borrowed historically from the code of the printers, and reinforced through the course of a century in which it was believed that all contributions to a paper carried more weight if they remained anonymous. There are important codes concerning accuracy which descend from the craft-protectiveness of the shorthand reporters: shorthand did more to establish the professional respectability of journalism than any other single factor: the reporter who recorded the *ipsissima verba* of a political speaker and passed it on to his readers carried with him an aura of extreme authority. Shorthand was the mirror held up to nature indeed; for centuries men had tried to perfect a viable form of universal shorthand. From the 1820s, under its glamour, the journalist established himself as a member of an honourable profession; he was no longer the hired hack of tradition. The self-protection of the reputation of reporters as a group helped greatly to establish journalism as an autonomous career.

A third group of beliefs which contribute to the congeries of assumptions we employ today derives from the various relationships which journalism has enjoyed with the audience. For a very long time newspapers were competing to make headway into an enormous and unexplored market; new readers were found among non-readers. But from the point at which the newspaper had virtually saturated the primary market – about the turn of the present century – the relationship changed. The newspaper market was not mainly to be captured by the skilful and repetitive colonisation of opinion, but by more varied forms of showmanship. The newspaper, whether popular or middle class, was turning into one of the new media of mass entertainment; the newspaper owners were obliged to manage their way through great demographic blocs, their newspapers' identities changing with the forces of social change, with the evolution of new social groups and especially with the emerging aspirations of the working-class reader. This has taken place in a period in which the newspaper has become, in Britain especially, part of the apparatus of big business, corporate capitalism, call it what you will. With the new difficulties of the mass newspapers in Britain as a viable industrial undertaking, with the growing concentration of press ownership, and with the urgent need for capital to transform the production system of the newspaper from the mechanical to the electronic, new forces are emerging in the newsroom, which promise to impose new assumptions upon the old ones.

The various traditional mystiques associated with the collection and distribution of news are disappearing: the electronic media are much more accessible to the audience than the old printed media. The politics of the last part of the twentieth century is a politics of groups; the large ideological parties are gradually coming to take second place to another set of organised pressures in society, groups demanding specific pieces of social change, making specific demands for preserving or altering the status of groups. Western societies present the spectacle sometimes of disintegrating under the weight of overlapping demands which in the past would have been rationalised within the ranks of a major political party. These developments (which should of course not be exaggerated) are requiring quite new roles for the media, and new functions and new loyalties on the part of the journalist. It is possible to argue that we are approaching a new journalism of opinion in which the hard fact is collected to support the claims of a given group conducting a short-term *ad hoc* contest with the rest of society. This involves new kinds of specialism in the journalist and new forms of ethical commitment. Let us take, for example, the case of Scotland, which in the era of North Sea oil, is increasingly aiming to demand a completely 'new deal' in British society. The role of the journalist in Scotland, in explaining the fascinating developments in attitude and consciousness among all the social groups of that country, is a very important one; he was to find quite new formulations of his professional beliefs to accommodate this new and very long-running story. His job, if he is working for a national newspaper, is to influence its policy through accurate information, but also to establish his credentials with previously non-newsworthy groups.

In Northern Ireland, in the period after 1969, journalists found themselves confronted with quite novel moral problems of reporting; there, they had to describe a sort of civil war within a part of their own audience of readers and the problem of whether one should tell all the truth all the time when this could cause one group of readers to do immediate violence to another, became extremely vexed. It affected the selection and arrangement of news as well as the professional ethic of the reporter; the temptation to 'play down' a story for the sake of saving the lives of people whom one might know personally was very powerful. Sometimes the temptation became a duty, though this involved a conflict with other professional duties; sometimes it involved an instruction from an editor, which brought out tensions within the newspaper organisation. Above all, these dilemmas were visited upon the broadcast journalist whose audience was a simultaneous audience composed partly of the factions involved in the fighting. In conflicts such as these, one can observe the inherited corpus of attitudes undergoing a process of ultimate trial. The historian of the future could well decide that the last decade has imposed more problems for the journalist, and brought about a more rapid evolution of his professional code than any period since the Napoleonic Wars. One can be certain, however, that the fundamental archetypes of what press freedom and independence mean will remain, even though the physical vehicles of journalism are being drastically transformed.

Chapter 12

State Intervention and the Management of the Press*

History provides many examples of trends which have begun as a trickle of sporadic anomalies, and of major transformations which are composed of an accumulation of long-established trends. The history of the relationship between the newspaper press and the governments of western democracies affords us an illuminating example of this principle. Looking back over the last century there is now clearly visible a growing tendency for government to take the crucial decisions which underpin the prevailing structure of the newspaper and other information industries; such a trend runs counter to the notions generally accepted in democratic societies enjoying press freedom as to the appropriate relationship between authority and journalism and has therefore tended to be, as it were, overlooked as a matter of exceptional circumstance involving for example, the control of newsprint in wartime, the establishment of national news agencies, the subsidising of party newspapers, the manipulation of government advertising. In fact, the anomalous intervention of

* Published originally in James Curran (ed.), *The British Press: a Manifesto* (London: Macmillan, 1978). © Acton Society Press Group.

government in the transactions which constitute the newspaper industry can now, in the age of the 'new technology' and the increasing use of telecommunications in the press, be seen to have turned into a major international trend, occurring with increasing force of example everywhere in Western Europe and, indeed, elsewhere. What has still to be made clear is the way in which this trend is now turning into a major transformation, which in due course, may result in a situation in which it is considered normal for government to control the provisioning of society with printed and other media, without, of course, entailing day-to-day government control of the content, although the two roles may turn out to be hard to separate. It does not necessarily follow from this that the 'freedom of the press' which has long been thought to be inseparable from the essential private sector position of the newspaper will disappear; on the contrary, there are signs that those societies most aware of the changes taking place are also those most concerned to see that journalistic and informational freedoms are enhanced and updated to take account of the other changes. At least, that will be the argument of this essay.[1]

There are four major spheres in which public policy and media provision converge, in which circumstances provide the spur for government to intervene in the privately owned industries of the press. The four are telecommunications, monopoly supervision, the provision of information on the processes of government, and the organisation of political debate. Decisions taken at the level of society as a whole in all of these areas have gradually broadened the scope of the role played by authority in the governance of the press. In some cases there are ancient traditions legitimising intervention, in others there are modern economic emergencies which have invited official intervention. Throughout Western Europe, with a few important exceptions, government is, in the late 1970s, already being looked to as the primary guarantor of the press's existence. There are instances where a traditional monetary support to the press, so entrenched as to have become ignored, has been taken into the limelight in recent years and newly established as a legitimising precedent. There are other cases where a traditional government support has been re-examined with a view to its being withdrawn and redistributed differently within the press industry.[2] There are also important cases where government is intervening very directly in the transactions between advertisers, readers and newspapers in order to redress by administrative means the free working of the very same market mechanisms which have traditionally been thought to be the mainstay of a free press, but which are now coming to be seen as the underminers of journalistic diversity. What is becoming clear is that each act of intervention necessitates further acts, especially where intervention is designed to compensate for damage inflicted upon existing private press institutions by historic market changes or by government activity in other spheres (for example the inauguration of commercial radio or television). But in its broadest context, we are seeing a single complex of institutions private, public and mixed, evolving in modern societies as mediators of information and entertainment, mutually dependent, mutually abrasive, with functional overlaps and newly emerging demarcations. There is thus a kind of cultural–informational complex growing at the heart of modern societies, which does not in itself spell any kind of doom but which profoundly alters the way in which we should think about the role of government and the press.

In the case of Britain, there is one important distinction from most of the other countries of Europe in regard to the increasing power of government over the newspaper and periodical press: whereas all the countries of Western Europe are aware of what is happening and are taking steps to adjust to the new situation, British politicians, administrators and newspaper editors and publishers continue to think and speak as if nothing had changed, as if the press in Britain were utterly unsubsidised, as if media policy over the last quarter century had left the press in the same essentially private position as before the Second World War, as if the changes in the structures of ownership had not fundamentally altered the relationship of the press with society as a whole. In fact the British press has become one of the more heavily subsidised newspaper systems of Europe, enjoying a wider diversity of state privileges and concomitant risks than most other societies.[3] The divisions of the market in Britain between different enterprises are such as to have warranted, in the context of other societies equally dedicated to press freedom, further measures of official intervention to safeguard political diversity. One further contrast between Britain and other societies is that in the former nearly all discussion of intervention as a means for reforming or rededicating the press has been the prerogative of the left. Ideas for redistributing advertising revenues, for aiding the entry of newcomers to the newspaper market, for changing by statute the relationship between journalists, owners and editors and for encouraging co-operative ownership and control of newspapers, have nearly all emerged from the left and died within the left to a chorus of public disapproval. In many European societies the construction of national media policies, encouraging co-operative ownership, redistribution or advertising, the subsidising of newspapers as a branch of party activity, all in the context of improving the laws protecting journalistic activity against interference or hindrance by government or administration and guaranteeing the presentation of information by government to the press, have generally been a matter of national consensus, schemes for improvement emerging from parties of the right as well as the left and centre. At the same time it requires to be emphasised that in such societies (such as Norway, Sweden, France, Italy, Finland, Switzerland) a much higher proportion of the press itself is owned or operated by parties of the left who thus are concerned with intervention as a matter of practical administration as much as of ideological commitment.

In many European societies telecommunications was one of the earliest of modern public utilities to be subjected to national monopolies. It was also the first area in which international institutions took a major role in defining functions and in sharing a kind of sovereignty with national governments.[4] Britain was unable to participate in certain international conventions on the telegraph and telephone because she, unlike her partners, had not nationalised the telegraph at the same time as France, Prussia, Belgium and other countries.[5] Thus Britain was absent from the great international gathering at Paris of 1865 which created international standards for telegraphy and established Morse as the international language of the air. In the 1880s, international telephony started up, necessitating further action at governmental level, and within twenty years the birth of wireless telephony (and an accompanying scramble for patents) encouraged the German Government to take the initiative in establishing international standardisation and therefore governmental supervision of all the apparatus, institutionalisation and allocation of the electromagnetic spectrum. Throughout the second half of the nineteenth century, therefore, the newspaper press was coming to rely more and more for its informational input on a series of contrivances over which government held control.[6] Reuters' control of the telegraph installations of several foreign countries was short-lived. The papers of the provinces had come to see, in the 1880s, the distinction between operating a news agency which supplied content and operating the telegraphs themselves which were becoming national resources with multiple applications. Reuters was able to develop as a supplier of information for business as well as newspaper purposes and gradually passed into the direct ownership of the newspapers themselves, as did the Press Association. However many European countries came to face a choice between reliance upon a foreign source of international news and the construction of their own (necessarily subsidised) national news agencies. The establishment of a news agency, like the acquisition of a parliament, a flag and a currency, became one of the *sine qua non* of modern European nationhood. Thus, in the aftermath of the Versailles Treaty a cluster of new news agencies emerged, which all depended upon one form of subsidy or another, and have done so ever since. By this means Government in those countries has been able to develop a major role in providing the input, the basic content of the papers circulating within their boundaries.

Telecommunications services thus came to serve as one of the early channels (and excuses) for government subsidy to the press. In France for example subsidies are given direct to newspapers to reduce their telephone bills and telegraph costs. In Britain reduced telegram rates to provincial papers were once a mainstay of the non-metropolitan press, enabling it to survive the arrival of the big national dailies in the age of the railway;[7] this form of subsidy was soon whittled away, however, until it finally disappeared with the triumph of national over small-town papers. In countries with large and difficult terrain the story has been different: Norway,[8] for example, has decided that its essentially small-town press is to be preserved (it has never developed a national press) together with the political diversity upon which it is predicated. In order to deter the development of large regional or national papers and to preserve small newspapers with adequate information from outside the country, the

Norwegian Government decided to defray the entire telecommunications costs of the national news agency, N. T. B. Each
subscribing newspaper pays N. T. B. a fee based upon its
circulation rather than upon its distance from Oslo, the capital.
In this way a small newspaper within the Arctic Circle can
receive the same news from N. T. B. at the same cost per head as a
paper in Oslo.[9] For N. T. B. the subsidy is a subsidy to the
communities which benefit rather than to itself. It provides an
apt example of the way in which governments have found
themselves alone available to guarantee the media policies
required by a nation as a whole.

In the case of France, telecommunications and other subsidies
began in the 1880s, not as a means for keeping newspapers alive
(they were then at the beginning of a period of exponential
growth as an industry) but as a means of guaranteeing the *reader*,
the new citizen of industrial society, with adequate information
upon which to exercise the franchise.[10] It was a policy designed to
create popular knowledge following the Press Law of 1881 rather
than a tool for manipulating the market for newspapers; between
1880 and 1914 France increased the number of newspapers
circulating per thousand of the population from 73 to 244 (a
higher number than prevails in the late 1970s) and total
circulation from two and three quarter millions to nearly ten
millions (close to today's total).[11] The early subsidies were thus
part of a process of social decision-taking in France which
enabled its press to achieve, by international historical comparison, a very early 'peaking-out' in newspaper development.

Today the A. F. P., France's national agency, operates without
apparent subsidy, which it enjoyed in previous decades. Since
1957 France has helped the A. F. P. by obliging all *mairies*,
prefectures, embassies and other official institutions to take out
subscriptions to A. F. P., thus guaranteeing an income adequate
to its needs as an international agency.[12]

The relevance of these examples of government involvement in
telecommunications is considerably enhanced when one con-
siders the implications of rapidly arriving systems of satellite
printing. Already several Paris papers are partly printed in
provincial districts by modern telecommunicated devices. Fourteen French newspapers are working on systems of fascimile
printing. Five Scandinavian papers, several Italian and four

British newspapers are all operating page transmission systems to remote printing plants.[13] These systems make it possible for the markets within which morning and evening papers circulate to be less dependent upon geography and public transport. With the arrival of printing via communication satellites distance is eliminated altogether as a factor within cost:[14] it becomes as cheap for a Hamburg newspaper to print copies remotely in Munich or Paris as in Limburg or Berlin. The arrival of these telecommunications devices could thus transform the historic markets of the press throughout Europe; language areas alone, rather than zone or city, will become the natural boundary for the printed word. However, this new facility depends upon three new earth resources: satellite capacity, which is a matter for inter-governmental and industrial arrangements within regions, geo-stationary orbits and microwave spectrum allocation which are subject to international treaty. The new newspaper market system of the 1980s and 1990s will thus depend permanently upon government. In time the satellite may come to *feel* as available as newsprint or telephone time, but in reality it will become quite rapidly a moderately scarce resource permanently dependent upon skilful diplomatic initiatives and dextrous international dealing, especially when the developing countries begin to demand more satellite and orbital privileges for themselves.[15] One question which has already arisen to reinforce this interconnection between governments and newspaper in-dustries is whether the existing telecommunication subsidies will apply to remote printing by satellite and terrestrial link; in the case of France, the answer has already been given – yes.[16] Newspapers will be able to claim back part of the costs of remote printing as an entitlement within the national newspaper subsidy system. At a still later stage when home facsimile and teletext services become general, a large part of the information input of the press will be disseminated not merely to remote printing plants but direct to the reader's home by over-the-air links. Telecommunications services will thus have passed through three stages: first in providing information to the newspapers, second in helping the newspaper through its stages of production and finally in sending out the material to the audience.[17] Govern-ment agencies will come to operate as the essential enabling institutions, through whose hands all the transactions which comprise a newspaper must pass. A national agency will be the inevitable intervening mechanism between all information and its reception.

The newspaper has always been designed to meet the needs of two separate markets: advertisers and readers. In the period since the establishment of adult suffrage and the creation of mass marketing economies the newspaper has come to play a dominant role in the mediation of both forms of information. Without it the whole world of sport, for example, could not have been developed, still less the efficient distribution of new models of manufactured consumer goods. It was in the inter-war years in most European societies that newspaper diversity reached its peak: at that cultural moment it was possible for two strata of newspapers to exist side by side, the new post-Northcliffe 'demographic' papers and the much smaller political papers identified with specific political groups and often subsidised covertly by those parties or more openly by the owners of profitable mass distribution papers.[18] Contraction in the diversity of owners as well as in plurality of titles brought about demands even before the Second World War for government intervention.[19] During the war years the entire newspaper industry was socially controlled simply as a result of newsprint rationing and this form of control created an overall scarcity of titles and indeed of circulation too, to the extent that all papers were profitable and had difficulty in meeting all the needs of advertisers.[20] In Britain the consumption of newsprint did not regain the levels of 1939 until well into the 1950s,[21] and at this point the newspaper industry, freed from controls, was having to face the new rivalry of commercial television, as well as fundamental changes in the structure of advertising. With the abolition of retail price maintenance, manufacturer consumer advertising began to decline, the trend towards classified advertising began to accelerate; changes were occurring in the age structure of the readership of certain of the mass papers (*Daily Herald* and *News Chronicle*). The concatenation of new circumstances meant that certain categories of newspaper enjoyed a period of rapid growth (quality Sundays, provincial dailies and weeklies) at the expense of other categories. Overall circulation began to fall.[22] Middle-class spending power was able to command media in a way which working-class spending power was not. The result was a spate of vertical and horizontal mergers within Britain's press, combined with one or two closures. The Monopolies Commission investigated several of the more important of the mergers, in particular that involving the combination of *The Times* and the *Sunday Times* in a group which already owned major provincials.[23]

Much of the ensuing public discussion revealed that large areas of opinion believed newspaper concentration to be inimical to the public interest. In a period dominated by the factors alluded to above, however, there was little that public policy could achieve other than to investigate and to obtain assurances from prprietors. Thus, Lord Thomson gave undertakings to the Monopolies Commission that it was not his policy to interfere with the editors of papers under his control.[24] The owners of the *Daily Mirror*, on acquiring its competitor, the *Daily Herald*, gave a public undertaking to keep the paper in existence for seven years.[25] Thomson was fortunate in holding large amounts of stock in Scottish Television, most of which he was permitted to keep after the refranchising of the commercial television companies in 1967; newspaper groups were allowed to acquire sometimes substantial holdings in other television companies (for example Southern T. V.).[26] Public policy found it impossible to grapple with the problem of concentration; at the point of merger it was generally too late for intervention and the 'public interest' in the preservation of titles could only be met by the extraction of promises from proprietors.

In other societies monopoly control systems have experienced similar set-backs. In the Federal Republic of Germany any merger between two newspaper interests which brings their combined annual turnover to the level of 25 million marks must be reported to the Kartellamt;[27] a combined circulation of 60,000 to 80,000 daily would be sufficient to reach this figure. However, in no case hitherto reported has this led to the ending of a proposed merger. The Kartellamt is generally faced with the choice of allowing the merger or letting one of the papers collapse. In December 1975 the *Westdeutsche Allgemeine Zeitung* (700,000 circulation) merged with two smaller papers and created a virtual social democrat newspaper monopoly from Hesse across the Ruhr and as far as the Dutch border.[28] The number of separate editorial entities in Germany has dropped from 225 in 1954 (when the post-war reconstruction of the press was complete) to 122 in 1976.[29] In terms of visible titles the number of papers has dropped from 1500 to 1200 in that time, but increasing numbers of papers are only notionally distinct, their contents being shared by groups of papers. In the same period the average circulation of German papers has increased from 60,000 to 158,000.[30]

German press policy, like that of virtually all other developed societies confronting the diminution of newspaper titles or editorial entities, has observed the failure of admonition as a tool and has seen that the only apt alternative lies in direct subsidy to those papers which cannot survive the historic tendencies of the market. The German newspaper industry planned to set up a Press Foundation with the German Government to produce unpoliticised grants of cash to the press, but the plan was not put into effect.[31] Denmark, Austria and Switzerland, traditionally countries with a huge diversity of newspapers and firmly disposed against the introduction of subsidies, went through a veritable newspaper carnage during the late 1960s and early 1970s. At the end of the war Denmark had 150 papers but today has only 45.[32] Austria has watched four of its nineteen daily papers gradually acquire 50 per cent of the entire market between them and has been able to respond only with modest subsidies.[33] Switzerland, where the multiplicity of newspapers is an inextricable element of its unusual system of direct consultative democracy, its citizens voting on innumerable issues themselves, has watched hundreds of its tiny newspapers disappear since the end of the Second World War.[34] Where there were 300 papers with circulations below 5000 there are now only 160; where there were only six papers with more than 50,000 there are now twelve.[35] One element in public policy which has acted as a brake on the tendency towards the large conventional local or regional daily in Switzerland has been the Swiss Government's decision not to introduce commercial radio; thus, in its efforts to hold back the tide of mergers Switzerland has stumbled across the important contemporary fact that media policies exist negatively as well as positively. Government control over telecommunications is in certain circumstances a powerful anti-monopoly regulatory weapon.

A direct connection between television advertising and the

viability of newspapers has been drawn in several smaller countries; in the Netherlands arrangements were made to pass a certain proportion of television commercial revenue over to the press, as 'compensation' for damage caused to the latter by the existence of the former.[36] Complex calculations were made as to the amount of advertising which newspapers would have collected in the first years following the introduction of commercial television. Gradually the system disappeared when the causal connections became difficult to draw and when the revenue position of a large part of the press was evidently restored. In Belgium, however, the whole of the newspaper subsidy allocation is described as 'compensation' not for revenues lost to the press but for the simple existence of rival editorial entities in television.[37] Thus, the Belgian Government has formally 'admitted' that by setting up broadcast services at all, it has damaged the interests of the newspapers; 200 million francs are distributed annually in lump sums, broken down equally among the separate registered editorial entities.[38] In countries which have eschewed commercial television, on principle, such as Sweden and Norway, the connections between media are not established in compensatory terms. There, local monopoly is simply recognised as an undesirable consequence of certain developments in the market for which society must take responsibility, and this brings us to the third area of public policy, the intervention of the state in guaranteeing the freer flow of information within society.

The first country in which public discussion focused on the connection between concentration in press ownership and the ability of the press to fulfil its democratic functions was the United States. The early post-war Commission under Robert Maynard Hutchins[39] formulated a set of roles which newspapers undertook on behalf of society, and concluded that these could not be adequately fulfilled with an inadequacy of newspaper coverage. It asserted a clear role for the state in guaranteeing that the *roles* were performed. The Hutchins Commission's line of thought was rejected for quarter of a century although it helped to influence the thinking of Britain's first post-war Royal Commission on the Press[40] which led to the establishment of the Press Council, an instrument which has subsequently been re-imported, in a different form back into the United States. The same themes, however, have cropped up all over Western Europe in the period of newspaper financial difficulties when country after country has instituted investigations into whether and how the state should help support the enterprises of the press. In countries in which the norm for the newspaper market consists in two or three newspapers of different political persuasions competing locally, the growth of concentration and therefore of local monopoly appears to be much more serious than in countries where plurality is supported by the presence of large national titles. Sweden, for example, in the early 1960s saw extreme dangers to the flow of information within society in the movement towards local press monopolies. The sense of emergency developed there and in Finland and Norway much more quickly than in Britain with her numerous national press.

Where state financial intervention in the press is established on the basis of the general difficulties of the newspaper industry, subsidies tend to develop of a 'general' kind. Sums of money can be distributed, as at times in Italy and in France,[41] on the basis of newsprint consumed; money can be provided to help defray the costs of distribution. But when the state is considering aid on the argument that diversity of outlet is an essential prerequisite to the free flow of information when it logically follows that the financial aid must be organised in such a way as to guarantee the desired results, that is the preservation of dying titles, newspapers which are losing the battle for life in a particular market. Swedish press policy after its first Parliamentary Commission (1963)[42] was to pass out moneys through the political parties represented in Parliament; it was soon seen, however, that this tended to over-emphasise the party loyalties of individual papers. The subsidy continued as a subsidy to party activity rather than to the press and a second Commission (1967)[43] brought about another form of subsidy, cheap loans for technical improvements and aid with the costs of newspaper distribution. The wave of financial difficulties which hit the Swedish press in the late 1960s, however, was such as to render these new forms of aid nugatory. A series of closures took place and it became clear that money would have to be found to help the second and third papers *against* the first papers, community by community. The Centre and Social Democrats accepted this dramatic switch of policy, the Liberals and Conservatives opposing it; within five years, however, the

Liberals came round to supporting the idea of selective subsidy and the Conservatives greatly modified their opposition.[44] The 1972 Press Commission argued that national policy must be based upon the needs of representative democracy; diversity of media did not fulfil these needs, which demanded a representative press as such. The press served to facilitate communication between groups and scrutinised the holders of power among its various functions. Sweden thus came to develop and strengthen her laws relating to freedom of information: journalists are *obliged*, under the latest press law, to preserve the confidentiality of their sources. Government departments, including the Prime Minister's office, are *obliged* to open all of their files to the press. The dangers to the press of the libel laws have been greatly softened. At the same time the 1972 Commission recognised that these roles could be fulfilled only if press subsidies were directed at minority papers. Newspapers needed to be free politically and this entailed a *slackening* of the dependence upon party-oriented subsidy. They fulfilled purely economic functions also and these required local diversity. Under the new Swedish subsidy system, a Press Support Board receives an equivalent in money terms of a 6 per cent tax imposed by the Swedish Government on all forms of advertising in the country; all newspapers are taxed on advertising revenues received over and above three million krone per year. The Press Support Board then pays out the money to newspapers occupying less than 40 per cent of the household coverage in their particular zone of distribution, the zones being mapped by the independent Press Support Board. The Board is also empowered to help new titles come into existence and all changes in ownership tending towards the creation of newspaper chains must be reported and investigated. However, working collaboration between papers is encouraged; competing papers are provided with additional help if they agree to use the same system of co-operative distribution and if they agree to use new technical processes jointly. Thus Sweden has come to provide the state with a dual role in the press, that of guarding against interference by authority and that of guarding against a dimunution of titles. So far since the new policies were adopted scarcely any papers have closed.

Italy is another example of a society in which state intervention, now of ancient lineage, is seen to be inadequate to meet society's current expectations of the press's role; the state is being invited to take stronger measures of financial support, in the context of stronger measures to guarantee the functions of the newspaper. State involvement in Italy goes back to the days of Mussolini when journalists became a kind of registered profession with restricted entry and with enormous financial and functional privileges.[45] Journalists to this day have enormous salaries and enjoy travel concessions by air and rail; they also enjoy rights within their newspapers as members of Editorial Committees who have to be informed of any impending changes in ownership or management; they also enjoy a wide measure of intellectual rights over their written copy which may not be altered without their permission.[46] The newspaper industry also enjoys other privileges: the price of newsprint is regulated by a state commission on paper[47] and the number of news-vendors throughout the country is also controlled in order to avoid wastage of copies.[48] The Italian newspaper works within a complex mesh of controls, all designed to ensure its freer operation. Italians read fewer newspapers per head of population than any other country in the developed world and it is difficult to decide whether this is a result of or the cause of the system of controls. In the context of the present international financial difficulties of the press the Italian newspaper enjoys one serious disadvantage: the presence of the newspaper in the 'basket' of goods which comprise the cost of living index means that there is enormous pressure imposed by the Italian Government on the special Commission which controls the prices of those goods which have been removed from normal market forces to keep down the cover price of newspapers. Thus the Italian press is constantly having to demand permission to increase its price to meet its current losses entailing an endless spiral of intrigue and counter-pressure. The newest and most comprehensive plans for press subsidies in Italy (the Arnaud proposals)[49] involve strengthening journalistic autonomy as well as providing larger sums of direct aid, paid out according to newsprint consumed: under the Arnaud plan no newspaper owner would be allowed to acquire more than 40 per cent of the national newspaper market (although regional monopoly would not be prevented, since it has already almost occurred) and all journalists would have a say in advance of any takeover. The journalist would be given the same immunity in court in protecting confidence as the priest and the doctor, and his rights of intellectual controls of his copy would be extended. But perhaps the most significant of all the proposed changes is that which encourages the formation of journalist co-operatives to take over control of failing papers: wherever a paper is due to close an opportunity must be provided for the journalists employed to inherit the paper and any resulting co-operative will henceforth enjoy additional subsidies across the board (covering newsprint, telecommunications, distribution, etc.). At the time of writing it is not known whether the Arnaud proposals will become law.[50]

The interconnection between subsidy systems and ownership systems was an inevitable development in European national press policies. Public policy intended to prohibit monopoly and maintain diversity falls down, as we have seen in the case of Germany, when prevailing financial circumstances offer no practical alternative to newspaper closure. Businesses cannot be obliged to live if their owners desire to go out of business. The discussion of co-operatively owned newspapers and of 'newsroom democracy' in various forms is now over ten years old in Europe, and it was inevitable that at some stage the development of this movement and the development of subsidy systems would become interconnected, as they now have been in the Arnaud proposals. Scandinavian policy would also support such developments, although none has yet occurred. Italy, however, has one very successful newspaper co-operative in Mantua[51] where the local newspaper has been owned by its staff for several decades and where the newspaper itself is three centuries old. The co-operative is effective morally and financially and the resulting newspaper is indistinguishable in general format and function from its contemporaries.

Perhaps the most interesting feature of the Italian discussion and situation is, however, the institution of a powerful Editorial Committee within each newspaper enterprise, designed to safeguard the editorial integrity of the paper against sudden takeovers and changes in management or line. It appears inevitable that the enhanced role of the state in providing the revenue for the newspaper form will entail the reopening of the whole gamut of issues affecting editorial rights. We have seen in Britain how the legalised closed shop for journalists has evoked an intense debate over the rights of the editor, even where he remains directly the 'property', as it were, of the owner. Where the power over life and death of a newspaper is held by the state, much more fundamental questions arise as to the powers of the editor *vis-à-vis* the owner as well as *vis-à-vis* the staff. It is inconceivable that subsidies can grow much further within the context of increasing chain ownership in Scandinavia, Germany, Britain, France and Italy without this particular Pandora's box being reopened. It is open to question, furthermore, whether the opposition by publishers to the idea of subsidies in Germany and Britain is partly motivated by a desire not to open up this vista of questions, which would pass over to government a much fuller set of responsibilities to guarantee internal structures of control within the press as well as the general spread of titles.

However, it is the fourth area of public involvement, that of guaranteeing party debate, which has taken root most deeply in Western Europe. Across the whole of central and northern Europe, including Scandinavia, one can discern geological strata of newspaper formation from period to period, in accordance with the establishment of political parties.[52] Ireland, Belgium, Norway, Sweden and Finland are perhaps the countries whose modern press continues to evince most clearly the outcrops of this political geology. Let us take Finland, where the first newspapers sprang up after the Language Ordinance of 1850, part of the aftermath of the great trans-European national movement of 1848. When Finnish consciousness developed further in the 1860s a group of liberal papers were founded; then came the Young Finland movement with another group in the 1890s, the Labour movement with its agitational papers at the turn of the century, followed by the Agrarian Party and its newspapers. Before the First World War Finland saw a new group of illegal papers spring up under severe political repression and with the peace of 1918, the Young and Old Finnish movements and their presses were transformed respectively into the Progressive and Coalition Parties; then came the great divide in the labour movement, causing a split between socialist and communist papers. In the 1930s came the development of politics on the far right with an appropriate press. With the firm if belated establishment of Finnish nationhood came the media counter parts: a national news agency, a national radio corporation and a national advertising industry.[53] Even in the 1950s the small population of Finland (5 millions) enjoyed 130 newspapers, and today still has nearly one hundred, divided among eight distinct political groups, plus the independents. Now the important point to observe is that the papers which survived the first carnage within the earliest political groups to emerge have in general the greatest survival power. In fact the *Helsingin Sanomat*, the largest circulating paper, which reaches many towns far away from Helsinki every day, was until the 1930s one of the Liberal organs; today it tries to serve a variety of non-socialist political audiences as the leading independent journal. Since the end of the Second World War, the Agrarians have increased the total circulation of their papers (from 219,000 to 383,000 per day) and the Conservatives have increased theirs very slightly (from 346,000 to 377,000) but the Social Democrats and the Communists have retained very small circulations (128,000 and 110,000 respectively) even though the former has become a major political grouping in terms of voting strength. The independent group of papers (including the ex-Liberal, *Helsingin Sanomat*) has almost tripled its circulation, from 505,000 in 1945 to 1,319,000 in 1972).[54] The big independent paper has become the largest circulating paper in Helsinki and the most important *second* paper in every other town of the country. What this brief analysis is designed to show is the principle that when party formation is the basis of newspaper formation, the older newspaper groups have the chance to hold onto their market and build on it long after the parties they adhere to have given way to more modern political alignments.[55] Thus, throughout the Nordic countries the Social Democrat papers (and the Agrarians in some areas) are the hardest hit even though they enjoy enormous electoral support. It is not surprising therefore that political support can be generated for government to take over the role traditionally performed when necessary by political parties of subsidising party organs. In the conditions of the modern consumer market the demand for government support takes the form of a more generalised cultural policy – that the 'state' must support the continuation of party political activity through the press if private industry, through advertising, is no longer minded to do so.

Many countries have adopted measures of support for political activity as such.[56] Several (including Sweden at an earlier stage) have built their newspaper support systems upon their party support systems. Finland is the society in which this tendency has gone furthest and where large quantities of cash are distributed to the press via the parties. This method has the additional convenience of denying funds to the wealthy independent papers, and there is fierce debate as to whether the traditional postal subsidies (reduced rates on newspapers charged by the Post Office) should not be removed altogether and redistributed in cash terms through the parties to the party papers, causing very severe damage to the circulation of the *Helsingin Sanomat* and other independent papers (not all of which are wealthy).

A very special strain is put upon newspaper industries which have been traditionally dependent on partisan loyalties among their readers in the conditions of modern consumer economies. In a country like the Netherlands with fourteen political parties, a multi-party press is essential; the country's broadcasting system is also predicated upon a supposed necessity for political and confessional groups to enjoy autonomous editorial outlets.[57] However the demands of advertisers in the last decade in the Netherlands, as elsewhere, have been for audiences of a 'demographic' rather than a confessional nature. Party papers circulating throughout the geographical terrain of a nation are handicapped by high distribution costs as well as by other new advertising disadvantages: their readership is not homogeneous in advertisers' terms; it is increasingly expensive to deliver papers to it. The Netherlands, therefore, has a tension between growing regional papers without strong commitments and shrinking national papers with large but scattered readerships.[58] Proposals have been put forward for a special *Bedrijfsfond*, or enterprise fund which would assist papers to adopt the new techniques. Prevailing public philosophy is opposed to comprehensive Scandinavian-type subsidies, although socialist opinion is now veering towards certain forms of direct subsidy, distributed according to rational, neutral criteria. In Germany proposals for similar grants have foundered upon an inability to discover what such criteria should be; Germany, however, has a unique press system with many quite different types of newspaper within its borders which are difficult to fit into the same kind of subsidy system.[59] The German press has been rescued largely from the current wave of newspaper disasters through the sheer efficiency of its management and its ability to negotiate new technology into a large number of its papers with the willing support of unions and workers.[60]

There is a fifth area of public policy which provides governments with powers over the financial governance of the press on a scale not previously thought desirable. In all countries which have adopted Value Added Tax (which includes all within the E. E. C. and several outside it) newspapers have been given certain tax advantages. The Republic of Ireland is the only exception.[61] In Germany VAT is halved on newspaper sales.[62] In France it is reduced to 2.1 per cent, a figure which enables the paper with small amounts of advertising (on which VAT is charged at the full rate) to recoup the taxes it pays on its editorial content and on the purchase of equipment.[63] Everywhere else VAT is reduced to zero on newspaper sales. In Britain alone is VAT zero-rated on advertising revenue as well as on sales.[64] VAT provides a government with endless opportunities to manipulate the finances of the press as a whole; it provides it also with a permanent responsibility for monitoring the revenue position of the press and registering structural changes. In Britain the total amount of money saved by the press (or for the press by government generosity) amounts to a sum approaching £100 million per year, although the state itself loses roughly half that figure in revenue foregone. The press of Britain, by virtue of its much-prized zero-rating on sales and advertising, enjoys not only a colossal fiscal advantage, worth between 5 and 10 per cent of total revenue, but leaves the British Government with a permanent and powerful manipulative weapon. In many societies government advertising (which is everywhere of enormous importance to the press) is being distributed to all newspapers irrespective of readership. In Norway, for example, it is now national policy for government to buy advertisements in all papers within a given market, even if it would not do so on business grounds alone.[65] Government advertising in that and other societies has thus come to take on the character of a subsidy to the press and one carrying considerable potential for embarrassment and manipulation. In this area as in others the balance between aid and interference has to be most carefully weighed. Public policy has developed to the point at which the state has taken on the role of providing the possibility for a newspaper to exist; where the press formerly depended on two markets, the reader and the advertiser, a third has now been added, the state.

State intervention has reached a stage at which a new formulation is required for the traditional press ethic based upon a total separation of powers between authority and media. We can no longer pretend that information or media enterprises are utterly private businesses existing at the convergence point of supply and demand. Somewhere at the level of society as a whole the great decisions are being made, willy-nilly, not of what shall be said today in this paper or that, but of how many different kinds of paper shall exist and what level of interaction there is to be in the ownership and control of newspapers and broadcasting installations. It would appear to be important, therefore, that the whole range of interventionist decisions taken by governments should be moved further towards the light, so that implicit policy may be made explicit, so that society may in some ways participate in the making of the policies which ensure a particular spread of media in a given society. It is not merely a switch from the secret to the open; it is a switch from the muddled and haphzard to the planned and avowed. It is not in itself a threat to the traditional freedom of the press, but it presents a very powerful case for the re-examination of the traditional ethic of journalism. We are witnessing a turning-point in history which removes the media from the private to the public sector of society. It is no longer as clear as it once was exactly what the public sector now is and what its responsibilities truly consist in. We are not at the end of a discussion about press freedom but at the beginning of a completely new recognition of the nature of the problem.

Chapter 13

The Long Road to Objectivity and Back Again – the Kinds of Truth We Get in Journalism*

When we pick up a newspaper we bring to the task of reading it a series of habitualised assumptions – that the events it describes will have actually occurred, that those to which it ascribes the greatest importance are likely to commend themselves to us as being worthy of priority, that information concerning goods for sale will be presented differently from other information, that information placed in specific categories will indeed belong to them (sports, business, entertainment, stock prices) and that the whole of what appears will have passed through a process of collection, checking, arrangement and general consideration consistent with the previous practice of the paper. In other words we approach the newspaper product having absorbed certain routines of comprehension, accepting the special codes of the newspaper genre; these are presumed to follow the routines and codes used by the journalists and compositors who create the

* Published originally as chapter 1 in James Curran (ed.), *Newspaper History: studies in the evolution of the British Press* (London: Constable, 1978). © Acton Society Press Group.

paper. This might make the newspaper sound a very settled product, unchanging in its intentions and presuppositions; in fact, it is in a permanent state of flux, its working practices and controlling mechanisms constantly shifting with the altering varieties of news demanded of it, the altering fashions and interests (which it seeks both to record and foster) of its audience, and the altering techniques and sub-departments of the profession of journalism itself. In recent years we have come to use the word objectivity to describe the most enduring quality expected of journalism; sometimes we speak of being objective as of a technique, sometimes as a glorious goal, occasionally as an external purpose which the journalist is supposed to serve. Recently the idea of objectivity has become subject to various kinds of criticism, some of it severe: it has been accused of being intellectually impossible, or impossible within the modalities of journalism. Alternatively it has been accused of being fraudulent altogether, a 'strategic ritual'[1] used simply to defend journalism against its host of critics and inquisitors. What have been the expectations held of the journalist in other periods and how has he coped, in self-defence and in professional self-rationalisation?

So many of the terms in which the journalistic pursuit of the realities of the world have been described have remained constant while their meanings have changed that this question is indeed tricky to deal with. Jacques Amyot, introducing his edition of the *Lives of Plutarch*, cautions us against those writers of history who 'cover and cloak their own passions' and then lists for us the properties which are necessarily required of a story writer, as these:

> That he set aside all affection, be void of envy, hatred and flattery: that he be a man experienced in the affairs of the world, of good utterance and good judgement discern what is to be said, and what to be left unsaid and what would do more harm to have it declared, than do good to have it reproved and condemned: forasmuch as his chief drift ought to be to serve the commonweal.[2]

It might be the voice of Lord Derby reproving Delane of *The Times*, insisting that journalists ought to 'maintain that tone of moderation and respect even in expressing frankly their opinions on foreign affairs which could be required of every man who pretends to guide public opinion, and which is naturally expected from every man who does not seek to inflict the most serious evils upon his own country and others'.[3] It is in essence the same message as that sent by the newspaper owner Lord Northcliffe to the Editor of the *Daily Mail* on 16 December 1916, in the midst of war: 'I should like a very gentle leading article calling attention to the many Roman Catholics who have done so much in the War on land and sea. Any attempted intervention by the Pope would stir up hell in this country. Cardinal Browne's attention should be called to this. Call him "His Eminence". The article should be very gentle, nice and correct.'[4] Yet Northcliffe would probably have approved of Delane's attack on British unpreparedness for war with Russia; might have seen no reason for so nicely glavering an irresponsible pontiff. The professional codes of essayists and journalists have never become those of a fully fledged profession. The journalist has always enjoyed the wavering status of a court follower who is never quite accorded the full status of courtier. Each sliver of the infinity of reality at which the reporter thrusts his attention reaches the reader through a haze of motives and intentions – those of journalist, subject, editor, censor, printer, government – which are all the more insistent for being less evident.

Journalism emerged historically with periodicity of publication. Only when postal service, printing capacity and supply of material were all sufficiently and consistently developed to the point at which regular weekly, thrice-weekly, or daily appearance could be assured, did journalism come recognisably into existence. That was early in the seventeenth century, when printing was, but journalism was not, an acknowledged occupation. The enlargement of scale made possible by the changes in printing techniques and organisational rearrangements of the Jacobean period caused writers to think and think again about the nature of that 'truth' after which they now so copiously and conspicuously strove. For John Donne truth stood

> Upon a Hill
> Cragged and steep[5]

obliging the writer to perambulate constantly in searching for it. For Montaigne there was no technique ready to hand which helped the conscientious seeker, only tradition: 'Let us consider through what clouds and how blind-fold we are led to the knowledge of most things, that passe our hands: verily we shall finde, it is rather custome, than science that removeth the strangenesse of them from us.'[6] Journalism and philosophy were in the same predicament: some formal authority was essential in guiding the innocent towards the truth. Any statement fit to be believed required an official provenance and the say-so of the writer was clearly insufficient, since he had no means of checking his own statements. Only with a *dual* communication system, when the same news flows along more than one channel at a time, can the journalist acquire his own specialism in the telling of accurate news. Journalism does not become professionalised, or even occupationalised until it requires the essential tool of double-checking; until then it remains a mere appendage of printing, or in its grander forms, a sub-branch of diplomacy. At the moment of the outbreak of the first Civil War Samuel Pecke and John Colês in their *Perfect Diurnall* promise their readers: 'You may henceforth expect from this relator to be informed onely of such things as are of credit, and of some part of the proceedings of one or both houses of Parliament fit to be divulged, or such other news as shall be certified by Letters from the Army, and other parts, from persons of speciall trust . . .'[7] Pecke was in fact in gaol while his partner published this. The avidness of readers for news of the political events of the moment was far greater than the authorities' willingness to allow publication. Every publication contained an implicit intention; it was in no one's interest to print anything which did not carry a political implication. The possibility of such a thing existing – merely to satisfy the lusts of the market – was not in the air. To the extent that market forces might render a counterfeit or un-authorised publication worthwhile, a strict licensing system was in existence.

Licensing is quite different from censoring (though in the Civil War, both processes occurred in varying degrees). Licensing implies a perceived obligation in the eyes of authority to prevent the people from being deceived. Printing belonged within the royal prerogative. Richard Atkyns[8] felt that, in his restoration pamphlet on the history of printing, he had amply 'demonstrated that Printing appertaineth to the Prerogative Royal; and is a Flower of the Crown of England'. This power to allow or not to allow the management of a printing press was 'intire and inherent in Your Majesties Person, and inseparable from Your Crown'. The Kingship entailed the notion of supreme magistracy and the king alone, argued this rather extreme theorist, could control the flow of printed matter. It was not to be delegated. 'If the Tongue, that is but a little Member, can set the Course of Nature on Fire; how much more the Quill, which is of a Flying Nature in it self, and so Spiritual, that it is in all Places at the same time.'[9] The argument may appear far-fetched to us today, but it is, of course, precisely the argument used throughout Western Europe in the twentieth century, for the control of broadcasting; a scarce natural resource (the electromagnetic spectrum) can be entrusted to the government alone, which possesses an essential and complete right to control the air waves, and therefore must take steps to ensure that the power to use the air, if delegated, is placed in the hands of those who will not misuse it.

The seventeenth century was a world which presented the writer with two possible dictions: truth and lies. One could not know very easily where truth lay and so authority (whether governmental, traditional or spiritual) had to lead the way. The argument against licensing the press, when such was offered, was not an argument against censorship, it was directed solely against a process which prevented truth and lies engaging in open encounter. The classic Miltonic case against licensing in *Areopagitica* is for freeing the contest, so that truth could put untruth to flight.[10] In order to re-establish a prerogative-based regime Charles II created an official newspaper, the *London Gazette*, which was published weekly 'by authority' and gave an official presentation of the events which had most recently been reported to London from abroad. The editorial centrality was the office of one of the two Secretaries of State through whose hands the information passed from diplomats, merchants, travellers and spies.[11] The task of the official editor was to arrange these in some sort of coherent sequence and to maintain the flow of correspondence. The guarantee of accuracy lay only in the filtering process and in the quality and authority of the informants. The *Gazette* reached England as a form rather later than Holland, Italy, France and elsewhere; it carried with it, in its stylish design and composition, a feeling of superior reliability: it was, to use the term of a later day, official. The reliability of one source was passed on through the various media which absorbed the material. When the licensing system failed and printing spread throughout the country in the first decade of the eighteenth century, the London papers became the exclusive source of material appearing in the new provincial weeklies. The new out-of-town papers aimed to provide 'a faithfull abstract of all the newspapers of note'[12] and no attempt was made by a country printer, for some time, to do more either to provide local interest material or to authenticate the material he offered his readers. The *Northampton Mercury* once felt it necessary to explain its technique to its readers:

> We hope our candid readers will not condemn our Mercury for the many falsities that have of late been inserted therein, as we took them all out of the London Printed Papers, and those too the most creditable.[13]

The provincial newspaper provided a similar service to that received by the client of the contemporary coffee-house who could read, for the price of his coffee, an enormous array of newspapers, all supportive of different factions, none attempting to be comprehensive. Licensing broke down precisely because the ending of the biological succession to the throne left England with a supreme authority based upon *opinion*. The monarch could not be sustained through Divine Right, except in a merely sentimental way; the institution of monarchy (and the particular dynasty) required for its survival more than merely passive acceptance; it had now in addition to command *opinion* and as the world of eighteenth-century politics emerged in London, the business of the London newspapers underwent a fundamental change. Its task was to support the intrigue-ridden, corrupt and factional political system; opinion could be sustained through persuasion and thus it was that the greatest essayists and pamphleteers of the day became the greatest successes in the profession of periodical publication. The preoccupation of the journalist lay quite outside the accurate reporting of facts; there were no facts more important, nor more urgent than the fate of factions; it was these that provided the revenue, the market and the intellectual compulsion behind the product. The journalist, as a *soi-disant* professional processor of information did not yet exist: the professional writer did, however, exist, in some profusion, able to command sufficient sums for theatrical work as well as novels or fiction to live without direct patronage. Money could be made by running a weekly journal, partly for profit, partly for payment by a group of politicians. Parliament had become a place within which the affairs of the nation were discussed; the power lay outside the Chamber as well as in it and Parliamentary discussion required to be spread through the new political world. Ministries might rail against this paper or that, might prosecute for trivial infringements of the complex laws of seditious libel, but political life had come in large part to depend upon its dissemination and extension into the medium of print.

There were, however, very few job demarcations within the newspaper or journal between different sections. The editor was a mere processor of the material; the printer was juridically and practically in charge, although he was not necessarily the sole or even the part owner of the enterprise. There were political writers who contributed articles, there were advertisers and there were correspondents who sent in material and wrote what they wished. There existed as yet no professional or occupational group whose task it was to provide an unblemished version of events. There were no techniques as yet developed within the business of writing by which any form of 'reportage' was manufactured within the journalistic enterprise; accounts of events were taken from foreign journals, from private newsletters, from hospitals, prisons, markets, courts and great houses. Most material which reached the medium of periodical printed papers was placed there by its *source*, or direct from its source.

In the trial of John Tutchin for publication of libel, the following piece of dialogue occurs:

> *Prosecutor*: When a copy is brought to you to be printed, do you print that copy always exactly?
> *Printer*: As near as I can, I do.
> *Prosecutor*: Or do you . . . alter it?
> *Printer*: I have altered it often times to make it safe.
> *Prosecutor*: Then you do take it on you to alter?
> *Printer*: To strike out a line, never to alter his sense.
> *Prosecutor*: Do you not insert anything?
> *Printer*: Yes, frequently a word.[14]

The printer, it was, who preserved the right of the writer to express his views by suppressing the writer's identity. The responsibility for content was placed in the hands of a professional group whose task was distinctly not to act as editor or even sub-editor in the modern sense. The printer held open to society the right of media access. Crabbe describes the anonymous correspondents of the mid-century as fawning upon the printers:

> These are a numerous tribe, to fame unknown,
> Who for the public good forego their own;
> Who volunteers in paper-war engage,
> With double portion of their party's rage:
> Such are the Bruti, Decii, who appear
> Wooing the printer for admission here;[15]

The only guarantee of accuracy throughout the century was provenance – at least until the advent of James Perry, an editor (in the modern sense) *avant la lettre*. The first daily paper in the language, the *Daily Courant*, which took the enormous risks of such prolific appearance because of the intense interest in the preliminaries and conduct of the Marlborough wars, opened its columns with the following undertaking:

> It will be found from the Foreign Prints, which from time to time, as Occasion offers, will be mention'd in this Paper, that the Author has taken care to be duly furnish'd with all that comes from Abroad in any language . . . at the beginning of each Article he will quote the Foreign Paper whence 'tis taken, that the Publick, seeing from what country a Piece of News comes with the Allowance of that Government, may be better able to Judge of the Credibility and Fairness of that Relation: Nor will he take it upon him to give any Comments or Conjectures of his own, but will relate only Matter of Fact; supposing other People to have Sense enough to make reflections for themselves.[16]

Between the province of the printer and the author often employed by him to compose the material of the paper there existed no division of labour by which anyone took it upon himself to test the provenance, still less the facts. The press throughout the eighteenth century was at pains to provide a variety of versions of unproven material for the benefit of ideological fractions. 'They all receive the same advices from abroad', writes Addison, 'and very often in the same words; but their way of cooking it is so different, that there is no citizen, who has an eye to the public good, that can leave the coffee-house with peace of mind, before he has given every one of them a reading.'[17]

The very titles of the papers expressed their function as *carriers* of observations and 'freshest advices', rather than original material. There were *Posts* and *Flying Posts*, *Pacquets*, the *Post Man* and the *Post Boy*, *Courant* and *Mercury*. The symbol of the forward-looking paper of the century tended to be the post and his trumpet, or the pacquet-boat which ferried the news to Dover. Daniel Defoe, it is true, adopted in the course of his feverishly productive years in journalism many of the techniques which were later to become associated with the journalism profession. He collected material, often of a sensational nature, about the earthquake in Lisbon, about the events of the plague year in London, but these were remote events which he never saw himself, though he sometimes wrote as if he had; he was a popular historian rather than a people's journalist; he made no clear distinction, even in theory, between his activities as spy and political agent in Scotland and those which led to his amazingly copious copy in the *Review*. The journalist was not yet a man who went to *look*, though occasionally he might by chance *see*.

There was one great exception to this, the coverage of Parliament. This is not the place to examine the details of the controversy and legal actions which led to the opening up of Parliament to reporting in the last decades of the century.[18] Despite the evolution of a politically educated body of opinion in London and the country, reporting of Parliament remained a breach of privilege and was subject, long after the ordinances of the Long Parliament, to a further enactment in 1705 of a Standing Order prohibiting the entry of strangers into the Chambers: this remained in force until 1845, though greatly modified in its impact, and it was this – the exclusion of those without direct business in the House – that brought about the great ructions of the 1770s. It occasionally even happened that a Member would be excluded if he had been known to make a note of the proceedings for the benefit of the press. Libel proceedings could be taken against newspapers for material they drew from debates, even though Parliament was privileged. In 1813

Creevey was fined £100 for a libel which consisted in sending his own speech, as delivered in the Chamber, to a Liverpool newspaper.

Even when reporters' presence came to be tolerated in the crowded and noisy Gallery (contemporaries said it was sometimes like a cockpit)[19] they were not permitted to take notes. The great advantage possessed by William 'Memory' Woodfall, editor, printer and forsooth sole reporter of the *Morning Chronicle*, was that his power of recollection enabled him to sit in the Gallery without moving for twelve hours at a time, occasionally throughout the night, and then move on to his printing house to compose a hasty record of the proceedings. Although Woodfall was credited with prodigious, indeed miraculous feats of verbatim recollection, his reports were in fact little more than rapid paraphrases. Samuel Johnson's reports in other papers were, on his own admission, largely imaginative concoctions.[20] As it became easier for reporters to gain and retain admission to the House, and as they were not prevented from taking notes, some of them took to various forms of private shorthand. Many of them were young barristers for whom the House was practice in listening for long hours to acquire the art of recall. Politicians who actually wanted their words disseminated would sometimes pay for the purpose and hand their original manuscripts over to the press. Woodfall was accused in 1773 of taking £400 per annum from Fox and Sheridan to ensure they were reported at greater length than Pitt and Dundas.[21] The contemporary practice of allowing anyone with cash to insert material in a paper (and to have material taken out or 'corrected' by contradiction later) partly embraced coverage of Parliament itself. Even T. C. Hansard used the existing system; he had no reporters of his own for many years and no formal shorthand; he would send round to the member concerned the longest comprehensive version of each speech and invite him to make corrections before the final text of the debate was prepared.[22]

It was, however, the advent of shorthand which transformed the business of reporting into a kind of science. Shorthand was the first of that long series of journalistic techniques which at first seem to promise the reader the complete recovery of some semblance of reality. A fully competent shorthand reporter seemed to have acquired an almost supernatural power and shorthand was invested with the same kind of social optimism as the microphone and the television camera in later times. By presenting the reader with the *ipsissima verba* of a speech it seemed at first that reporting was capable of providing a true mirror of reality. Not everyone thought this, however. John Campbell, one of the *Morning Chronicle's* Parliamentary reporting team who later became Lord Chancellor, argued that longhand notes transcribed in tranquillity provided a better idea of the speech. The reporter must thoroughly understand the subject.

> He should take down notes in abbreviated longhand as he can for aids to his memory. He must then retire to his room, and looking at these recollect the speech as it was delivered, and give it with all the fidelity, point and spirit, as the speaker would write it out if preparing it for the press. Fidelity is the first and indispensible requisite, but this does not demand an exposure of inaccuracies and repetitions.[23]

A distinction must be drawn between the old-style cultured reporter of Parliament of the late eighteenth century whose longhand reflected his education and intellectual predilections and the brasher reporter of the Napoleonic period who experimented with various forms of shorthand and dazzled his readers with his skills. He would be sent to report the House in a system of relays, working for an hour or so collecting notes and then rushing back to his printing office to write them up. It was in fact the system of relays more than the system of note-taking that made daily publication of debates possible. Tyas, the most famous reporter of his time, who later covered Peterloo for *The Times* (the first event to which a number of reporters were *sent* by their editors)[24] was not really a shorthand reporter in the modern sense; he had developed an abbreviating system of his own, which he alone could transcribe; it was said that speakers in the Commons actually competed for position in the order of speakers when Tyas was due to appear in the Gallery.

John Gurney had perfected a system of shorthand in the 1750s; he was a clockmaker by trade but spent much of his time as a reporter in the Old Bailey and fathered a line of Gurneys who practised their eponymous system for more than a century in Parliament itself. It was Gurney's system of brachygraphy which the Dickens family learned: John Dickens (father of Charles) and

John Henry Barrow (Charles' brother-in-law) both worked at the business of Parliamentary reporting for newspapers. Charles Dickens, when he refers in a much-quoted passage to having 'tamed the savage stenographic system', was alluding to Gurney's brachygraphy, the fifteenth edition of which came out in 1824; Dickens used it in the Law Courts and after 1832 in the reporting of Parliament for the Whig paper, the *True Sun*.

The acquisition of various systems of shorthand, leading up eventually to the universally applicable system perfected by Pitman, gave reporters their true mystery. It separated the correspondent from the reporter. It meant that a man could specialise in observing or hearing and recording with precision. It was the promised ability to recover the dimension of reality in reporting that turned it into an occupation. One of the most important divisions of labour within the business of newspaper-making had taken place, important because it appeared to satisfy a readers' demand; it gave the reporter an aura of neutrality as he stood between event and reader; it gave him the chance to feel that he represented the interests of the newspaper's clients; it connected the task of reporting to the perspective of experimental science; it gave the writer a tool which enabled him to aspire to the status of the engineer and the philosopher. The reporter had become part of the new world of the early nineteenth century, a world of individual and collective progress. The reporter by presenting an undisputed reality to his customers was involved in the business of social governance and social change.

For the rest of the century it was possible for a reporter adept at shorthand to set up in business and offer his skill to editors and lawyers. One manual shorthand of 1869, for instance, offers the young reporter advice on how to proceed with his career:

> . . . a young man, without money and without introductions, who wants to obtain a professional position as a shorthand writer in London, must reckon upon sharp work before he succeeds. Probably he will turn his thoughts, first of all, to reporting to the newspapers. If he can get a warm introduction to a good-natured editor (and most editors are good-natured) he may possibly have opportunity afforded to him of testing his abilities, and glide, not so painfully, into a recognised situation. But under ordinary circumstances, the aspirant, allowing him

both skill and energy, must fight hard for his object. If he has the courage and perseverance to keep on sending in reports of meetings to all the papers in London, for the chance of getting one or two inserted, and all the while does his work well, he will probably make good his footing at last.[25]

The newspapers of the mid- to late-nineteenth century consisted in very large measure of shorthand reports of speeches, political, religious, scientific, educational. The basic image which emerges from the newspaper of the period is of a man on a platform speaking to rows of listeners and reaching a wider public *via* the shorthand reporter. The reporter became, as it were, the principal brokerage for the substantial discourse of society. No wonder Walter Bagehot called it 'The Age of Discussion'[26] and people saw the platform as a principal engine of civilisation. The agitation over the Reform Bill in 1831 was attended by riot and disorder; the agitation over the repeal of the Corn Laws a decade and a half later was conducted throughout the nation by means of the platform and the press, two interconnected institutions, indeed symbiotic institutions, which depended upon clear notes being taken by teams of reporters.[27] In the mid-nineteenth century the reporter and his notebook (occasionally even her notebook) bore something of the magic of the new television teams of the 1960s, moving from riot to battlefield, demonstration to sit-in, while being widely accused of causing the scenes which they recorded and reproduced. In the 1840s and 1850s the new generation of reporters were credited with having helped to cool the tempers of politics and enabled, as it were, a national 'village' to develop within which social change could proceed through argument and debate. It was, however, still possible to accuse the press of a vulgar despotism, of setting itself up to act as a 'moral gens-d'armerie'[28] a corrupt and licentious would-be censor of vice. The greater dignity which was ascribed to the press once it had acquired a quasi-formal role within the constitution was not universally acknowledged. In Britain society clung to the laws of libel, amending them always too little and too late for the aspirations of the newspapers. Libel was society's only protection against the indiscriminate pursuit of its material on the part of the press. The reporter had to be very severely restrained from roaming too freely with his notebook. The reporter had developed the skills, but others were to decide where he was to employ them; in Parliament, perhaps, in the Law Courts, yes, in recording the prices of the stock exchange and the traffic at the ports, certainly, but the journalist's very routines channelled and confined his skills and talents. His role within politics was to be circumscribed by the general lines of a silent pact between editors and authorities. 'Without aid from the press', says an anonymous opponent of the press in the *Quarterly Review*,

> conduct grossly reprehensible must be known to the friends and relations of the party, that is, to all those on whose good opinion he sets a value; and the additional censure of thousands for whom he cares nothing, can have few terrors for one who has already steeled his feelings against the scorn and aversion of kindred and connexions . . . We believe, therefore, that the attempt to write down the follies and vices of society is, in truth, hopeless and visionary . . . we doubt the services of personal vituperation, and the exposure of individual conduct, by way of correction or example.[29]

The leeway acquired by journalism was very narrow; its ability to ferret truth was not accepted as a valid duty, not yet. The kind of accuracy which it was invited to pursue related to public events. The newspaper had indeed become an *estate*. Burke said so; Sheridan said so; Jefferson had proclaimed the moral role of the press. But this meant merely that it occupied an important political role, in making possible the existence of a political power which was not physically contained within Parliament. The press could record public events, it could enliven debate among the politically involved but as a means of social communication it was, in the eyes of many, a non-starter. It had a part to play in the political *Gemeinschaft*; it had no acknowledged role within the wider growing *Gesellschaft*. The social structures were too solid to admit of any new agency. Journalism was kept from communicating between classes, from spreading its truths in such a way as to allow the crowd to set up in judgement against the governing classes. Their curiosity was to be slaked, if at all, by the illegal unstamped newspapers, which began to circulate in greater profusion, the tighter the laws to tax and contain the ordinary press.

What we have seen is a transition from a journalism which could merely observe the distinction between truth and lies in a general way and a journalism which recognised a special relationship between itself as an activity and certain categories of events and information. The techniques of collection employed by newspapers and the observance of the role that their information played in society gave journalists an *outlook*, a specialised role within the social observance of reality. But the very division of labour which gave rise to the reporter with his specialised approach to certain material proposed a further and more complicated problem. The reporter serviced a medium; unlike the author or the printer he was not and could not by his nature be his own boss. There was another figure who sent him into the world, who detailed him to observe this event or that. The evolution of the editor is a key development in the shaping of journalism as a tool for registering reality.

It was not until 1802 that the term editor was used to describe the man in charge of a periodical publication. Until then the word is indeed occasionally used, but only of a supplementary employee working to the printer. The grander papers of the late-eighteenth century had established an editorial figure as one who was supposed to collect paid material from the public, who would often stand in for the printer when facing outraged members of the public; he was distinctly not the man in charge. In 1777 it was said in the trial of one William Dodd, a preacher charged with forgery, almost as corroboration of the allegation, that he had 'descended so low as to become the editor of a newspaper'.[30]

However, the newspaper was becoming medium-sized if not big business. Newspapers employed men to parade through the streets advertising them. Their circulations rose into the thousands per day. Their columns regularly contained separate departments. *The Morning Chronicle* collected so much advertising revenue during the editorship of James Perry that he was often hard pressed to find room for all his Whig propaganda. It was in fact Perry who led the way to the modern editorship. Together with Daniel Stuart and John Walter II of *The Times*, he professionalised the *management* function of newspaper editorship as much as the production function; with Perry the demarcated role of editor, as the supreme functionary short of the owner was established. (John Walter II, of course, was himself the owner

and brought on the young Thomas Barnes as a highly professional editor to run *The Times* during his (Walter's) absence in
parliament.) Perry had run the *Gazetteer* for a brief period, and
had managed to beat 'Memory' Woodfall in the art of Parliamentary reporting by hiring a team of young barristers to
report the debates in relay. He moved to the *Morning Chronicle*
with the undertaking to further the cause of the Whig party. He
kept the paper for nearly forty years and turned it into a
considerable capital asset. Daniel Stuart in the same period
performed a similar transformation task on the *Morning Post* and
afterwards the *Courier*, which later he was able to sell for a fortune
large enough to retire. The difference between these men and
their predecessors was that they presided over offices large and
talented enough for editorial decisions to cover one story or
another to be made. Perry even sent a man to watch over the
events in France after the Revolution. Until then, a newspaper
had been usually synonymous with a man. It was a kind of book
or essay published in daily or thrice weekly parts. Defoe had
written weekly pamphlets called the *Review*; Abel Boyer worked
for a printer and was disguised, as it were, under the periodical's
title *Post Boy*. The *Spectator* was a similar title, and indeed *Mr
Punch*, of much later date, was a kind of hangover from this
system. There was the presumption if only by amusing fiction,
that one man wrote everything. In the revolution wrought by
Perry, Stuart and Walter the newspaper became an organisation,
presided over by a man skilled in delegation, arrangement,
judgements about the world of various kinds. It was the
combination of professionalised editor and professionalised reporter that opened up the complex of problems we have come to
label as those of the 'media'. With these two roles separated out,
the newspaper became a means, perhaps the principal means, by
which social reality became clearly delineated. The departments
of the newspaper reflected the routines of the various sub-groups
which grew up within the profession. Within these routines there
lay all manner of professional codes and duties. When the
agencies took over the major task of collecting accounts of
Parliamentary debates, the lobby men took over, a great crowd
of journalists who seldom heard a debate but who, remunerated
as handsomely as any member of any profession at the time,
roamed the Houses of Parliament, talking to members freely and

creating a picture, an image of the political reality which emerged from the aggregation of parliamentary activity. The idea was born that beneath the straight reliable account of what was happening in the formal affairs of Parliament, there lay a half-secret, half-conscious world consisting of what was 'really' going on 'behind the scenes'. Reporters who once felt that, with shorthand, you could capture the essence of the real, now slipped slowly downwards through the professional scale of status, their places at the pinnacle being taken by those who extracted truth from a cloud of obfuscations put up by politicians. Thus it was in other areas of life. The *story* lay behind the account of an event; it lay somewhere in the minds of men, however; it could be found and recorded in print, given tenacity and space.

The telegraph and the telegram created further divisions and demarcations. They meant, for one thing, that reporting from more places became more possible though much more expensive. These devices helped to raise ever higher the quantity of fixed capital entailed in owning and running a newspaper; rising circulations increased the variable costs, as did the possibility of adding to one's staff and creating ever more departments within the paper. The telegraph helped to intensify the distinction made between reporting and 'appreciating'; the split which had taken place within the Parliamentary journalists was followed through in other categories of material, especially in foreign affairs. A telegram, its provenance often elaborately explained in sub-headings, would bring the announcement of a royal birth, a battle, a crisis, the outlines of a speech. The task of evaluation, discussion, explanation would come much later, often through the postal service. The telegraph created, most certainly, a global village, but it raised more issues than it resolved, when readers troubled to ask themselves whether they were being given a complete and balanced account.

The telegraph created a pressured world within journalism. It made possible the idea that a daily newspaper should encompass the events of a 'day'. Such boundaries hardly correspond with the conceptual and cognitive categories accepted elsewhere, but henceforth daily journalism operated within a new tense, as it were, of the instantaneous present. The latter half of the nineteenth century brought out more new kinds of publication than any generation before or since, all adding to the various extensions and limitations imposed upon the professional techniques of journalism and the development of its outlook upon reality. 'The journalist judges for himself what is uppermost in the public mind', wrote Besant at the end of the century, 'Each able writer has a test of his own for knowing what new subject the public will be interested in reading about at the morning or the evening meal, and he goes to work to produce that. The market is large.'[31] The London journalist had two dozen *daily* outlets from which to choose. His task was to insinuate himself into the lives of his readers, to wrap himself around their being, to fulfil unconscious interests, to lead them into experiences beyond their horizons and their pockets, to open up social space to them.

The penny-a-liners of the time when shorthand alone was a qualification sank in the social spectrum. Shorthand became less and less necessary to the London journalist. The press agencies supplied the papers with all the news they required of a 'routine' character. Dickens lived to see the day come and go when every paper of note sent its own man by stage coach to cover every major meeting in the country. By the 1890s the telegraph had provided sufficient economies of scale for reports to be sent anywhere in the country, delivered to a sub-editor's desk at ten or fifteen shillings a column.

In the newspaper office, the 'story' became the basic molecular element of journalistic reality, a structured nugget of information, the basic unit through which the reader was to be presented with events. The techniques of journalism became analogous to those of fiction, and lay partly in the ability to discern those elements which could be made into a transmittable artefact. There was a convenient division into 'hard' and 'soft'; there was the clear underlying recognition of the audience as a market. The specialism of the journalist, and especially of the editor, lay in knowing what the market required. Reality was categorised into pages, home, overseas, political, women's interest, sport, the City. Special new kinds of event were developed which had not previously existed in human cognition, such as the 'crisis', the 'horror', the 'human story'. Events acquired 'angles', or rather special elements which made them more easily communicable within certain sectors of the market.

The 'New Journalism' of the 1880s, building on the experience of the Sunday press of the mid-century, was the first step along the road to the Northcliffe revolution; it recognised that journalism took place within an ever-burgeoning market. The interest of the reader was an unplumbed well, which could be explored and re-explored for ever. Journalism became the art of structuring reality, rather than recording it. Though it developed a mission (and a defence) of 'objectivity' in the twentieth century, this claim has continued to spawn as many new debates as it resolves. The element of ideology which the journalist in a formal sense left to the leading article and excluded from the 'news' has never truly disappeared. In the decision to report lies the ideological mission. The journalist looks, metaphorically speaking, now to his right, now to his left, as he searches for the senses in which his account will be accepted within the rubric of objectivity. In performing this very task he weaves the tapestry of reality which society accepts – or rejects – as being a true image of 'things as they really are'. The journalist has come to supply the needs of a large social machinery which defines the interim phases of reality. The techniques of journalism have come to consist in skilful filling of pre-defined genres, each of which stands for a certain definition of the audience's needs. For a century now the ideological content of journalism has lain in the way in which the media which contain it have tried to amass and approach their audiences. The task of indoctrination, as it were, has been taken from the journalist and given to the product.

The confidence with which the newspaper pursued its newly defined set of roles grew noticeably until the Second World War. Problems only began to arise after the firm establishment of radio and television news and their acquisition of certain roles for themselves within the spectrum of journalism. Alfred Harmsworth claimed that journalism now provided 'scope for every type of brain';[32] there was writing for the well-read man, sub-editing 'for the man of detail', and management for the man of business. The age of specialism left its mark firmly upon the world of journalism. The specialist correspondent moved close in on his sources and became an expert in his own right within a given field. He was faced, therefore, with all the perplexities of the academic scholar, all the extenuating circumstances which stood between reality and vigorous judgement of it. His colleague, the non-specialist 'general' reporter, was free to pounce upon his subject, declare it to operate against the public interest, define

the nature of the public interest and therefore form the available
policies of officialdom. Hidden away from the world of journalism lay that of administration, the civil service, whose powers
were circumscribed by the growing activities of the media. There
grew up demarcated administrative and other interest groups all
concerned with public policy and all at some stage dependent
upon acquiring the attention of the press. 'Every extension of the
franchise', declared Harmsworth, 'renders more powerful the
newspaper and less powerful the politician.'[33] With the mass
newspaper was born the politics of the image, the need to perform
before democracy rather than argue with it. An army of
professional press agents filed solemnly into the world of politics,
making greyer, if that were possible, the area which lay between
the reporter and his prime subject. Harmsworth set the main
boundaries of journalism for the bulk of the century; he saw that
his kind of newspaper demanded a new form of specialist training
of its journalists, which socialised them away from the other
constituencies of public life. Journalism should not be a stepping
stone to any other profession, unless it was statesmanship itself.
'The curse of Fleet Street is not the drinking man, but the man
who has failed in the City, or the army, the man of mature years
can no longer master journalism.'[34] Northcliffe spoke the kind of
nonsense which made millions.

The issue which confronts journalism in the twentieth century,
which transmutes it stage by stage into different forms, is whom the
journalist is to represent. The newspaper has acquired a public
role within the private sector. Its economics have narrowed its
political representative capacity. The market is not as differentiated a phenomenon as the electorate, and the journalist finds
himself being asked why he does not adopt the standpoint of a
given section of the population though offering his wares to it.
The provincial paper, with one political line, has come to occupy
a monopoly position within every city from which it originates
and has therefore to serve a multi-ideological constituency. The
mass daily papers from London have approximate though not
identical problems.

On the one hand the journalist offers his 'objectivity' as the
solution, the promise to fulfil the demands of complete truthfulness within the prescribed categories. The speech will be written
as spoken, the prices recorded according to the deals made, the

battles will be described as they have been fought. Perhaps. But who directs the attention of the reporter from one arena to another? What forces motivate the feature writer to weep for one cause and scoff at another? The techniques of recording sounds and pictures and transmitting them to waiting audiences themselves help to shape the realities as did the shorthand system a century ago. The uncertainties attendant upon reporting in the late twentieth century have thrown to the winds the careful confidence which the newspaper form acquired between 1880 and 1920. It was then seen as the engine of political freedom, the means by which the Victorian state had achieved its security and flexibility. Charles Pebody starts his history of British journalism with the proud statement:

> The history of the English press is the history, if not of English liberty, of all those popular forces and political franchises which have given strength and solidity to English institutions; renewed the youth of the state; made England, with its ancient monarchical institutions, with its feudal relics, with its aristocracy, and with its established church, the greatest state in the world: . . . raised the tone of our public life: made bribery and corruption impossible, and welded together the whole British Empire with all its races, all its religions, into a compact and powerful mass, which moves, when it moves at all, with a force, a unanimity and a decision that constitute Public Opinion one of the marvels of our time.[35]

That is indeed a very long way from the world of the three post-war Royal Commissions which have been obliged to discover ways in which the reader might be protected against the journalist and the newspaper rendered more 'socially accountable'. The journalist's profession has brought with it into the late twentieth century a little of the eighteenth-century rationalism into which it was, as an occupation, born. It has grafted onto this a large quantity of Victorian objectivity, of Mr Gradgrind's 'Facts, hard facts', and has attempted, with this scanty and fraying intellectual equipment, to sustain itself through the era of Einstein and Heisenberg, of rationalised doubts and relativities. Institutionally, the press has continued to require the assistance of a rationale which protects it against the kind of assailant who claims that no knowledge can be certain, still less comprehensive.

The training of journalists is shielded against the extreme doubts about the nature of factuality inherent in modern science. The investigative journalist, the vogue of the 1960s and 1970s, finds that in examining public life from a standpoint of extreme moral doubt, he is pushing against a very shaky structure. Every institution of society contains, it appears, as many morally doubtful elements as secure ones. Journalism could go on for ever 'cleaning up' public life without ever finding the task complete, while finding its own criteria of cleanliness constantly changing. The activity of journalism takes place in a world with two quite different value systems, perhaps more; in it the journalist finds his 'facts' vanish into opinions as he tries to take them across the frontiers of east and west. The clarity of purpose which absorbed and concentrated the energies of English journalism at its peak a century ago has gone and will never return.

Chapter 14

Technology, Distribution and Editorial Control: their Interactions in the Evolution of Journalism*

The newspaper and the novel were the first cultural forms to emerge directly from printing; they were both essentially publishing phenomena and developed in England in the aftermath of the expiration in 1695 of the Licensing Act when printers, no longer limited in numbers by statute, were free to flourish – or perish – according to the behaviour of the market.[1] Journalism has thus a similar relationship to printing as pop music to the phonograph or the film to photography: it depends upon an industrial activity, it involves the creative individual as a worker within a fairly complex process of manufacturing and distribution. The journalism is, as it were the 'software' supplied to fill the 'hardware' of the newspaper system, and it thus serves as a pioneer example of the working of modern mechanical

* Published originally as chapter 7 in James Curran *et al.* (eds), *Mass Communication and Society* (London: Edward Arnold/Open University Press, 1977).

media. Unfortunately the newspaper is only now beginning to be studied historically as a *media* system;[2] most of those interested in the history of the press have been hitherto concerned with the newspaper either as a component of 'Whig' history, concentrating on those elements which illustrate the great tide of public freedom swelling from the eighteenth century onwards,[3] or else as a component of a kind of 'Whiggism-in-reverse', bringing out those elements which illustrate the increasing amiseration or exploitation of the new mass readership.[4]

Part of the interest in journalism in Britain lies in the sheer unbroken continuity of its tradition. From the 1620s onwards one may be certain that each generation of journalists has consciously acquired its professional skills from the previous one; the tradition can be traced even beyond Archer, Bourne and Butter who were the first to assemble items of European news into a single periodical publication in running form in the English language; they borrowed this clever publishing idea from the printers of Amsterdam.[5] Their typographical devices, journalistic expedients and tone of voice, even, can be traced through the vigorous partisan journalism of the English Civil War and even into the period after the Restoration when the newspaper was placed under the most stringent monarchical scrutiny. Until then the publication of all news was considered to be part of the royal prerogative, an unimpeachable aspect of the Divine Right of the King, but this doctrine began to fade when William III, no longer a biological heir, ascended the throne.[6] With the ending of the traditional system of licensing which limited the legal number of working master printers – as a means of controlling the whole medium of print – the publishing industry began to develop very rapidly; none the less, the actual techniques of printing remained relatively static, and Caxton would have recognised his converted wine press in any newspaper office until the end of the eighteenth century.

The government developed a method of controlling news despite the ending of licensing by placing an ever-growing series of taxes on the press: there were taxes on the paper used in publishing news, on each advertisement, on every newspaper copy. Many forms of journalism developed out of attempts to evade the taxes (like the essay form of the *Tatler* and the *Spectator*, which, by being regular publications but *not* containing hard news, could avoid paying the tax) and all news publications altered in format as a result of the tax. The newspaper still developed rapidly in the era of Queen Anne and her successors because of the growth of mercantile and trading life, because small towns all over the country were developing complex local economies of their own which depended on advertisement, and because of the growth of a political class profoundly involved in the activities of Parliament and government. The government used the revenue from taxation as a slush fund to bribe newspapers and journalists to work in the official interest. Power in Britain, in the aftermath of the Glorious Revolution, rested upon *opinion* not upon Divine Right, and the newspaper, corrupt, vindictive, biased but in essence uncontrollable by the Crown, was the vehicle for creating and reflecting opinion, and sustaining the wide spectrum of factions into which the political class was subdivided. The battle for the freedom of the press which was fought out during the century was a battle for the right to report the affairs of Parliament, and to mitigate the battery of legal constraints and inhibitions to which the press was shackled.

Throughout this period the number and diversity of social groups with physical, financial and educational access to the press was growing. The arrival of Frederick Koenig in London during the Napoleonic War led to the first of a series of revolutionary developments in printing and newspaper production which were to continue throughout the nineteenth century. The advanced stage coach, improved roads and the train helped to expand the lines of distribution of the press and release it from the dependence on the coffee-house which had been the chief means of circulation since Cromwellian days (and highly consistent with the role of the newspaper as a facilitator of factional rather than *party* Politics). The nineteenth century saw at first a major bifurcation within the readership of newspapers between, on one hand, a middle-class press, fully taxed, expensive and legal, which concentrated on developing contact with major demographic groups which were nationally spread and were developing an increasing political consciousness, and on the other, a cheaper working-class press which secured extremely large circulations but little advertising and worked under the particularly irksome constraint of being illegal because unstamped and untaxed. With the ending of the stamp tax, however, in 1855, it was the middle-class newspapers (the *Daily Telegraph* in particular) which were the first to grasp the opportunity of circulating among the growing group of newspaper-reading skilled workers. Thereafter, every major development in the formation of press publics involved the amalgamation of groups previously differentiated according to class or political predilection, into broader, more heterogeneous audiences. The newspaper sought out more variegated material. The newspaper enterprise changed from the joint stock system of the late eighteenth century, in which the shareholders included the printer and the principal advertisers, into the large family firm of the nineteenth century with access to larger blocks of capital to buy equipment for printing and reproducing illustrations, to pay the high costs of the telegraph, transport and squads of reporters and correspondents.

The end of the nineteenth century saw the perfection of technical and distribution methods to the point at which a truly mass newspaper could develop, encompassing a wide enough range of content, styles and audience-attracting material to hold together the first regular national audiences of a million at a cover cost of $\frac{1}{2}$d (the *Daily Mail* by 1912). Until then only the Sunday newspapers, traditionally concentrating more on scandal and crime than the daily papers, had reached out into that vast hardly tapped waiting audience. There had been several 'New Journalisms' in the later nineteenth century, clustered around the styles pioneered by the *Daily News* (1846), the *Daily Telegraph* (1885) and especially the *Pall Mall Gazette* (1865) and they had been concerned with puncturing the hidebound traditionalism of the longer established papers such as *The Times* and the *Morning Post*. Each thrust forwards had involved devising ways of making the content more palatable to an additional group of the population.[7]

The enormous leaps in circulation which took place between the World Wars turned the daily newspaper into a universal medium which henceforth was concerned with penetrating not a non-newspaper public but the public of rival papers. Newspapers devised forms and political positions which would help them each make inroads into the readership of other papers. The family firm gave way to multi-ownership in large corporations, although many papers continued to have single owners; with the

demise of the *News Chronicle* and *Daily Herald* in the 1960s no
newspaper remained which avowedly belonged to a single class.
Sometimes the traditional tones of radicalism remained but only
transmitted by the homogenising voice of modern circulation
management. The twentieth century has seen the solidification of
a dichotomy between the 'quality' and the 'popular' in journalism, competition taking place mainly, though by no means
entirely, between newspapers within one group rather than
between the two.

I have merely hinted at some of the major 'formations' through
which the newspaper and journalism has passed, although a
comprehensive list would be extremely long. Each new system
involves a shift in one or more of five partly separable dimensions.
First of all, each of them has been characterised by a different
grouping of the audience and a different way of grouping towards
a larger or different intended audience. Then, in each, the
journalist has been coping with different levels and arrangements
of material which has necessitated his developing lines of contact
with different kinds of news sources. Third, the journalist has
been obliged to devise or acquire new techniques for actually
performing his work (such as shorthand, typing, translating).
Fourth, the state of the available printing technology has itself
developed in ways which have helped to change the fundamental
stance of journalists towards their readers. Finally, perhaps most
importantly, each new formation of the newspaper as a media
system has brought about a new structure of editorial control,
leaving the journalist, in his various forms, working within a line
of management stretching up towards a board of shareholders or
perhaps an eccentric single owner or (in earlier days) the king
himself. These five dimensions are *in part* determinants of the
nature of journalism as the 'software' to their 'hardware'; but
they are themselves, of course, the results of many other strands of
social, technological and political history, and have developed
along lines of mutual interaction as well as being influenced by
the journalism which they encase. Examination of each of these
five dimensions throws a certain light on the ways in which the
profession of journalism has developed through its three and a
half century tradition and might as we shall see help to show how
journalism is evolving in the period immediately ahead.

Even in the earliest versions or predecessors of the newspaper one can discern these five elements. The *Mercurius Gallo-Belgicus* was a Latin news periodical which started in 1594 and circulated throughout the Holy Roman Empire.[8] The printers of Cologne, always a prudent and far-sighted body of men, had perceived a method for distributing information concerning military, political and other events via the six-monthly trade fairs at which merchants and other groups of influential people would gather. The fact of *regularity* of publication was the prerequisite for creating a constant public whose needs and interests the publishers would then attempt to satisfy. The *Gallo-Belgicus* was the first publication in history to have a regular title and consistency of printing, which meant that its audience would learn to *expect* it. The sources of the *Gallo-Belgicus's* information lay in the network of postmasters which existed throughout the Empire, efficiently passing along their routes all important news about the movements of armies and important personalities. The available technology for producing *Gallo-Belgicus* was a press essentially constructed for the making of books and so this earliest news publication appeared as a book and its writers thought of themselves as book-writers specialising in the compiling in a single publication of a quantity of news stories which might otherwise have been published as a series of separate broadsheets. Their professional techniques consisted in recognising news of importance when it arrived and translating it into Latin. Although we know little about the week to week workings of these early newsmen we do know that their work was publicly supervised and criticised; their operation grew within a craft hierarchy which sprang from the traditions of printing, with political pressures feeding back and tending towards a form of control. The *Mercurius Gallo-Belgicus* was well known in England and John Donne took it to task in an epigram:

> change they name: thou art like
> Mercury in stealing, but lyest like a Greeke.[9]

Our five dimensions are thus delineable in this very ancient though sophisticated news service and between them they constitute a set of determining constraints which provided the journalists (if we may call them that) with the basis of their professional and trade outlook. The picture of the world which the compilers of the *Gallo-Belgicus* serviced and sustained passed through the mesh of conceptual and physical equipment which constituted its media system. I shall try to provide an historical sketch of each of the five dimensions, taking a specific, almost random, case study as demonstration of each of them.

I

One is easily sometimes tempted to assume that the audience for newspapers has simply expanded generation by generation until reaching total social saturation in the present century. Statistically that is perhaps true, although not all new newspapers have tried merely to maximise their sales; there have often been specialist papers which increase their profits by concentrating on a single wealthy market, narrowing their editorial focus to exploit a smaller market more expertly both for sales and advertising. The journalist on a given publication rapidly learns to recognise, conceptualise and internalise the supposed needs of the particular target audience of his paper. He speaks as if through a proscenium arch of his newspaper office to a public which has been gathered through the tradition and the promotion system of the newspaper concerned. It is the distribution system and the advertising sales system which feed back into a media institution and its employees the picture of the audience for which they are writing.

There are, and have often been, papers which are purely ideologically motivated – journals of opinion – and with these the audience is more tightly delineated from the start; the provincial papers of the late nineteenth century, for example, struggled to acquire and maintain special local audiences sharing a liberal, radical or conservative outlook, which their journalists recognised and indeed identified with. W. T. Stead, Wickham Steed, Alfred Spender all learned the business of journalism as young men on provincial Liberal papers, where their experience as communicators within a particular political constituency provided them with the qualifications necessary for their first London posts. Spender spent some years at his uncle's paper the *Eastern Morning News* before proceeding, in the early 1890s, to work on the *Pall Mall Gazette* and then transferring when the former was sold into the hands of a Tory, to a new Liberal paper the *Westminster Gazette*.[10] The reader's loyalty was acquired through political identification; the journalist's credentials, which remained with him throughout his career, were founded on his ability to grasp and internalise the outlook of a single political community. Yet the development of newspaper readerships as confessional communities was possible only when methods of distribution and sales had developed in a manner conducive to the paper reaching its target community on the right day and at the right price.

Until well into the last century it was impossible to separate postal systems from newspaper delivery systems. The Post Office undertook both tasks. The character of most newspapers emanating from London was designed for the London audience, since only a small proportion of total sales could reach the non-metropolitan public despite the steady improvement of postal services ever since the 1620s. Provincial papers, which started up in the first decade of the eighteenth century, tended to cover very wide areas geographically around their city of origination, too wide in fact to make the papers themselves at all reflective of the interests and problems of any single community. The particular case study I shall use in considering the impact of audience identification upon the styles of journalism consists in an account of how that necessary transition took place within the provincial press between a generation of papers which were non-London but not rooted in a particular locality to a new generation which were non-metropolitan and profoundly rooted in the affairs of a neighbourhood.

The London papers of the eighteenth century were mainly distributed through the hundreds of coffee-houses which had first been established during the political terror of the late 1650s as safe locations for political discussion. By the time of Queen Anne, London also had a highly organised distribution system through its many booksellers, street hawkers, coachmen, carriers and watermen. Wealthier readers outside London could have their papers sent by post, which would cost an extra 2d on the cover price, in addition to a ½d surcharge if the paper were brought from the posthouse to a private residence. Simultaneously, however, printers were moving out of London and setting up in rapidly expanding country towns. In fact in the early eighteenth century newspapers began to spread throughout the English provinces; their content consisted mainly of summaries of the

London papers which were delivered twice weekly by stagecoach and private transport – 'a faithfull abstract of all the Newspapers of Note' was how one provincial paper advertised itself and another used to refer proudly to its success in providing 'the quintessence of every Print'.[11] What hampered for some decades the development of a real provincial journalism based on events occuring within each town of publication was the small size of the available readership. In order to maintain sufficient readers to cover his production costs a printer would sometimes employ a roundsman who would walk through the countryside delivering the paper to known subscribers within a very wide radius. The *Northampton Mercury* said its 'newsmen' would cover forty miles on foot once a week. The *Manchester Magazine* said that one of its roundsmen walked 100 miles every week on a circuit which took three days to complete. If the weather was bad and the men were unable to set out, publication would occasionally be delayed. There were also street hawkers and specialised delivery systems in the larger towns, but so long as a given edition had to be sold in towns as far apart as Oxford, Northampton and Lincoln, there was little chance of a vigorous local journalism developing. By the 1750s, however, it was becoming possible for printers to engage in intensive distribution within a single town; population had increased and with it the kinds of business activity which depends on advertising. Shops would consider it worth advertising in a paper which could be guaranteed to reach a significant proportion of the buying population in its catchment area, and the growth of advertising made it possible for the printer to concentrate his efforts more within a given area.

With the growth of distribution it was difficult for the printer to add the cost of delivery to the cost of the paper, as had always been the practice with newspapers in London and the provinces. In the 1740s, for example, the newsmen employed by the *Birmingham Gazette* started to be paid a proportion of the cover price of copies sold and this increased the pressures on the printer to provide the kind of material which the newsmen could easily sell. If the paper had little to appeal to readers the newsmen would threaten resignation because this endangered their livelihood. The distribution system acted thus as a constraining pressure on the editor and his tiny staff. The provincial press accordingly began to recognise its target audience more clearly as these and similar pressures accumulated. From the mid-eighteenth century onwards the content of English provincial papers begins to reveal a certain liveliness and originality: the occasional cartoon appears and there is a vigorous growth of political comment when the great Parliamentary schisms of the mid-century began to work up partisan loyalties among the emerging country readership. Above all, however, the provincial press found itself training editors who saw *news* in the affairs of a small town, which until then had appeared merely irrelevant to the concerns of a newspaper. The first indigenous country journalism sprang from the conceptualisation of the new urban audiences of the north and west and midlands from the 1760s onwards.

II

It might seem merely obvious to say that journalism depends upon the available sources of news. Much of the literature of the press, however, takes it for granted that to journalists within the English tradition, the same range of matters have always been of equal relevance. In fact, journalism in any given period has functioned mainly as the processor of certain available kinds of material. The demand for a particular kind of information (say, news of the Thirty Year War) is generated through a society which has a particular interest in the events concerned. (In this case, Londoners disapproving of their king's failure to support King Ferdinand.) The flow of information from event to news medium becomes organised when a suitable medium is set up to circulate it (in our example, the printers of Amsterdam and their counterparts in London creating the first weekly books of news). At the newsroom or printing shop end of the process the journalist seeks out the flow of information from ambassadors, spies, mercenaries, imperial postmasters, merchants and continental news-sheets. The journalist had never merely stared out of his window at a total reality; he is only given his desk and chair when an input system already exists. The newspaper is not a mirror of reality, but the realisation of the potential of its sources. It may build great influence out of its eloquent advocacy of a cause; it may stimulate new interests and realisations within its audience; it may cause new kinds of information to reach its audience and new sources of information to be organised; but its chief characteristic lies in the selection, arrangement and reformulation of information passing to it through regular channels.

The wire services of the nineteenth century emerged as collectors and pre-processors of information; their customers were newspapers and editors of vastly differing political persuasions and they therefore helped to generate the idea that at the root of all news there lay 'hard facts' which could be discovered and disseminated in a value-free manner.[12] A successful newspaper like *The Times* rejected John Julius Reuter's service as long as it could: it seemed that to rely on people outside immediate editorial control to supply news would endanger the intellectual and ideological integrity of the paper; the growth of a fiercer competition between London papers and the enormous expense involved in maintaining coverage of all the events on which British readers now wanted to be informed, brought about after a time the capitulation of *The Times*. The paper agreed to print the news offered by Reuters and later of other agencies.[13] The wire service and the agency were of course indispensable to the provincial press in its competition with London-based papers which were constantly trying to take over the lucrative newspaper market in the growing Victorian cities. By means of the telegraph a provincial paper could receive a complete flow of foreign news and also publish in full the speeches of local politicians in Parliament, two elements with which they were able to hold their own against metropolitan newspapers. The telegraph, therefore, both threatened the security of the provincial press and gave it the opportunity of developing its own special services.

One episode which aptly illustrates the way in which an alignment of news services helps to determine the character of a particular form of journalism is that of the London press of the early Restoration when, for about a decade, the figure of Henry Muddiman, the 'King's Journalist', dominated the world of London journalism.[14] His career and the special system of news flow which he perfected and partly devised aptly illustrates the way in which the character of journalism is heavily influenced by the nature of its sources.

If you look at a typical English or continental newspaper of the late seventeenth century you cannot fail to be struck by the enormous geographical scope of the news. The paper covers but a single sheet but it contains carefully filed material from a score of European cities, arranged in brief, bleak paragraphs each with its clearly marked provenance, the city of origin and the date on which the information was first sent out. Domestic news leads the paper but is very scanty; it consists of news from Court, royal proclamations and other official material, plus a good deal of shipping and commercial news. The flow of material around England was clearly (or apparently) inferior to the network which produced up-to-date intelligence on places as far afield as Muscovy and Naples, Istanbul and Berlin.

The dominant news publication in England in the 1660s and 1670s was the *London Gazette* and its methods of operation had been developed from the papers of the late Commonwealth and the immediate Restoration period.[15] Under Cromwell, Secretary Thurloe had built up a system of Eurpean intelligence which had kept the English government among the best informed in Europe ('Cromwell kept the secrets of all the princes of Europe at his girdle'), and Charles II was determined to maintain the system, though with different men. In addition Charles and his Court brought back with them from Breda an acquaintance with the new generation of European Gazettes: Paris had its *Gazette* and the *Nouvelles Ordinaires*, Brussels the *Relations Veritables*, and Amsterdam, for decades the central entrepôt of European news, produced the *Gazette D'Amsterdam* and the *Oprechte Haarlemsche Courant*. They were stylish publications, bearing with them a sense of modernity and efficiency. When the Court retired briefly to Oxford to avoid the plague raging in London in 1665, Charles seized the opportunity to start an *Oxford Gazette* which later became the *London Gazette*; in charge of it was the most experienced news collector and editor of the day, Henry Muddiman. What concerns us here, however, is simply the means by which Muddiman and his rivals and immediate successors procured their information.

The prerogative of the king over the publication of news applied only to printed material. The Stationers' Company was obliged by law to supervise the whole trade of printing and publishing and ensure that only duly licensed material was handled by the booksellers (who were also members of the Company). The Stationers, however, could not be trusted to perform this task wholeheartedly since it tended to restrict their own trade and therefore, in 1663, a special Surveyor of the Press was appointed, the notorious Sir Roger L'Estrange, an old Cavalier who had served the king faithfully throughout his period of exile. L'Estrange's men guaranteed that the illegal rivals to the official news publications were rooted out. L'Estrange's reward for his labours was an exclusive privilege to publish news, 'All Narratives of relacons not exceeding two sheets of paper and all advertisements, Mercuries, Diurnals and Books of Publick Intelligence', as the official proclamation put it. L'Estrange was an odd choice for exercising this privilege since he was a strong opponent of general publication of political news, thinking that it gave the people 'not only an itch but a colourable right and licence to be meddling with the Government'. He proved, however, to be most efficient in destroying the network of anti-Caroline propaganda, but was confronted with the more long-term problem of how to set about the dissemination of necessary intelligence around the governing groups in society.

There was at that period a secondary system by which news travelled around the country, a system of written newsletters, copied out by a small army of scriveners and composed by a single man who enjoyed access to the full flow of political information entering and leaving Whitehall.[16] Henry Muddiman, originally chosen to take charge of publishing news by General Monck in the months between the death of Richard Cromwell and the return of Charles, sat at the centre of a web of contacts throughout England and Europe. At the heart of the Restoration system of government there were the offices of the two Secretaries of State, one of whom handled relations with the Northern (i.e. Protestant) countries, the other with the Southern (i.e. Catholic) countries. Muddiman worked for the Under-Secretary at the Southern Department and his job was to monitor the governmental intelligence network, making certain that the agents were kept working efficiently. He enjoyed a privilege of free postage in order to perform his task and the Letter Office was at certain periods kept under the general supervision of one of the Secretaries of State; Muddiman was allowed to exploit the free postage privilege to send out his own handwritten newsletters to a string of correspondents throughout the country, who paid £5 a year directly to Muddiman as a subscription: the newsletter could be supplied free to members of the intelligence network, so that a kind of collective European news agency existed, creating an international coterie of well-informed men.

The printed *Gazette* and the handwritten newsletters developed a symbiotic relationship. Muddiman would send out newsletters of domestic news to subscribers in Britain and receive from his counterparts on the continent their domestic newsletters which provided material for his printed *London Gazette*. The continental editors in their turn incorporated the material from the English written newsletters in their printed news publications. There were therefore two kinds of audience, one which paid for a relatively inexpensive but authoritative printed medium of international news and another, wealthier or more privileged, group who received the handwritten news on affairs at home, some of whom helped to supply that news as well. At the centre of this apparatus sat Muddiman, his wealth growing with the years, as trade in and with Europe increased and created an expanding demand for both of his news services. He was not left to enjoy his position unhampered for long, however. There were constant rivalries between the two Secretaries of State, their subordinates and the men at the Letter Office upon whose good (and free) postal services the whole machinery of intelligence depended. At one point Muddiman was forced to resign his office and transfer himself to the department of the other Secretary starting a rival paper to the *London Gazette*, the people at the Southern Department, anxious to steal Muddiman's remunerative list of correspondents, had started opening his mail in order to filch the addresses. The 'mercury' women who hawked the printed papers around the streets had to be bribed and fed in order to keep the paper before the public. It was not a stable system but it was a very effective one in collecting and disseminating news; it made a small supplementary income by providing space for half a dozen or so advertisements in each weekly or bi-weekly edition; tea, coffee, books, lost servants and stray animals were the mainstays of the advertising section, although they also played a part in the business of maintaining law and order by helping the tracing of criminals, pickpockets and stolen goods.

Muddiman's professionalism and political position arose from his particular technique for organising his sources. His outlook was international as that of the European news agencies of the last century. The typographical layout in which he published his material was the archetypal *Gazette* which acquired an aura of authority and reliability which other news publications had never achieved, whether emanating from a government department or not. Muddiman's predecessors had operated in the greyer area between pamphleteering and intelligence. He made a profession of unadorned intelligence, as pure and devoid of comment as the politics and standards of the time allowed. The journalistic revolution over which he presided consisted in the novel organisation of an input system of information.

III

The profession of journalism has been marked by a seemingly endless process of re-demarcation of specialisms and sub-professions. Every new mechanical device (telegraph, typewriter, wireless) has tended to summon into existence a new schism within the business of journalism, or rather, act as the defining catalyst for the emergence of a new brand of journalism. But the devices need not be mechanical, they can relate to a special skill not directly related to a piece of machinery.

One important qualification of a journalist in the early seventeenth century, for instance, was an ability to understand Dutch, because that was the language in which most of the information arrived, via the weekly pack-boat from the Hague. Several of the writers of the newsbooks of the period (until the *Gazette* news was published in the form of a book) were referred to as 'Dutch captains' because the main source of Dutch-speaking Englishmen were soldiers who had enlisted as mercenaries in Holland and been invalided out. Leader writers of a much later date would be more likely to have to understand ancient Greek than Dutch! The growth of reporters as the most important subdivision within journalism in the nineteenth century demanded a whole range of new skills, involving powers of observation, of validation of statements and of rapid accurate recording of information acquired – which had come to be desired.

One of these was shorthand, which did more than any other single phenomenon to establish the stereotype of the journalist as provider of hard facts. With the help of a training in this new skill a reporter in the nineteenth century could at last hold a mirror up to nature, and provide not merely an elegant paraphrase of a speech but also the exact reproduction of the words of a politician or agitator, a judge, prisoner in court or minister of the Crown. Shorthand created an aura of high prestige around the journalist. In the last decades of the eighteenth century, Parliament had been reported by great feats of memory. William Woodfall of the *Morning Chronicle* and William Radcliffe of the *Morning Herald* could carry the substance of an important debate direct from Parliament to the printing room, dictating copy to two compositors at once.[17] When James Perry took over the editorship of the former paper he transformed Parliamentary reporting by employing a team of young barristers, who would attend the House in relays, returning to the printing house in time to produce their report in sections for the morning edition. In the days of 'memory' Woodfall, the reports would have to await his convenience and would continue for some weeks after the end of the Parliamentary session, so that readers would have to wait for the final votes and debates of the Parliament until long after it had finished sitting.[18]

Several journalists had perfected forms of shorthand of their own invention, including John Tyas, the great reporter of *The Times* (see Chapter 13).[19] Others learned the Gurney system of brachygraphy and were able to acquire for themselves an aura of infallibility, which became important in the development of the profession. In the 1830s O'Connell charged some of the reporters in the Parliamentary Gallery with deliberate misrepresentation of his speeches; they responded by announcing a boycott of O'Connell, collectively refusing to publicise him until he had apologised, which he duly did, to the proprietors of *The Times*.[20] 'There is scarcely a gentleman on our establishment who is not by education and habits the equal of any Member whose opinions he is engaged to record', replied *The Times* in its editorial columns.[21] The fight between O'Connell and the reporters broke out again the following year but skirmishes of this kind only served to emphasise the growing status of the journals, which had been considerably aided by the acquisition of the shorthand skill.

With the coming of Pitman and the first easily acquired and transferable shorthand system, a new era in reporting was brought about. The freelance journalist was conjured into being,

who could ply his trade from home without belonging to the staff
of a particular paper; the demand for the reports of public
speeches and lectures was insatiable among Victorian newspaper
readers or, at least, among newspaper editors. A journalist would
find out where interesting speeches were being made, and armed
with a shorthand notebook, make his report and walk late at
night through the newspaper offices of Fleet Street until he found
an editor interested in having the article. Shorthand was the
lingua franca of the freelance, it democratised the profession, in a
sense. It provided it with a 'mystery'.

IV

As far as the production of newspapers is concerned all the
nineteenth century was the era of great advance between the
start of the newspaper as a form and the present day, when we are
on the brink of another series of major changes in the method of
production. Between the *Gallo-Belgicus* and *The Times* of Thomas
Barnes, nothing fundamental changed in the method of producing news periodicals. It was extremely heavy work and each
sheet of paper required an immense muscular effort on the part of
several men; the formes had to be inked with messy inking balls;
circulations were limited by the sheer limitations of human
physique. The Victorians saw a dramatic switch to mechanical
systems of production, the rotary press arrived and multiplied
production per hour ten-fold; steam engines were attached to
printing presses and brought about a further exponential
increase in the productivity of printing labour. Every few years
fresh developments enabled circulations to grow faster, definition
of print to improve, and illustrations to become easier to
reproduce. But each major improvement helped wholly new
forms of publication to be brought into being, and with them new
branches of the profession of journalism. *Punch* (1841) and the
Illustrated London News (1842) were the first successful and lasting
pioneers of illustrated journalism, the former bringing the
draughtsman-journalist into being and the latter the artist –
reporter. A new method of production often dovetailed into a
newly emerging audience or a new grouping of existing audiences and the fusion could result in a publication proclaiming yet
another 'New Journalism'.

The technical advances of the last century seldom resulted from a random serendipity on the part of the inventors. On the contrary, each development tended to occur after a long period of thwarted endeavour to bring about the required change. In the years of the Napoleonic Wars, for example, the presses could not cope with the increasing demand for copies. *The Times*, already the largest circulating paper of London, had been looking for a mechanical improvement in the existing Stanhope press which would enable it to increase its daily edition without having to bring an extra machine into use. In the first decade of the century it had sometimes had to place three machines together producing the same material from three separate settings of the copy. Frederick Koenig arrived in London from a printing office in Leipzig in 1808 and within three years brought about the most important revolution in the industry since Caxton. He had already wasted several years trying in vain to persuade printers in Germany and Russia to adopt his scheme for power printing before he met Thomas Rewsley, a London printer who commissioned him to build a machine, which was perfected in 1811. The proprietors of the *Morning Chronicle* examined the contraption and rejected it; John Walter II of *The Times* saw it and ordered two more to be made. In November 1814 he succeeded in producing an edition of *The Times* with the Koenig machine and his paper rapidly thereafter climbed to a position pre-eminent in the newspaper world of London, its circulation unbeaten until after the mid-century. It reached production figures of 8000 copies per hour and was able to build up a circulation equal to that of all other London papers combined.[22] It was this pre-eminence which, anchored to the aspirations of the burgeoning middle class, made the term 'public opinion' almost synonymous with Liberalism for half a century. Charles Pebody, writing of the press in 1882, says 'public opinion, during the past forty or fifty years has been in the main what the Newspaper Press has made it, and the Press has been so overwhelmingly Liberal that, until a few years ago when all the press suddenly turned Tory, a Tory Government has been practically impossible.[23] Pebody was exaggerating, but without doubt the basic values of journalism between the Napoleonic Wars and the Crimean were heavily influenced by the fact of *The Times's* unassailable supremacy in circulation. The journalist found himself with a dominant professional doctrine of confrontation with government rather than subservience or cooperation with it; the journalist increasingly spoke of himself as part of a 'Fourth Estate' which exercised social power as a legitimate by-product of the circulating of information.

Journalism had most conspicuously acted out this role during the battle for the Reform Bill, in the course of which the London press emerged as an independent political power. Until that moment newspapers had tended to hitch themselves to one politician or faction or another but in the struggle of 1831 the press in general, led by *The Times*, set up shop for itself, joining forces with Grey, Brougham and Russell. The press moved in again during the Corn Law Repeal agitation to enable Peel successfully to defy his own party. Pebody later concluded: 'Parliamentary minority plus the press is more powerful than Parliamentary majority without the press'. For the rest of the century the press behaved as if it shared power with the government during the Parliamentary sessions, but exercised the prerogative of Parliament during the recess.

There were many social and political trends which reflect themselves in the 'Fourth Estate' self-image of the press; indeed it was an exaggerated notion which totally failed to take account of the enormous readership of the unstamped working-class press circulating among a larger social group which was, however, unenfranchised and played no part in the formal activities of the Parliamentary system. All the same, it is apt to point out the relationship between such evolutions in the ideology of the press and the development of appropriate production technologies. The arrival of the steam press released a series of social forces and made possible a newspaper public which could aspire to a political power synchronous with the broader lines along which political information was enabled to circulate.

Another example of the sudden impact of a long retarded technological development upon journalism is the appearance of the first cheap wood-pulp paper in the 1880s. There had been a frantic search for new ways of making paper since the peace of 1815, a search which became ever more intense in the 1850s when the newspaper started to become a major world industry. France, Prussia and Rome actually prohibited the export of rags in 1857 when American provincial newspapers started to generate so

great a demand for paper that the price on the world market
rocketed upwards. America was obliged to obtain rags from
India, China and Japan and even then, during the Civil War,
American newspapers were obliged to more than double their
prices. There were periods when the London papers thought it
would be impossible to hold their prices (even after the abolition
of the newspaper tax in 1855) and maintain the existing
circulation structure of the newspaper. The newspaper as a
commodity is extremely sensitive to minor fluctuations in price
and operated on extremely small profit margins per copy. In
1867 the first plant making paper from wood pulp was installed
and within four years the price began to fall again, from 30 cents
per pound in 1865 to 3 cents in 1870 to one cent in 1880.[24] It was
the abolition of the newspaper tax, added to the extremely low
price of paper which enabled Newnes in the 1880s and
Northcliffe in the 1890s to work towards the modern mass
newspaper. In reading the new popular journalism of the *Daily
Telegraph*, then the *Pall Mall* and *Westminster Gazettes*, then the
new evening papers of the end of the century (the *Echo*, the *Star*,
and the *Evening News*), then hard upon their trail, the *Daily Mail*
the *Daily Express* of Northcliffe, one can feel the hot breath of
owners and editors scrambling after readers as they had never
done before. Throughout the provinces little chains of halfpenny
daily newspapers had sprung up, forerunners of the *Mail's* first
effort as a *national* halfpenny daily. The whole accent of
journalism had changed from that of the schoolmaster to that of
the huckster. Decreasing costs of production as a result of a series
of technological breakthroughs, long awaited, turned the newspaper into a source of enormous profit; the journalist became
entertainer first and teacher second. He had to grab his reader
before he could address him, because his typical purchaser was
no longer a man who had leisure to wait. The subject matter of
news was transformed, not merely because the market had
changed and enlarged to include social groups interested only in
trivia, but because the nature of the newspaper as a marketed
industrial commodity had altered. Henceforth the newspaper
was sold as it was written; its copy was its packaging. It would be
bought for its front page layout, or for its publicity stunts, or its
free offers or competitions. Gradually over the century to come
the whole output of the newspaper press was to be brought within

this system, including the provincial and 'quality' dailies which sought to survive by joining in the fray, the skills of journalism at all levels changing to encompass the new task.

V

The fifth and last of my five 'dimensions' emphasises the importance of the lines of management within a newspaper enterprise and between a newspaper enterprise and the society it serves. In the seventeenth century the central tension lay between the Royal Prerogative and the Stationers' Company whose members, controlled, checked, searched, limited in numbers, were the only people allowed to indulge in the business of news publication. In the next century the government exercised its controls through the taxation system and through the highly restrictive libel laws; the 'editor' emerged as the responsible official of a newspaper, a duty previously pertaining to the figure of the printer.[25] The editor was a new demarcation within the printing fraternity but made increasingly powerful within his particular enterprise because of his responsibilities in law. The owner at that time was a shadowy figure, anxious to shift the risks of the libel system to other shoulders, normally consisting of a co-operative of small businesses.[26] The nineteenth century saw the editor rise to a peak of importance in Barnes and Delane of *The Times*, where a financially successful owner was willing to place his publication virtually at the mercy of a skilled and experienced though still anonymous employee.[27]

As newspapers became more profitable but also more prone to risk as enterprises, an important set of tensions began to develop between owners and editors especially during the last three decades of the century. The notion of press 'freedom' centred around the freedom of the editor whose personal ideology had to be identified with that of his paper. The freedom of the editor from all but the most long-term of proprietorial instructions seemed to be the prerequisite of journalistic independence. The working journalist remained anonymous and utterly dependent on his editor. It is worth taking up the classic example of a nineteenth-century editorial career, that of Sir Edward Cook,[28] and examining his role within the spectrum of the press of the time. The editorial figure was the point at which the whole ideological integrity of a newspaper rested. The area in which newspapers competed was that of politics. It was the political persuasion of a newspaper which anchored it to its regular audience and every political grouping took pains to see that it had a newspaper owned and possibly subsidised by one of its leading adherents. If you look at the spectrum of the daily press of late Victorian times, it is clear how the pattern had emerged. First came *The Times*, read by the whole of the governing class, rather dull at this period and not as wealthy as in the past, but solid and reliable, expressing always a national standpoint. The *Morning Post* was the organ of the aristocracy: it favoured a populist Toryism at home and pure jingoism abroad. The *Standard* was the organ of the business-minded Tories; it spoke for the City rather than the counties. The *Daily Telegraph* was well established, the first of the penny dailies: it supported the Liberals but in foreign affairs clearly preferred the imperialist wing of that party; its readership had been built up partly as a result of its well written articles, relatively popular in tone and covering a wide area of subject matter. The *Daily Chronicle* was read by the educated working class; it was firmly radical in tone with a touch of jingoism in its treatment of foreign affairs. The *Daily News*, founded originally by Charles Dickens, was a paper of traditional liberalism and was slowly slipping in reader support. Two new papers had come onto the scene, the *Pall Mall Gazette* and the *Star*, exponents of a New Journalism (as Matthew Arnold had chosen to label it), each of them selling in the evenings at a halfpenny; they had hit the newspaper scene of the 1880s with a loud trumpet blast, and they were out to abolish the terrible dullness of the press and give their readers what they wanted to read. These papers had pioneered the interview, their columns contained cross-heads, their machinery was the new improved Hoe and Walter Presses, they employed the latest devices for printing illustrations and they eagerly accepted the new cheaper woodpulp paper which suited their printing machinery. The *Star* in fact was printed very elegantly on green paper. They pioneered sensationalism in news coverage, but both realized that their audience was interested mainly in politics. The *Pall Mall Gazette* was independent in politics, under its Liberal editor W. T. Stead, but the *Star* was more avowedly Radical.[29]

Now the total circulation of all eight of these papers was under half a million a day, though all of them ran at a profit or existed on a small political subsidy. They all reported Parliament in some detail and were clearly divisible into two sections, one in which carefully written neutral news was provided to feed their readers' judgements and a second which was devoted un-ashamedly to partisan editorialising. Their whole existence depended upon their ideological function within the national political spectrum. The editors lived by their public political identity. Yet the papers were run as business enterprises: problems would arise when the ownership of a paper switched from one political persuasion to another or if, in the course of time, issues arose on which editor and owner could not agree. The editor owned no capital; he existed as an experienced newspaper man of a given politics and if he was sacked he could be employed only in a paper of similar scope.

The *Pall Mall Gazette* had been originally founded by George Smith, the publisher, and the first editor had been Frederick Greenwood, both of them unswervingly Conservative in politics. In 1880 Smith suddenly lost interest in the paper and sold it to a keen Liberal, Henry Yates Thompson, who fired Greenwood and hired W. T. Stead (a young successful journalist from the *Northern Echo*) and John Morley, both of them equally staunch Liberals. Stead eventually became sole editor and made the paper the primal force in the New Journalism, but later handed over the editorial chair to E. T. Cook, who had no sooner settled into this now most influential position, than its owner announced the sale of the paper to a Conservative, W. W. Astor, for £50,000. Cook and most other members of the staff walked out in a body and were invited by Sir George Newnes within a brief period to start a new rival Liberal evening paper, *The Westminster Gazette*, to be printed on sea-green paper. In 1895 Cook went on to edit the *Daily News*, but within a few years a new set of tensions broke out within Liberal ranks; Cook was an Imperialist Liberal and supported the Boer War; the *Daily News* changed hands and passed into the possession of a pro-Boer (i.e. anti-Imperialist) Liberal; once again Cook had to pack his bags and find employment elsewhere. The years of his maturity had been spent playing a kind of ideological musical chairs with a series of proprietors. There are similar career patterns to be detected among leading Conservative journalists of the period. The whole stance of a paper circulating among a mainly politically-minded class depended upon the political identity of its leading contributors. Only with the coming of a much broader readership did this phenomenon begin to recede.[30] Only in the present century have people seriously argued that a paper has a social duty to provide for the whole spectrum of available political views; the main popular daily of the 1950s to 1970s has operated in the knowledge that its readers vote in different ways. The political views of editors are far less important than they were even fifty years ago. The *professional* code of the editor, and journalists as a whole, has thus been profoundly influenced by the evolution of the distribution methods of newspapers and their successive delineations of appropriate markets.

A medium of communication is a set of technical possibilities, the physical manifestation of which involves the convergence of a series of trends and impulses in society. The various parts of a medium are sustained through mutual and societal pressures. The journalists, like the other parts of the machine, are constantly re-professionalised, as it were, to new tasks, as each formulation of a medium succeeds its predecessor. We do not live at the end of that great evolution. Indeed we can see in the 1970s another 'new' journalist coming into being, a professional trained to supply material to the new electronic apparatus which is already taking over the production of many newspapers and will spread rapidly between now and the end of the century. A journalist who sends his copy into the central newspaper computer through a video display unit will inevitably be quite different from a shorthand reporter whose material was typed, dubbed set and printed. The journalist of the 1980s might want more *control* over his material; for one thing he might prefer to work at home, his V. D. U. attached to his telephone; for another, he might wish to control the fate of his copy more completely than was formerly possible. There is also the possibility that the new electronic process will enable newspapers to come into being with less founding capital in future than has been necessary for the last forty years, and this could bring new titles into existence and turn back the tide of amalgamation. Of course, the opposite could equally well happen. We might be left with one or two enormous and prosperous newspapers, each much larger and covering a vaster territory of information and ideologies. The kind of analysis offered here is not a basis for prediction, but simply a method for helping to recognise some of the basic processes which lie behind the evolution of media and the professions which service them.

Conclusion

A Telecommunications Future?

Chapter 15

Needs, Wants, Demands, Luxuries and Scarce Natural Resources*

During the last two centuries, when mankind has been increasingly occupied with the process of industrialisation, we have come to associate the process of development with the idea of invention. Each important stride has been made in the wake of a specific discovery or new mechanical contrivance. Society has become dependent upon these apparent gifts and has turned them rapidly from new luxuries into essentials. Today, we can no longer hope to feed and clothe the population of the planet without the machinery which has evolved decade by decade. Each stage in the process of industrialisation has left people believing that at last scarcity was being left behind; that at last there would be enough of a particular commodity for certain basic needs to be satisfied effortlessly and forever. But, although mankind has frequently felt itself standing on the very brink of abundance, it has never in practice managed to abolish scarcity. We cannot say with confidence that we have a sufficient supply,

* Published originally as chapter 3 of *Vision and Hindsight: The Future of Communications* (London: International Institute of Communications, 1976). © I. I. C.

forever, of anything. New wants and desires have always overtaken the expanded supply provided by the new invention.

We are probably on the brink of another major expansion and transformation of human capacities in the field of telecommunications. We can be certain of the potential because the process of 'invention' is already complete; in a sense, we know how to transfer to computers and modern transmission systems a whole host of human activities hitherto conducted through painful human physical and intellectual effort. We can imagine and foresee a world in which many of the basic processes of education, business, industry, banking, as well as the distribution of news, information, personal correspondence, scientific and medical knowledge and a vastly expanded flow of cultural and entertainment material, are all disseminated by means of a new generation of telecommunication devices, many of which already exist somewhere in embryo form and some of which have already been demonstrated.

What we have not yet invented is the means of human organisation to maximise this potential. We have not yet found the means by which mankind can share out the basic natural resource – the electromagnetic spectrum – upon which many of them depend. We still have to discover how to fit these and future inventions into human society, how to organise priorities nationally and internationally and how to overcome the problems of transition. In many cases, these social problems of transition and organisation are far more intractable than the primary technological invention of the new devices themselves.

For some societies, the new gadgetry could provide services which are thought by others to be absolutely fundamental; the newer satellites, for example, can provide telephone services in remote parts of the globe where the telephone has been a most unlikely practical possibility. The same resources could be used by already developed societies to provide extremely sophisticated information or entertainment services. Is the video-telephone less important to the Parisians than a national postal service via telefacsimile for Indonesia? If so, how is this global priority to be expressed? How can the real or imagined needs of one society be made to take precedence over the real or imagined needs of another? Should areas of the spectrum be set aside, perhaps for a generation or two, to lie fallow, as it were, while society develops more capacity to exploit them, even though society already has a clear, achievable and useful goal which can be reached immediately by using the same resource?

These questions cannot be pondered for very long: there is a revolutionary release of telecommunications energy occurring before our eyes and ears and nothing can stop it or delay it. Decisions which are being taken actively or merely passively as a result of inaction can have the effect of foreclosing on certain developmental options, in first, second and third worlds alike.

We therefore must consider very carefully as societies on different levels of development and with quite different views of social and international equity how needs and resources should be defined. In what sense does this or that nation have a need for a given allocation of the radio spectrum in order to allow its ships or its remote schools or its fourth television channel to operate? Is there in fact, such a thing as a fundamental telecommunications need? And in what sense is communications a resource? What obligations does a nation have towards the world as a whole to conserve the electromagnetic spectrum?

These questions of needs and resources revolve around political issues. For example, the world's merchant ships currently use long-wave frequencies. For some time these frequencies have been very congested. Sometimes a ship will have to queue for twelve hours to send an urgent message to shore. It is known that the world's shipping could be far more economically, efficiently and safely organised if ships used very short-wave frequencies. But many owners are unwilling to invest in the new devices. Their current equipment is often fully amortised; the new equipment is comparatively expensive. An added difficulty is that thousands of such vessels are technically registered in Liberia or Panama and there is no available governmental machinery which can oblige them to modernise their communications systems. Meanwhile ports are unnecessarily clogged and valuable oil is wasted while ships idle. To impose a completely rational telecommunications system on the world's merchant fleets would involve a degree of coercion which has no precise precedent, no means of enforcement and no established international authority. Examples of this kind are today multiplying. New technical opportunities render old forms of wastage more manifest and more painful. But the task of establishing individual and collective needs on the one hand, and of monitoring the rapidly evolving resources on the other, is extremely complicated.

In the last two decades a vast increase has taken place in the variety of activities which rely upon telecommunication resources. In some ways this expansion is similar to the revolution in business and educational activities which took place a century ago and which relied upon and emerged from the invention of apparently limitless quantities of cheap paper. When we were at the threshold of this present telecommunication revolution it seemed that, once again, mankind was looking upon an unchartered and limitless telecommunications ocean, in which satellites, coaxial cables, optic fibres and waveguide transmission systems, and the gradual exploitation of very low and very high frequencies of the radio spectrum, would constantly increase the available transmission resources of the globe beyond the level of desired use.

More recent events have taught us to see these resources in a quite different light. Although human ingenuity and capital can continue to expand them for the foreseeable future they will, in practice, always remain scarce and limited. Perhaps in a similar way to the paper revolution of the last century, the telecommunication revolution is going to bring with it problems of allocation and disputes of equity and political control which will ensure that the sense of abundance will be permanently denied to us even while enormous expansions are taking place.

The International Telecommunication Union; founded as long ago as 1865, has succeeded generation by generation in keeping the world from spectrum chaos by pooling the sovereignty of member nations. But it is now beset by a host of new and difficult problems. Eighty per cent of the world's telecommunications media are owned by only ten nations; the whole of the developing world accounts for less than 8 per cent. Somehow the I. T. U. has to cope in the next decade with the completion of a series of major tasks of reallocation. It is a period in which the expansion of telecommunications will be ever more closely associated with economic development.

The allocation of frequencies is a continuous process. The most recent I. T. U. conference – the allocation of the L. F./M. F. band in Regions 1 and 3 – took place in Geneva in 1975, and an agreement was drawn up which will come into force at the end of 1978. In 1977, a World Administrative Radio Conference was called to plan the satellite broadcasting service in the 12GHz band. To allocate the frequencies by which countries may provide themselves with extra television channels via geo-stationary satellites is likely to prove a very tough negotiation task indeed. Finally, in 1979, another World Administrative Radio Conference will revise the entire Table of Frequency Allocations. The 1979 W. A. R. C. is concerned with the allocation of the spectrum to different services – i.e., fixed, mobile and broadcasting – and to different countries. It will determine the framework and a great deal of the content of radio communications for the rest of the century. The 1979 conference will inevitably bring out the inherent tensions between developed and developing worlds. It may also reveal a rather crude division along geo-political lines, although the national and regional telecommunication needs of countries seldom reflect ideological patterns. For example, interesting parallels can be drawn between countries as diverse as Belgium and Sri Lanka in terms of their terrain, size and population. In some developing countries, a satellite could provide the first real national communication system of any kind; in others, it would be something of an additional luxury.

From the point of view of economic and social development, particularly in the Third World, there exist some extremely urgent informational needs. These needs will be a dominant factor of the 1979 W. A. R. C. Because of their urgency, all countries need to be helped to understand the potential benefits that the telecommunications resources offer for cultural and economic development.

Each country, of course, is sovereign, and different from all others in its national resources and its needs. The significant point, which is often not clearly stated, is that each country must therefore be well enough informed to chart its own resources, map out its own telecommunications needs, and formulate a series of logical and chronological demands. It would be a tragedy if the W. A. R. C.s dissolved into geo-political camps, all the adherents tending to assume they had opposing and exclusive needs. Only through extremely adept and sensitive planning, based upon the appropriate technical information, can countries make the best use of the negotiating opportunities provided by these important conferences. What is needed is a judicious mixture of intelligent diplomacy and highly technical information.

If we were now planning the telecommunication systems of the late twentieth century from scratch, our problems would be much easier. Almost all communication messages that are now broadcast over-the-air could be sent through cables, and the wavelengths currently used for fixed point-to-point radio and television could be primarily used for mobile services and possibly for emergency back-up services. If this had been done sixty years ago, what we have come to call the 'mass media' would probably never have developed at all in their present 'mass' forms; entertainment and information, if they had been disseminated along modern cables and fibres, would now be much more private forms of communication, involving more individual consumer choice and more tied down to specific local and regional areas. The spectre of one big mass audience would never have haunted the world, would never have confronted it with the profoundly vexing intellectual and institutional problems which beset today's broadcasting.

Yet now the pressure on the radio spectrum cannot be easily decreased; is indeed likely to get worse; and the problems of finding criteria for equitable access to it between nations is as difficult as it is urgent.

Radio and television can no more be abandoned in order to use their resources for some other economic or developmental purpose than the newspaper could be abandoned, or the postal services. All of these in their time were novel advances whose organisers were uncertain as to whether they would ever become established.

The whole process occurs under the shadow of our initial paradox. Between invention and exploitation the abundance vanishes. One finds a typical and immediate frustration in the increasing use of large-scale integration techniques for manufacturing the terminal equipment which is an essential part of the new transmission systems. Large-scale integration now makes possible a major redeployment of labour within modern societies. As a result, many industries which depend on the manufacture, use and movement of paper will find themselves in a crisis of 'role'.

Some are already finding that paper has its own inherent physical constraints. Many postal services are simply unable to cope with today's supply and demands for mail – for messages written on paper. Postal services are facing a series of new opportunities for the electronic delivery of written material and a new set of agonies of retraining or removing traditional postmen. Furthermore, transference towards electronic delivery will mean that new equipment needs to be placed in every single home for sending and receiving material.

Many new devices for storing and retrieving data – the new computer memories, printing equipment, the latest teletext services – depend increasingly on geo-stationary satellites, whose orbital belt 22,300 miles high is perhaps the scarcest and most expensive of all the new resources. The dependence on geo-stationary satellites is increasing over a whole range of activities that formerly depended on the physical movement of large quantities of paper and personnel.

These various opportunities of telecommunications open up the prospect of a major shift of social investment from the public sector to the private. In the future a much larger part of telecommunications investment will be brought and maintained in private groups (businesses, households). A very significant proportion will exist in homes. An earlier example of this process is the shift occasioned by the development of broadcasting, which switched investment from the theatre and cinema to the home in the form of radio and T. V. sets. The source of entertainment shifted from group neighbourhood viewing to family domestic viewing; the whole entertainment industry changed its structure as a result. (The development of hi-fi, super-8 film and video cassettes and discs is a continuation of this process.) We now face parallel developments in the postal services and in the press.

But changes in the method of distribution nearly always bring about changes in the nature of the items being distributed. We might see in the press, for example, a retreat from the idea of the newspaper as a medley of material which may interest different sections of its readership to very different degrees. Since the development of the mass circulation press at the beginning of this century, newspapers have tried to appeal to ever wider readerships and have tended to amalgamate more and more ranges of material within a smaller number of publications. The newer editorial policies of some magazines, on the other hand, have aimed at more specialist markets. The electronic delivery of printed material is likely to continue the magazine along this increasingly specialist path and to narrow down its ranges of material to suit the needs of smaller groups of readers or even individual readers. Consumers may begin to pre-select their areas of interest; advertisers will be able to focus more narrowly on the kinds of reader they want. The changes in telecommunication and in the manufacture of terminal devices could thus lead to a change in the nature of news and other published information as well as in their distribution. Subtle and far-reaching changes could take place in the ways in which information is created, collected and shaped for its readers.

One major area of priority, it is now clear, must lie in the development of means to make the most of each frequency band. There is a variety of ways in which the world's resources of spectrum can, as it were, be stretched. For instance, data, voice and image signals can be sent in digital forms, which use much less space. They can be switched in 'packets'. New multiplexing by multiple access frequency and/or time division have the same result. It is also possible to effect great economies by the more skilled use of power levels in transmission and in new methods of controlling the magnetic field covered by a given signal. As telecommunication engineering marches further towards the receding goal of abundance it will become feasible to explore the hitherto unusuable parts of the spectrum, including visible light waves and X-rays.

Mankind will proceed, via expansion and better exploitation, from scarcity to scarcity in the search for abundance.

Today's technologists are 'stretching' the spectrum in a series of uneven developments, each of which is prompted by the demands of society (including the technologists' own) for a particular service to be expanded or improved. But society also impresses its own image on the technology itself. Marconi's discoveries of certain uses for Hertzian waves led first to the improvement of ship-to-ship and ship-to-shore communication, then to the expansion of military and official communication services and only after a quarter of century to the development of radio as a mass entertainment medium. The 'mass audience' phase was retarded, if that is the right way of looking at it, because the manufacturing capacity, the administrative and marketing machinery, and the perception of society's needs for further media of information and entertainment, were not yet ready. Nature is always ready to support development. Human society takes longer to make up its mind, and to change it. Furthermore, by staking out its options too rapidly in one generation, society can often multiply the technical troubles of the next generation. Hindsight, alas, is the only exact human science.

Hindsight reminds us of the paradox of apparent abundance and actual scarcity. We are today in a position similar to that reached in the last generation of the nineteenth century when means had been discovered (and fully developed by industry) to produce paper from wood pulp at a fraction of the price of the paper produced from old rags (itself based on the limited human resource of cast-off fabric). At first, the forests of Northern Europe and Canada seemed limitless; usable trees were found more quickly than demand increased. It was thought that trees could be grown and the production of paper increased without stint. A revolution in human communication took place in the 1870s, 1880s and 1890s. Cheap textbooks made mass education cheap and easy to supply. Bookstalls spread as rapidly in those years as radio stations were to in the 1920s. Whole new industries for the making, handling and shipping of paper sprang up and prospered. The newspaper expanded its readership to those who could pay only a halfpenny a day.

The vision of abundance did not last long. Countries like the United Kingdom and France which were no longer able to supply their own paper needs became very dependent on countries (including some colonies) from which they had to import wood pulp. The revolution occasioned by cheap paper ended in a series of shortages with industrial, political and economic complications. The vision of abundance had been genuine; it had seemed that no society could possibly expand its needs to the extent of using this new resource to its limits. But by 1914 the dream was over; and another natural resource of mankind, confronted with the spectre of rising costs, joined the list of those which demanded constant and patient international negotiation.

So it is with the electronmagnetic spectrum and the new

services that increasingly rely on it. The 'abundance' which some techno-prophets proclaimed only a decade ago is already evaporating. We are seeing a series of shortages. The resource which Marconi developed for Victorian ships to use for navigation and which seemed as limitless as the ocean on which they floated, has now become the very sinew of a land-based society, a prerequisite for industrial activity as much as human leisure, and an essential condition for the fulfilment of much of modern human expectations in the fields of education, transport, medicine and interpersonal communication.

The new developments in telecommunications bring with them a perplexing set of social and political dilemmas, especially in the area where the jurisdictional limits of public and private spheres overlap. The telephone handset provides an interesting example of some of the new problems. In most countries it is made by private firms and paid for indirectly by private subscribers. Many of the new facsimile, data and teletext services, however, depend on a different terminal unit. The entire development of these new services (and the concomitant decline of the manual services they supplant) will depend on the development and dissemination of new types of telephone terminals. What priority will this be given? How will countries co-ordinate the various codes and systems on which effective interconnection depends? What proportion of gross national products will be consumed by the task of converting the tens of millions of telephone handsets into the more advanced units that are required? Until a very large proportion of terminals in any given region or country has been changed, the new services cannot function properly, and those who want and begin to need them will be unable to gain the full benefits. It is not the same as individually, home by home, exchanging an old kitchen mangle for a modern washing machine. All telecommunication devices are to some extent interactive and economies of scale are reached only when the hardware has been installed on a very broad front.

Yet even when this is achieved there remains the problem of individuals and groups who are outside the system because of personal desire, poverty, geographical location or other reasons. These people – to whom radio and television sought to offer a kind of cultural and social enfranchisement – will tend to find themselves even more tightly excluded. On a wider scale there is the problem of the country which is poor or remote or changes late to the new systems. The more sophisticated the devices, the harder it will be for the laggard nation to catch up; and the more dependent it will be on the technology developed and manufactured by other countries. The inequalities that are generated by a period of intensive innovation are sometimes vexingly irremediable.

One final question permeates these technical, economic and social issues. Are we on the threshold of a new extension of mass society or of some entirely new kind of human society? On the one hand, information of all kinds will become even more prodigiously available; the great dream of a democracy of knowledge and information with international dimensions might seem to be at hand. But the sheer quantities in which material is made available, and the manner in which the individual will be enabled to have as much as he likes, and avoid whatever he finds dull or irrelevant, will probably lead to a new kind of social divisiveness. The scarcity of the resources employed by radio and television have tended to guarantee that their content has a kind of universality of application. The mass newspaper developed into its mass stage precisely by dint of amalgamating many diffierent kind of material and many different kinds of audience into the new penny-a-time transnational reading public. The dream of the founders of the great broadcasting institutions was to provide information, education and entertainment to the whole of their public simultaneously and with equality. Of course, some parts of the audience would watch more of one genre than another. And different groups could derive quite different forms of satisfaction from the same material. But so long as the material was created on a high enough level of quality and interest, a kind of democracy of communication was thought to ensue. Many broadcasting systems created their own internally or externally imposed structures of balance precisely in order to guarantee that their radio and television services addressed themselves to the whole range of the audience, mass and élite, at the same time.

The new telecommunications environment opens up the possibility of a quite different line of development. Audiences will have the choice of much more material. This material, if broadcast, will be occupying a scarce international resource, the supply of which is becoming highly politicised. The pressure to provide material for a specific auidence, which is known to want it, will be very great. Since there will be no apparent abundance there can be no redundancy in the material supplied. It would seem possible therefore that the mass audience will come to manifest itself much more in terms of its component elements. The 'mass', will be likely to consume much less of the material available – which informs and educates. That, however, would not mean that the public will necessarily polarise into a mass versus and élite; information will arrive in sufficient variety and scale to satisfy a large series of overlapping élites and perhaps create new ones, serviced by the new telecommunications, with a largely 'entertained' section of the audience (smaller than the old 'mass') and a series of large but minority, more or less informed, audiences. In political terms, that would suggest a society falling woefully short of the liberal/democratic vision, but by no means the manipulated world of 1984. It would be a society which had evolved partly according to its desires and partly to its needs.

Notes and References

Chapter 1

1. Published as Tom Burns, *The B. B. C. – Public Institution and Private World* (London: Macmillan, 1977).

Chapter 2

1. Daniel Boorstin, *The Image: Whatever Happened to the American Dream?* (London: Weidenfeld and Nicolson, 1961) p. 3.
2. Marshall McLuhan, 'Candid Conversation', *Playboy*, March 1969, pp. 71–2.
3. Harold Mendelsohn and Irving Crespi, *Polls, Television and the New Politics* (Scranton, Pa.: Chandler, 1970).
4. Thomas Klapper, *The Effects of Mass Communication* (New York: Free Press, 1960) p. 8.
5. Published in Kurt Lang and Gladys Lang, *Politics and Television* (Chicago: Quadrangle Books, 1968).
6. Robert MacNeil, *The People Machine: The Influence of Television on American Politics* (New York: Harper and Row, 1968) p. xvii.
7. Jean-François Revel, *Without Marx or Jesus* (London: Paladin, 1972).

Chapter 6

1. Sir William Haley, 'The Central Problem of Broadcasting', (London: British Broadcasting Corporation, 1948).

Chapter 7

1. Lord Windlesham, 'Creativity and Control in Television', in *Politics in*

Practice (London: Jonathan Cape, 1975) p. 176.

2. In a speech delivered on 1 March 1977 at Goldsmiths College, London. Published as 'B. B. C. Journalism: The Relevance of Structure' in *COMBROAD* (April–June 1977) pp. 23–8.

3. *The Report of the Pilkington Committee on Broadcasting* (Cmnd. 1753, June 1962) was very critical of commercial television and recommended, among other reforms, that I. T. A. (now I. B. A.), the regulatory authority, should be empowered to make programmes itself where the private companies failed to cater for specific social needs.

4. Grace Wyndham Goldie, *Facing the Nation: Television and Politics 1963– 1976* (London: Bodley Head, 1977).

5. Tom Burns, '*Commitment and Career in the B. B. C.*', in *Sociology of Mass Communications*, ed. Denis McQuail (Harmondsworth: Penguin, 1972).

Chapter 8

1. J. Ellul, *Propaganda: the Formation of Men's Attitudes* (New York: Vintage, 1973) p. 261.

2. T. Pateman, *Television and the February 1974 General Election* (Television Monograph 3) (London: British Film Institute, 1975) p. 2.

3. M. Tracey, unpublished doctoral thesis, Leicester University, 1975, p. 490.

4. J. Ellul, *Propaganda . . .* , p. 19.

5. J. Trenaman and D. McQuail, *Television and the Political Image: the Study of the Impact of Television on the 1959 General Election* (London: Methuen, 1961).

6. M. Harrison, 'Television and radio', in *The British General Election of 1964*, ed. D. Butler and A. King (London: Macmillan, 1965) p. 156.

7. J. G. Blumler and D. McQuail, *Television in Politics: Its Uses and Influence* (London: Faber and Faber, 1968) p. 262.

8. Ibid. pp. 261–81.

9. C. Seymour-Ure, *The Political Impact of Mass Media* (London: Constable, 1974) p. 233.

10. H. Mendelsohn and I. Crespi, *Polls, Television and the New Politics* (Scranton, p. 2: Chandler, 1970) pp. 294–5.

11. Granada Television, *Prelude to Westminster?* (Manchester: Granada Television, 1974).

12. Lord Windlesham, *Politics in Practice* (London: Cape, 1975) pp. 146–7.

13. M. Harrison, 'Television and radio', in *The British General Election of February 1974*, ed. D. Butler and D. Kavanagh (London: Macmillan, 1974) pp. 146–69.

14. British Broadcasting Corporation, General Advisory Council, *The B. B. C. and the February 1974 General Election* (London: British Broadcasting Corporation, 1974) p. 19.

15. C. Dunkley, 'Overkill on television', *Financial Times*, 28 February 1974.

16. British Broadcasting Corporation, General Advisory Council, *The B. B. C. and the February 1974 General Election*, pp. 22–3.

17. British Broadcasting Corporation, General Advisory Council,

B. B. C. Coverage of the General Election September/October 1974: Summary of Public Reactions (London: British Broadcasting Corporation, 1974).

18. Lord Windlesham, *Politics . . .* , p. 148.

19. C. Curran, *A Maturing Democracy* (London: British Broadcasting Corporation, 1973).

20. M. Swann, *Problems in Broadcasting* (Annan address at the University of Leeds Television Seminar) (London: British Broadcasting Corporation).

21. M. Swan, *Problems . . .*

22. J. Dearlove, *The B. B. C. and the Politicians* (London: Writers and Scholars International, 1974).

23. Independent Television Companies Association, *I. T. V.'s Guide to Television for Parliamentary Candidates* (London: Independent Television Companies Association, 1974).

24. British Broadcasting Corporation, General Advisory Council, *The B. B. C. and the February 1974 General Election*, p. 21.

25. Granada Television, *Granada Goes to Rochdale: the First Series of Television Programmes on a By-election* (Manchester: Granada Television, 1974).

26. Granada Television, *A First Report on Constituency Television in a General Election: the Granada Election Marathon* (Manchester: Granada Television, 1974).

27. Granada Television, *The Granada 500: An Experiment in Collective Discussion of Election Issues* (Manchester: Granada Television, 1974).

Chapter 10

1. Quoted in Joseph Frank, *The Beginnings of the English Newspaper* (Cambridge, Mass.: Harvard University Press, 1961) p. 158.

Chapter 11

1. Edward J. Epstein, *News from Nowhere: Television and the News* (New York: Random House, 1973).

2. Bernard C. Cohen, *The Press and Foreign Policy* (Princeton University Press, 1965).

3. Jock Young, 'The Role of the Police as the Amplifiers of Deviancy', in *Images of Deviance*, ed., S. Cohen (Harmondsworth: Penguin, 1973).

4. John Dillingham in 'The Parliament Scout' (Jan 1647).

5. Rev. George Crabbe, 'The Newspaper' in *Collected Works*, vol. II (London: John Murray, 1834).

6. See *History of the Times*, vol. 2 (London: The Times, 1939) p. 151.

7. *The life and letters of C. Moberly Bell by his daughter, E. H. C. Moberly Bell* (London: Richards Press, 1927) p. 160.

Chapter 12

1. Much of the more detailed material relevant to the theme of this essay is to

be found in: Anthony Smith, 'Subsidies and the Press in Europe', *Political and Economic Planning*, vol. XLIII, no. 569 (June 1977).

2. For example, in the Finnish debate as to whether to redistribute the national sums expended on reduced postal charges. Parts I and II of the *Report of the Government Committee on Communication Policy*, 91 I, (1973) and 148 II, (1973), abridged (Helsinki: 1974) pp. 22–5.

3. See *Royal Commission on the Press*, Cmnd. 6810-1 (July 1977) Appendix C, and Final Report, para 11.17, p. 111.

4. *From Semaphore to Satellite, the History of the International Telecommunications Union, 1865–1965* (Geneva: I. T. U., 1966).

5. J. L. Kieve, *A History of the Electric Telegraph: a Social and Economic History* (Newton Abbot: David & Charles, 1973) pp. 119–53.

6. *From Semaphore to Satellite* . . . ; and see Edwin Emery and Henry Ladd Smith, *The Press and America* (New York: Prentice-Hall, 1954) pp. 386–94.

7. J. L. Kieve, *A History of the Electric Telegraph* . . . , pp. 216–29.

8. *Samarbeid i Dagspressen* (Norges Offentlige Utredninger, 1974) 5.1.

9. See comparison of balance sheets for different Norwegian papers in *Dagspressens økonomi* (Norges Offentlige Utredninger, 1973) tables 1–13, pp. 19–28.

10. *Rapport du Groupe de Travail sur les aides publiques aux entreprises de presse* – the Serisé Report (Paris: July 1972, p. 28.) (A French Government report.)

11. *La Presse Quotidienne* (Cahiers Français No. 178, Oct–Dec 1976) 'Un secteur en crise', table 3, p. 4. (A French Government report.)

12. P. Frederix, *Un siècle de chasse aux nouvelles – de L'Agence d'Information Havas à l'A. F. P.* (Paris: Flammarion, 1959).

13. I. P. T. C. Newsletter, no. 37 (May 1977) p. 11.

14. European Space Agency, *Remote Printing in Europe via Satellite*, vol. 1 'Summary' (London: Arthur D. Little Ltd. 1977).

15. *Telecommunications – National Policy and International Agreement, a Briefing Paper in preparation for the World Administrative Radio Conference of 1979* (cyclostyled document, International Institute of Communications, London) Sept 1977.

16. P.-J. Lévèque, 'Remote Printing for Paris Newspapers', in *I. P. T. C. Newsletter*, no. 37 (May 1977) p. 6.

17. Anthony Smith, *Telecommunications and the Press* (British Post Office, Long-Range Research Report No. 15, 1977).

18. See A. J. P. Taylor, *Beaverbrook* (Harmondsworth: Penguins, 1974) p. 95, and Colin Seymour-Ure, 'Changing Partisanship in the British Press, 1890–1970' (paper prepared for the European Consortium for Political Research Workshop on the Political Role of Mass Media, Strasbourg, March 1974).

19. Sir Norman Angell, *The Press and the Organisation of Society* (London: Labour Publishing Co., 1922).

20. J. Edward Gerald, *The British Press under Government Economic Controls* (Minneapolis: University of Minnesota Press, 1960).

21. Ibid. table 8, p. 43.

22. *Royal Commission on the Press, 1961–2* Report, Cmnd. 1811 (1962) table 7, p. 173.

23. Monopolies Commission, *The Times Newspaper and the Sunday Times Newspaper* (London: H. M. S. O., 20 Dec 1966).

24. Ibid. para 162.

25. Harford Thomas, *Newspaper Crisis – a Study of Development in the National Press of Britain, 1966–67* (Zurich: International Press Institute, 1967).

26. This was discussed by the Royal Commission on the Press, 1961–2, which concluded: '. . . in view of the statutory monopoly enjoyed by television contracting companies we consider it to be contrary to the public interest for such companies to be controlled by newspaper undertakings' (para 244).

27. *Bericht der Bundesregierung über die Lage von Presse und Rundfunk in der Bundesrepublik Deutschland* (Bonn: Presse und Informationsamt der Bundesregierung, 1974) p. 45.

28. *Frankfurter Allgemeine Zeitung*, 6 Dec 1975.

29. *Deutsche Presse-Agentur*, March 1976.

30. Deutscher Presserat, Tätigkeitsbericht 1975–76.

31. See speech of Federal Minister for Internal Affairs, Gerhart Baum, 15 May 1975 (Pressedienst des Bundesministeriums des Innern).

32. *Fact Sheet/Denmark* (Copenhagen: Press and Cultural Relations Dept of Ministry of Foreign Affairs, 1977).

33. *Pressehandbuch 1975* (Austrian Press Handbook) (Vienna: Verband Oesterreichischer Zeitungsherausgeber und Zeitungsverleger, 1976); and see article in Suddeutsche Zeitung, 3 June 1975.

34. Ulrich Saxer, *Medienpolitische Systeme: eine Analyse schweizerischer Medienpolitik*, Heft 1 (Publizistik, Drückerei und Verlagsanstalt Konstanz Universitätsverlag 1976).

35. Christian Padrutt, *Zur Lage der Schweizerischer Presse* (Zurich: Publizistisches Seminar der Universitat Zurich, 1975).

36. Report by the Nederlandse Vereniging van Journalisten (Amsterdam, 1975).

37. Centre du Recherche et d'Information socio-politiques (C. R. I. S. P.), *Morphologie des groupes et entreprises de presse (III)*, 9 May 1975, *Courrier Hebdomadaire*, no. 682.

38. C. R. I. S. P., Annex sur 'DOC' no. 103, 1976.

39. *A Free and Responsible Press – a General Report on Mass Communication* (University of Chicago Press, 1947).

40. *Royal Commission on the Press, 1947–9 Report*, Cmd. 7700 (1949) ch. XI.

41. The French newspapers received a once-only newsprint subsidy after the tremendous price rises of 1973. In Italy, the Ente Nazionale per la Celluloza e per la Carta (E. N. C. C.) distributes a subsidy to all newspapers according to newsprint consumed per page per thousand of circulation.

42. Statens Offentliga Utredningar (Swedish Government Official Report), *Dagspressens ekonomiska villkor*, 1965:22.

43. Statens Offentliga Utredningar, *Dagspressens situation*, 1968:48.

44. Karl Erik Gustafsson and Stig Hadenius, *Swedish Press Policy* (Stockholm: Swedish Institute, 1976) p. 52.

45. Federazione Italiana Editorial Giornali (F. I. E. G.) *Ordinamento della professione di giornalista* (Rome: Industria tipografica Imperia, 1965).

46. See Stefano Merlini, 'Ordine dei giornalisti, Contrattazione collective, liberta a dignita professionale dei lavoratori nell' azienda giornalistica', and Pietro Zanelli, 'Aspetti particolari del trattamento economico-normativo dei

giornalisti', both in *La stampa quotidiana tra crisi e riforma*, ed. Paolo Barile and Enzo Cheli (Bologna: Societa editrice il Mulino, 1976).

47. Andrea Orsi Battaglini, 'L'integrazione del prezzo della carta: logica di mercato e politica dell'informazione', in Barile and Cheli, ibid.

48. Carlo Macchitella and Domenico Sorace, 'I problemi della distribuzione', in Barile and Cheli, ibid.

49. *Disegno di Legge concernente nuove norme per la Stampa* – cyclostyled Italian draft law, 1977.

50. These have been subjected to various proposals for further amendment at the time of writing. For discussion on the Arnaud draft law, see *Il Sole-24 Ore* (Milan), 8 Feb 1977.

51. The *Gazetta di Mantova*.

52. Svennik Høyer, 'Temporal Patterns and Political Factors in the Diffusion of Newspaper Publishing – the Case of Norway', *Scandinavian Political Studies*, vol. 10 (1975) (Oslo: Universitetsforlaget and London: Sage Publications, 1976).

53. Allan Viranko, *Suomen sanomaelehdisto vakaanuttaa asemaansa, 1916–1966* (The Consolidation of the Finnish Press, 1916–1966) (Helsinki, 1970).

54. Report of the Government Committee on Communication Policy, p. 14.

55. S. Høyer, 'Temporal Patterns'.

56. Dick Leonard, 'Paying for Party Politics: the Case for Public Subsidies', *Political and Economic Planning*, vol. VLI, Broadsheet no. 555 September (1975).

57. For a description, see Anthony Smith, *The Shadow in the Cave* (London: Quartet, 1976).

58. *De Journalist* (Amsterdam), 15 Sept 1976.

59. Elisabeth Noelle-Neumann, Franz Ronneberger and Heinz Werner Stuiber, *Streitpunkt Lokales Pressemonopol – Untarsuchungen auz Alleinstellung von Tageszeiten* (Düsseldorf: Droste Verlag, 1976).

60. *Media Perspektiven* (Hamburg) 1977, no. 1.

61. Submission of the Dublin Newspaper Managers' Committee to the Minister of Finance, Dublin, June 1975 (prepared by P. A. Management Consultants (Ireland) Ltd).

62. To $5\frac{1}{2}$ per cent on all papers sold by subscription.

63. *Bulletin de Documentation Pratique des Taxes*, no. 10 (Oct 1976) (article on 'La Presse et la T. V. A.') and Sénat, 106, *Rapport au nom de la Commission des Finances*, par M. Jean Francou, 3 Dec 1976.

64. See *Royal Commission on the Press*, Cmnd. 6810 (July 1977) Final Report, para 11.13, p.111.

65. *Dagspressens økonomi* (Norges Offentlige Utredninger, 1973) pp. 48–55.

Chapter 13

1. Gaye Tuchman, 'Objectivity as a Strategic Ritual: an Examination of Newsmen's Notions of Objectivity', *American Journal of Sociology*, 78 (Jan 1972) pp. 660–70.

2. 'Amyot to His Readers', introduction to the *Lives of Plutarch, Englished by Sir Thomas North, 1579*, vol. 1 (London: J. M. Dent, 1896) p. 9.

3. House of Lords *Hansard*, Wednesday 4 Feb 1852.

4. A 'Message from the Chief' (Northcliffe's papers, Bodleian Library, Oxford) typescript dated 16 Dec 1916.

5. John Donne, *Collected Poems*, ed. Sir Herbert Grierson (Oxford University Press, 1933) p. 69.

6. *The Essays of Montaigne, translated by John Florio*, 1603, vol. 1 (London: J. M. Dent, 1898) p. 270.

7. Quoted in: Joseph Frank, *The Beginnings of English Journalism* (Cambridge, Mass.: Harvard University Press, 1971) p. 43.

8. Richard Atkyns, *The Original and Growth of Printing* (London, April 1664) title page.

9. R. Atkyns, ibid. (1664) dedication.

10. John Milton, *Areopagitica*, vol. II (Yale University Press edition, 1959) p. 561.

11. See Peter Fraser, *The Intelligence of Secretaries of State* (Cambridge University Press, 1956) pp. 9–34.

12. G. A. Cranfield, *The Development of the Provincial Newspapers 1700–1760* (Oxford: Clarendon Press, 1962) p. 28.

13. *Northampton Mercury*, March 1721, quoted by G. A. Cranfield, ibid. p. 29.

14. T. B. Howell (ed.), *A Complete Collection of State Trials*, vol. 14 (London) pp. 1106–7.

15. Rev. George Crabbe, 'The Newspaper' in *Collected Works*, vol. II (London: John Murray, 1834) p. 135.

16. *Daily Courant*, no. 1, 21 April 1702.

17. *Spectator*, no. 452, 8 Aug 1712.

18. Good accounts exist in Michael MacDonagh, *The Reporters' Gallery* (London: Hodder & Stoughton, n.d.) and in Robert C. Haig, *The Gazetteer, 1735–1797* (Illinois: Southern Illinois University Press, 1960) *passim*.

19. See A. Aspinall, 'The Reporting and Publishing of the House of Commons Debates 1771–1834' in *Essays Presented to Sir Lewis Namier* (eds Richard Pares and Alan Taylor (Oxford University Press, 1956) pp. 233–8.

20. M. Macdonagh, *Reporters' Gallery*, pp. 137–47.

21. M. Macdonagh, ibid. p. 269.

22. A. Aspinall, *'House of Commons Debates'*, p. 254.

23. M. Macdonagh, *Reporters' Gallery*, p. 339.

24. See D. Ayerst, *The Guardian – Biography of a Newspaper* (London: Collins, 1971).

25. *The Young Reporter, A Practical Guide to the Art and Profession of Shorthand Writing* (London: Lockwood, 1869) p. 27.

26. In a chapter of that title in Walter Bagehot, *Physics and Politics* (London: Cassell, 1872).

27. See Leslie Stephen, 'The Evolution of Editors', *Studies of a Biographer*, vol. I, 3 (London: Duckworth, 1898) pp. 37–73.

28. 'Libel State of the Press', anonymous in *Quarterly Review* (1827) p. 592.

29. Ibid.

30. See Leslie Stephen, *Studies* . . .

31. Walter Besant, 'Journalism', *The Pen and the Book* (London: Thomas Burleigh, 1899) ch 3, p. 248.

32. Alfred C. Harmsworth in a chapter appended to Arthur Lawrence, *Journalism as a Profession* (London: Hodder & Stoughton, 1903).

33. A. C. Harmsworth, ibid.

34. A. C. Harmsworth, ibid.

35. Charles Pebody, *English Journalism and the Men Who Made It*, Preface, (London: Cassell, Petter, Galpin, 1882) p. 5.

Chapter 14

1. I. Watt, *The Rise of the Novel* (London: Chatto and Windus, 1957) p. 214.

2. M. McLuhan, *The Gutenberg Galaxy: the Making of Typographic Man* (London: Routledge, 1962).

3. Typical are Alexander Andrews, *History of British Journalism until the year 1855* (London: Richard Bentley, 1859), F. Knight Hunt, *The Fourth Estate* (London: David Bogue, 1850), Fox Bourne, *English Newspapers – Chapters in the History of Journalism* (London: Chatto and Windus, 1887), T. H. S. Escott, *Masters of English Journalism* (London: T. Fisher Unwin, 1911) and, more recently, Harold Herd, *The March of Journalism* (London: Allen & Unwin, 1952) and Francis Williams, *Dangerous Estate* (London: Longman, 1953).

4. R. K. Webb, *The British Working Class Reader 1790–1848* (London: Allen and Unwin, 1955): R. Williams *The Long Revolution* (London: Chatto and Windus, 1961).

5. J. Frank, *The Beginnings of the English Newspaper 1621–1660* (Cambridge, Mass.: University of Harvard Press, 1971); J. B. Williams, *History of English Journalism until the Foundation of the Gazette* (London: Longmans Green, 1908).

6. J. H. Plumb, *The Growth of Political Stability in England 1675–1725* (London: Macmillan, 1969).

7. S. Morrison, *The English Newspaper* (Cambridge University Press, 1932) chs 13 and 14; F. Greenwood, 'The Newspaper Press', *Nineteenth Century*, May 1890.

8. M. A. Shaaber, *Some Forerunners of the Newspaper in England*, 1476–1622 (University of Pennsylvania Press, 1929).

9. John Donne, *Collected Poems*, ed. Sir Herbert Grierson (Oxford University Press, 1933) p. 69.

10. W. Harris, *J. A. Spender* (London: Cassell, 1946).

11. G. A. Cranfield, *The Development of the Provincial Newspaper, 1700–1760* (Oxford: Clarendon Press 1962); W. F. Belcher, 'The Sale and Distribution of the British Apollo', in *Studies in the Early English Periodical*, ed. R. P. Bond (University of North Carolina Press, 1957) pp. 73–101.

12. J. L. Kieve, *A History of the Electric Telegraph* (Newton Abbot: David and Charles, 1974).

13. *History of the Times*, vol. 2 (London: The Times, 1939) pp. 272–3.

14. J. Lane. *J. G. Muddiman: The Kings' Journalist 1659–1689* (London: Bodley Head, 1923); P. Fraser, *The Intelligence of the Secretaries of State and their Monopoly of Printed News 1660–1688* (Cambridge University Press, 1956).

15. P. M. Handover, *A History of the London Gazette 1665–1965* (London: HMSO, 1965).

16. P. Fraser, *Secretaries of State* . . .

17. M. MacDonagh, *The Reporters' Gallery* (London: Hodder and Stoughton, 1912) p. 269.

18. A. Andrews, *History* . . . , vol. 1, p. 196.

19. M. MacDonagh, *Reporters' Gallery*, p. 348.

20. *History of the Times*, vol. 1 (1935) pp. 311–15.

21. 23 June 1832.

22. C. Pebody, *English Journalism and the Men who have made it* (London: Cassell, Petter, Galpin, 1882) p. 107.

23. Ibid. p. 91.

24. D. C. Coleman, *The British paper Industry 1494–1860: A study in industrial growth* (Oxford University Press, 1958); D. C. Smith, 'Wood pulp and Newspapers, 1867–1900' in *The Business History Review*, 38 no. 3 (1964) pp. 328–45.

25. F. S. Siebert, 'Taxes on Publications in England in the 18th Century' in *Journalism Quarterly*, vol. 21 (1944) pp. 12–24; L. Hanson, *Government and the Press* (Oxford University Press, 1936); Leslie Stephen, 'The Evolution of Editors' in *Studies in Biography*, vol. 1 (London: Duckworth, 1898) pp. 37–73.

26. R. L. Haig, *The Gazetteer, 1735–1797: A study in the 18th Century English Newspaper* (Illinois: University of Southern Illinois Press, 1960).

27. A. I. Dasent, *John Thaddeus Delane: Editor of the Times* (London: John Murray, 1908); *History of the Times*, vol. 2.

28. J. S. Mills, *Sir Edward Cook, K.B.E.* (London: Constable, 1921).

29. H. G. Scalk, 'Fleet Street in the 1880s: the Old Journalism and the New', in *Journalism Quarterly*, Summer 1964, pp. 421–6; W. T. Stead, 'A Journalist on Journalism', in E. H. Stout, ed (John Haddon, 1892).

30. J. S. Mills, *Sir Edward Cook* . . . , pp. 192–205; J. W. R. Scott, *The Story of the Pall Mall Gazette* (Oxford University Press, 1950); W. Harris, J. A. Spender (London: Cassell, 1946) pp. 22–7.

Index

Annan Committee 39, 45, 47,
    54n., 55
  Kensington House Document
    76-7, 78, 81
Atkyns, Richard 180
Austria
  broadcasting control in 39
  press mergers 166

Barnes, Thomas 192, 215, 219
B.B.C. 5, 9, 29, 34, 46, 50, 52,
    56
  broadcasting in Northern
    Ireland 109-12, 114-20
  'Campaign Special' 99
  Complaints Commission 33,
    51
  'Election Forum' 92, 100-1
  'Irish Half-Hour' 111
  'The Money Programme' 92
  'Nationwide' 8
  'Panorama' 92, 94, 115, 119
    126, 127
  powers of 31
  question of power and
    responsibility 125-6
  'A Question of Ulster' 126
  'That Was the Week That Was'
    79
  'Tonight' 112, 127

'24 Hours' 119, 127
'World at One' 119
Beadle, Gerald 110
Belgium
  press subsidies from T.V. 167
  separate French and Flemish
    media 132
Blaew, William Jenson 48
Britain
  control of broadcasting and
    licence fee 29
  E.E.C. referendum 96, 139
  'fairness' in Northern Ireland
    broadcasting 125
  forms of electoral
    broadcasting 98-104
  subsidised press 159, 161
  system of broadcasting 45-6,
    82, 83
broadcasting
  advertisement financing 40,
    41, 44
  central problem 56
  codes of conduct 150-1
  continuous assessment needed
    46-7
  criticisms in last decade 38-40
  licence-fee financing 40-1, 42,
    44
  pluralism in finance 43-4

broadcasting—*continued*
  problems of electoral 97-8
  re-examinations in 1970s 4, 9
broadcasting institutions
  democratisation needed 31-5
  internal structures consequent
    upon social roles 77
  proposed National
    Broadcasting Centre
    51-2
Burns, Tom 9, 83

Campbell, John 187
Canada
  C.R.T.C. 52
  problem of broadcasting
    finance 41, 42
Cohen, Bernard 144
Committee on Political
    Broadcasting 102
community conflicts
  defining 131-2
  effect on news values 133,
    134-5
  in Watts County 130
Cook, Sir Edward 152, 219,
    221
Crabbe, George 144, 147, 184
Crespi, Irving 12
Curran, Sir Charles 77, 78

Daily Courant 184
Daily Express 109, 218
Daily Herald 164, 165, 203
Daily Mail 179, 202, 218
Daily Mirror 165
Daily News 202, 220, 221
Daily Telegraph 202, 218, 220
Delane, J.T. 178, 179, 219
Dickens, Charles 187, 188, 194,
    220
Eire
  financing broadcasting 41, 42
  Radio Eireann 110, 111
Ellul, Jacques 85
Epstein, Edward 144

Finland
  Helsingin Sanomat 173, 174
  newspaper formation and
    closure 172-3
  press subsidies 174
  question of press monopolies
    168
France
  A.F.P. news agency 162
  advertising revenue for
    broadcasting 41
  Audio-Visual Institute 52, 81
  creativity and management
    81-2, 83
  French Society for Production
    6, 81
  O.R.T.F. 6
  post-1972 reorganisation of
    broadcasting 6, 39
  problem of broadcasting
    control 29
  subsidies to press 161, 162,
    163, 168

Germany
  broadcasting control 29, 39,
    40, 55, 61, 68, 82
  development of press laws
    57-61
  Employers' Association of
    German Newspaper
    Trade 57
  freelancing in broadcasting
    69-71, 80, 81
  Hessischer Rundfunk 61, 70
  Journalists' Association 57,
    58
  legal demands on programmers
    62
  licence-fee collection 44
  N.D.R. 65, 70, 71
  national control of
    telecommunications
    apparatus 160-1
  newspaper mergers 165-6,
    171

Germany—*continued*

  political, producer and staff
      pulls on T.V. 62-4,
      80-1
  press efficiency 174-5
  'Proporz' system 64, 66, 68,
      69
  question of press subsidies
      166, 174
  R.F.F.U. 66, 71
  rise of producers' committees
      64-6, 67, 128
  sources of information on
      broadcasting 71-3
  trade unions in broadcasting
      66, 67
  Union of Journalists 59
  W.D.R. 61-2, 70
  Z.D.F. 61, 62, 64, 68, 80
Granada T.V. 103
  conflict with I.T.A. 121-3,
      124
  'Granada 500' 103, 104
  'World in Action' 119, 121,
      123, 124, 126
Guardian (Manchester) 122, 149
Gurney, John 187

Haley, Sir William 56
Hansard, T.C. 186
Heath, Edward 93, 94, 95
Helsinki Agreement xii, 143n.
Hill, Lord 45, 117, 118

I.B.A. 5, 38, 50, 51
  I.T.N. 120, 121
  'News at Ten' 8
  on live audiences 102-3,
      104
  powers of 31
  problems of broadcasting in
      Northern Ireland 120-4
  separation of powers under
      78
International Telecommunication
    Union 230

Italy
  broadcasting control 39, 40
  editorial committees 171
  press subsidies 168, 169-71
  R.A.I. 39, 40

Japan
  N.H.K. 41
  operation of licence fee 41
journalism
  advent of shorthand 186,
      187, 188, 213-14, 215
  'Fourth Estate' image 217
  objectivity 178, 195, 196
  Parliamentary reporting
      185-7, 214

Klapper, Thomas 13
Koenig, Frederick 201, 216

Leeds, T.V. Research Centre 51
London Gazette 181, 210, 212,
    213

MacMullan, Henry 114
MacNeil, Robert 14
Maguire, Waldo 114, 115, 117
    119
Marconi, Marchese 104, 234,
    236
Marshall, G.L. 110, 111, 114
Maudling, Reginald 186, 187,
    191, 192, 214, 216
media
  as effect of social change
      48-9
  changing values in 134
  community conflict and
      107, 129-40
  inadequacy of present news
      forms 139-40
  mass 48
  problem of access to 139
Mercurius Gallo-Belgicus 204,
    215

Morning Chronicle   186, 187,
     191, 192, 214, 216
Morning Post   192, 202, 220
Muddiman, Henry   209, 210,
     213
   newsletters   211-12

Netherlands
   organisation and problems
        of broadcasting   6-7,
        29, 78-9, 82
   party newspapers and
        advertising   174
   press subsidies from
        T.V.   167
   problem of financing
        broadcasting   41
New Chronicle   164, 203
Nixon, Richard M.   16, 18
Northampton Mercury   182, 207
Northcliffe, Lord   52, 150, 179,
     195-6, 218
Northern Ireland   139
   history and problems of
        broadcasting   108-16,
        156
   problems of press reporting
        155
   separate sets of news values in
        133, 135
   T.V. coverage   106-47
Norway
   N.T.B. news agency   162
   press subsidies   162, 167
   question of press monopolies
        168

Pall Mall Gazette   202, 205, 218,
     220, 221
paper
   development of wood pulp
        217, 218, 235
   social change and cost of   48-9
   war-time scarcity   164
Pebody, Charles   197, 216, 217
Perry, James   184, 191, 192, 194
Pilkington Report   38, 78

politics
   boredom and T.V.   104-5
   effect of T.V. on   12, 14, 19,
        86-90
   forms of T.V. programmes
        98-104
   in T.V. terms   22
   interrogating the politician
        21-2
   issues in 1974 elections   93-4
   phone-in programmes   85-6
        92, 101
   politician in mass age   15, 16
   problem of live T.V. audiences
        100, 101-2, 103
   T.V. coverage of 1974
        elections   84-105

press
   development of   48
   editors   152, 172, 191, 219,
        220, 221
   government advertising as press
        subsidy   175-6
   government as guarantor of
        158
   impartiality of   145, 146, 147,
        153
   licensing   180, 181
   management   219
   mergers   165
   news sources   208-10
   news values   144-5
   newspaper audiences   203-4,
        207, 220
   newspaper distribution   206-7
   present journalistic attitudes
        153-5
   question of responsibility   151
   satellite printing   162-3
   state intervention and
        management of   157-76
   technical improvements   201,
        202, 217-18
   VAT relief   175
   wire agencies   148-9, 161, 209
Press Association   161

Press Council 32, 167

Reuters 149, 161, 209

Sampson-Woodfall, Henry 147
Scott, C.P. 149
Scottish Television 102, 165
Southern T.V. 165
Spectator 192, 200
Stationers' Company 210, 219
Stead, W.T. 152, 205, 221
Steed, Wickham 205
Stuart, Daniel 181, 192
Sunday Times 116, 165
Sweden
    broadcasting control in 40
    press subsidies 167, 168-9
    question of press monopolies
        168

telecommunications
    congestion of frequencies 229
    international 160
    possible developments 233-4,
        237-8
    satellites 228, 233
    telegraphy 193, 194
    telephony 25, 49-50, 160
television
    assumptions of society and 21
    cognition—emotion duality
        11, 12
    constraints 29-30, 31
    controlling organisations and
        their values 27-8
    effect of camera on crowds
        14, 130
    effect on other media 4-5
    financing 38-44, 51
    freedom of expression and
        24-5, 30
    management 24-37
    management and creativity
        74-5, 79
    minority taste in 26

need for access 33-4
neutral ideology of 106-7
news balance 86
over-management 76
principal system of social
    regulation 17, 18
problem of programme-makers,
    power 55
problems of power of 5-6, 19,
    27
public's right to be entertained
    3-4, 9, 25-6
research into effects of 13,
    14, 16
social accountability 45-53
trial by ordeal 22-3
unreality and 11, 12, 14
Thames T.V. 102
'This Week' 120
Times, The 90, 165, 187, 192,
    202, 209, 214-20 *passim*.
    relation to its readers 147-8
Tyas, John 187, 214

Ulster Television 113-14, 115,
    120, 121
United States of America
    Federal Communications
        Commission 151
    Hutchins Commission 151,
        167
    influence of T.V. techniques
        4
    presidential debates 16, 22
    Watergate crisis 139

Vietnam war 16-17, 132, 139

Walter, John, II 191-2, 216
Wilson, Harold 8, 94, 95
Windlesham, Lord 75, 95
Woodfall, William 'Memory'
    186, 192, 214

Yorkshire Television 102